ENTER AT
YOUR OW
RISK!!

AUTHORIZED
20th Century Fox
TWENTIETH
CENTURY-FOX
Lou Adler /
Michael White,
S.A.
AUTHORIZED

By

**Bill Henkin**

HAWTHORN BOOKS, INC.

Publishers

*A Howard & Wyndham Company*

THE ROCKY HORROR PICTURE SHOW BOOK



Library of Congress Catalog Card Number: 79–63619

ISBN: 0–8015–6436–0

1 2 3 4 5 6 7 8 9 10

Book design by Edwin H. Kaplin

*To absent friends*

## ACKNOWLEDGMENTS

Many people provided information and insights that wound up in the following pages, in one form or another. A few of these people were particularly gracious and/or indispensable. For their invaluable aid thanks are due Lou Adler; John Beug; Skip Bruno; The Fly-By-Night Juggling Company (Michael Goudeau, Robert Lind, Frank Mitello, John Park); Phil Molar; Carol Murray; David Nochimson; Marni Scofidio; Queenie Taylor; and Michael Wolfson. At Twentieth Century-Fox: Rand Marlis; Tim Deegan; Pat Miller; Willie Navarro, and Frank Rodriguez. The consultation services of Sal Piro were particularly helpful in focusing this book, and his enthusiastic support of the project—and the film—made possible the inclusion of materials that would not have appeared here otherwise. Similarly, *Rocky Horror* fans all over the country, who have been unbelievably generous wih their time and efforts, proved all-important. Special thanks and a tip of the hat are due my editor at Hawthorn Books, Sandra Choron, without whom this book would still be just a good idea.*

B.H.

*You're welcome.—S.C.

# THE ROCKY HORROR PICTURE SHOW

*Starring*

Tim Curry—Dr. Frank-N-Furter (A Scientist)
Susan Sarandon—Janet Weiss (A Heroine)
Barry Bostwick—Brad Majors (A Hero)
Richard O'Brien—Riff Raff (A Handyman)
Patricia Quinn—Magenta (A Domestic)
Little Nell—Columbia (A Groupie)
Jonathan Adams—Dr. Everett V. Scott (A Rival Scientist)
Peter Hinwood—Rocky Horror (A Creation)
Meatloaf—Eddie (Ex-Delivery Boy)
Charles Gray—The Criminologist (An Expert)
Jeremy Newson—Ralph Hapschatt
Hilary Labow—Betty Munroe

The Transylvanians:

Perry Bedden
Christopher Biggins
Gayle Brown
Ishaq Bux
Stephen Calcutt
Hugh Cecil
Imogen Claire
Rufus Collins
Tony Cowan
Sadie Corre
Fran Fullenwider
Lindsay Ingram
Peggy Ledger
Annabelle Leventon
Anthony Milner
Pamela Obermeyer
Tony Then
Kimi Wong
Henry Woolf

Richard O'Brien—Original Musical Play, Music and Lyrics
Jim Sharman and Richard O'Brien—Screenplay

John Goldstone—Associate Producer
Lou Adler—Executive Producer
Michael White—Producer
Jim Sharman—Director
Richard Hartley—Musical Direction and Arrangements
Peter Suschitzky—Director of Photography
Graeme Clifford—Film and Music Editor
Brian Thomson—Design
Sue Blane—Original Costume Design
Richard Hartley—Incidental Music
David Toguri—Choreography
Ron Barron—Sound Recordist
Keith Grant—Music Recording

| | |
|---|---|
| Count Lan Blair<br>Mick Grabham<br>David Wintour<br>B. J. Wilson<br>Phil Kenzie<br>Rabbit<br>Richard Hartley | Principal Musicians |

Bill Rowe—Dubbing Mixer
Ian Fuller—Dubbing Editor
Rodney Glenn—Assistant Editor
Denis Lewiston—Camera Operator
Mike Roberts—Camera Focus
Terry Ackland-Snow—Art Director
Dick Frift—Construction Manager
Ian Whittaker—Set Dresser
Peter Robb-King—Makeup
(Based on original makeup designs created by Pierre La Roche)
Ramon Gow—Hairdresser
Richard Pointing and Gillian Dods—Wardrobe
John Comfort—Production Manager
Mike Gowans—First Assistant Director
Sue Merry—Continuity
Celestia Fox (UK) and Otto and Windsor (USA)—Casting Consultants
Ron Swinburne—Production Accountant
Wally Veevers and Colin Chilvers—Special Effects

THE ROCKY HORROR PICTURE SHOW
was filmed on Location at Oakley Court and at Bray Studios, Berkshire, England.

Post Production at Emi-Elstree Studios, England.

# CONTENTS

THE
ROCKY HORROR
PICTURE SHOW
BOOK

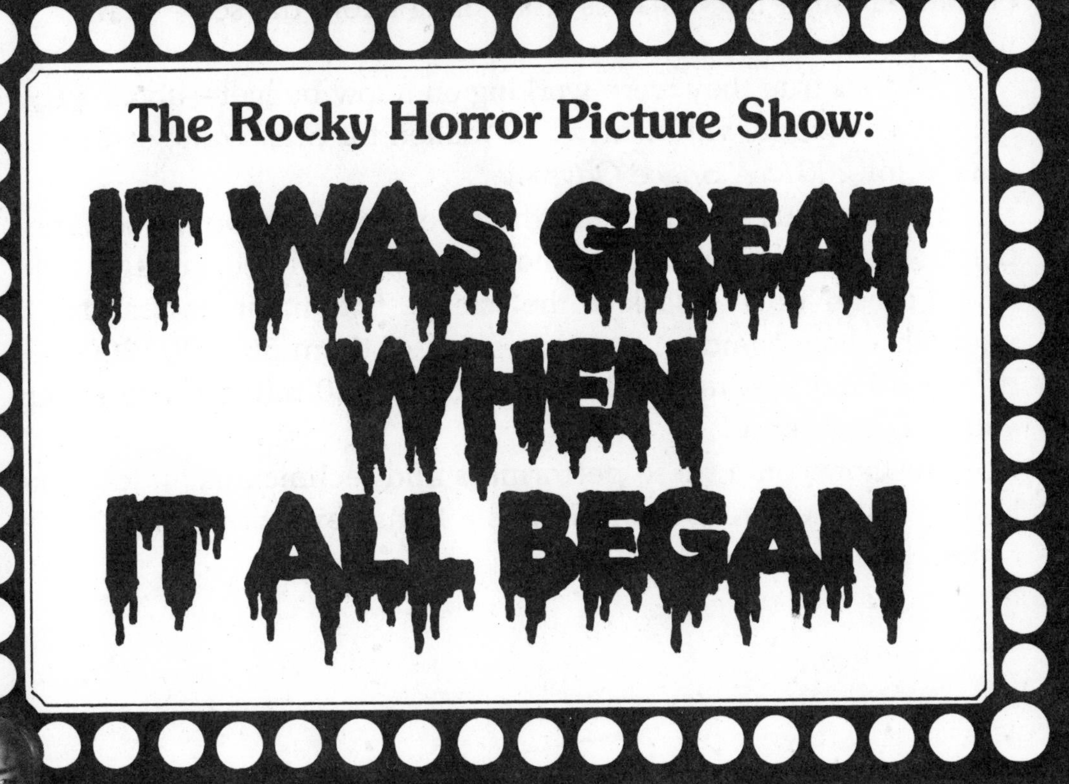

# The Rocky Horror Picture Show: IT WAS GREAT WHEN IT ALL BEGAN

*I would like, if I may,*
*to take you on a strange journey.*

You would, would you?

You may

How strange was it? It was so strange, they made a movie about it.

It seemed a fairly ordinary October, in 1974, when the cast and crew began to film *The Rocky Horror Picture Show* at England's Bray Studios—where such horror classics as *The Curse of Frankenstein; The Curse of the Mummy's Tomb;* and *The Horror of*

*Dracula* had been made by Hammer Productions—and on location in the castle used by General Charles de Gaulle as a refuge during World War II.

It's true that the filming of the birth of the character Rocky Horror just happened to fall on October 30, 1974, the 81st anniversary of the birth of Charles Atlas, and that the assembled performers sang the "Charles Atlas Song" from the score in the muscle-builder's honor.

And it's true they were working on a low budget—about $1 million, compared with nearly $12 million for *Star Wars,* or $18 million for *2001: A Space Odyssey.*

It's also true that the film they were making would become the biggest audience participation film in history, bringing hard-core Transylvanians back to the science fiction, single-feature, midnight show again and again—some of them 50, 100, 200 times and more—and would gross nearly $20 million within four years of its release.

But how could these performers and technicians on location know what the future held? It was a film they were going to remember for a very long time.

Twentieth Century-Fox executives visit the movie set. *Left to right*: executive producer Lou Adler; Ascanio Branca, assistant managing director, London; Steve Panama, advertising and publicity executive for Los Angeles; Emile Buyse, vice president for Europe and the Middle East; Percy Livingstone, managing director, London; and Stanley Bielecki of Avenue Studios, London.

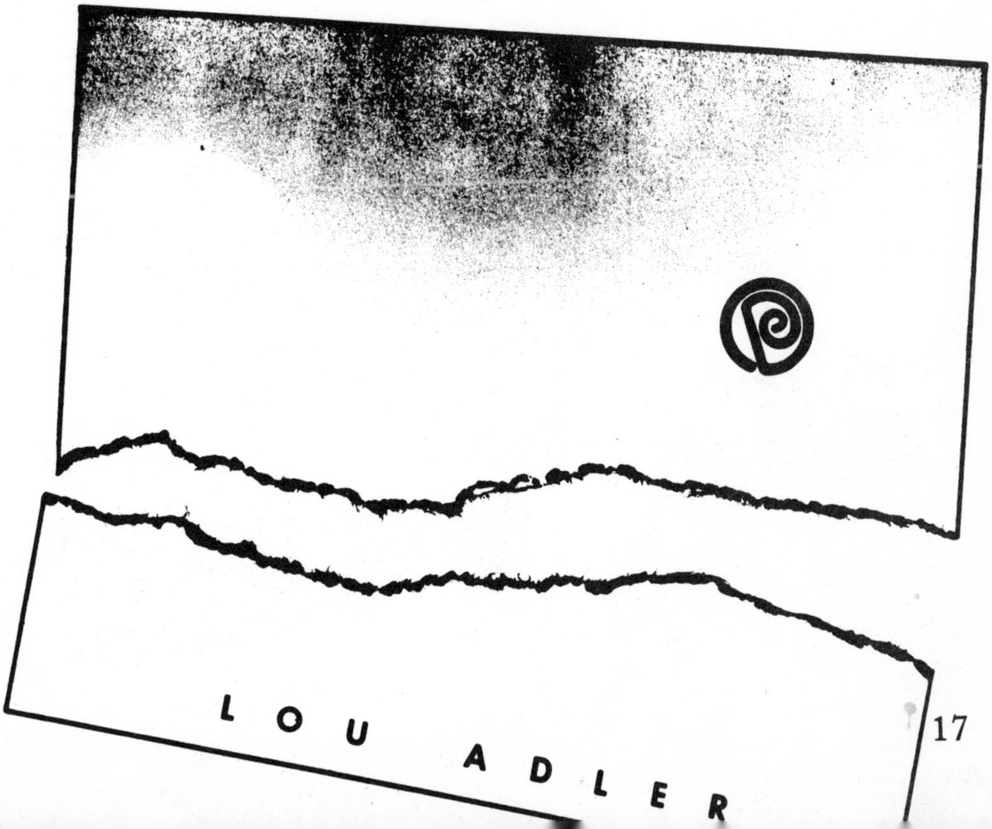

H
OD

LOU ADLER

Drawing by Dori Hartley

When Richard O'Brien wrote *They Came From Denton High* (which later became *The Rock Horroar Show,* which later became *The Rocky Horror Show)* in six months, he saw it as "something any ten-year-old could enjoy." But Michael White, a British producer and director whose previous ninety shows included *Sleuth* and *Oh! Calcutta,* saw possibilities in the musical satire, and mounted a stage production at the Royal Court's experimental Theatre Upstairs in June 1973. The show proved to be enormously popular. Soon it was moved from the 60-seat theater, first to a converted movie house, and later to the 500-seat King's Road Theatre. When the *London Evening Standard* took its 1973 annual poll of drama critics, *The Rocky Horror Show* was named best musical.

After the play had been running for about ten months, American producer and director Lou Adler saw it. At a party later the same evening he spoke with White about bringing the show to America. Adler had an impressive list of credits himself. He had co-produced the Monterey Pop Festival; his films included *Monterey Pop* and *Brewster McCloud;* and he owned Ode Records and the Roxy Theatre in Los Angeles. Adler envisioned the play as a film. An agreement was reached with Michael White in less than thirty-six hours.

First Adler booked *The Rocky Horror Show* into his Roxy Theatre. Then, when the show was running well, he pursued his film deal. He invited Gordon Stulberg, an attorney and then head of Twentieth Century-Fox to see the show. He did and so did his children. Adler loaded the audience with regulars—yes, there were *Rocky Horror* fans even before the movie—and Stulberg saw what happened. "I don't think he understood the motivation for the reaction," Adler recalls. "But from what he saw he was enthused enough to spend a million dollars."

Richard O'Brien, Patricia Quinn, and Little Nell were cast in the film to play the roles they had created for the original London production as Riff Raff, Magenta, and Columbia. Jonathan Adams, who had played the Narrator in the stage production, was cast as Dr. Everett Scott, while Meatloaf, who had played both Eddie and Dr. Scott on stage, retained the role of Eddie. Jim

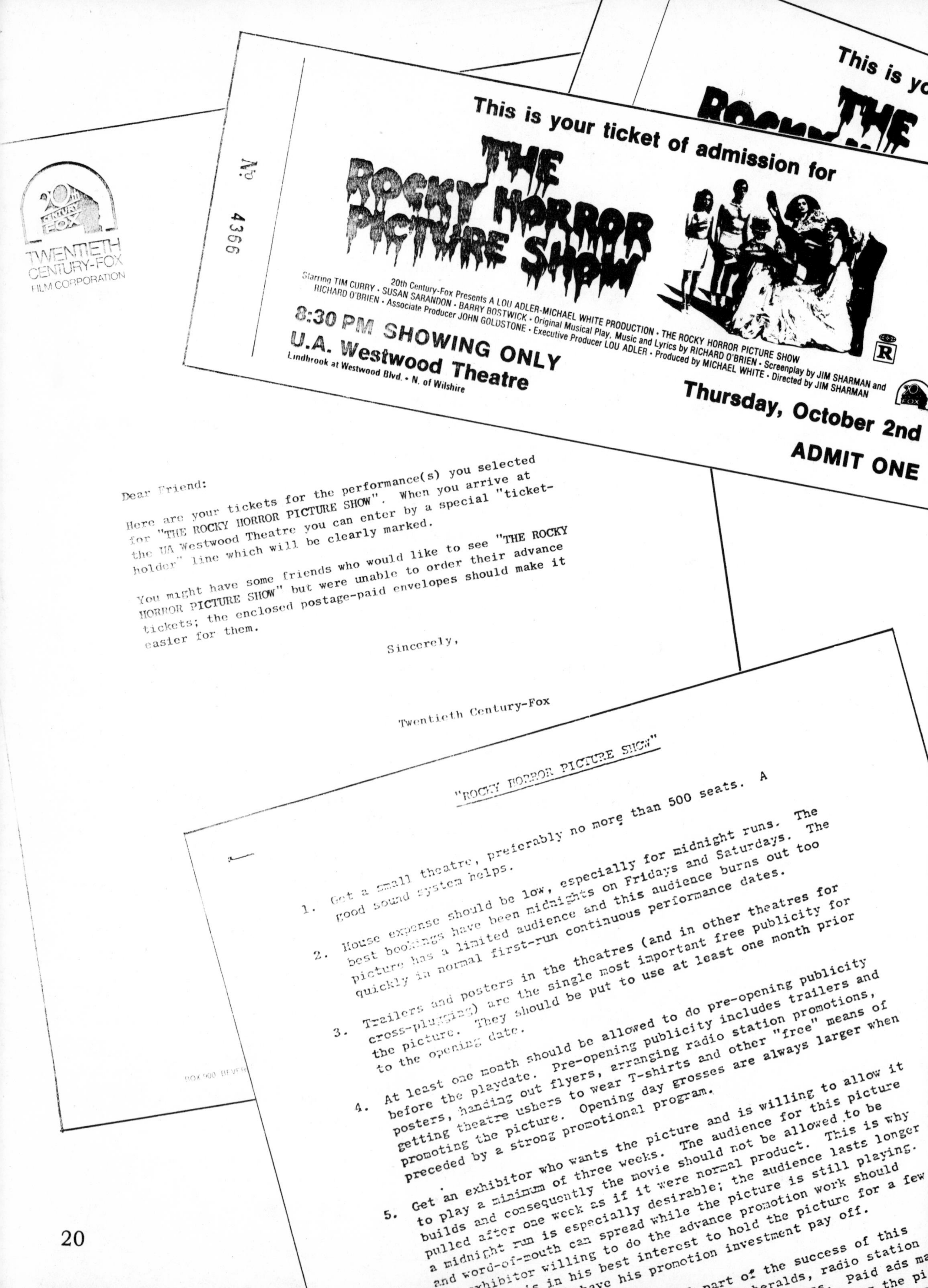

TWENTIETH CENTURY-FOX FILM CORPORATION

This is your ticket of admission for

THE ROCKY HORROR PICTURE SHOW

№ 4366

20th Century-Fox Presents A LOU ADLER-MICHAEL WHITE PRODUCTION · THE ROCKY HORROR PICTURE SHOW

Starring TIM CURRY · SUSAN SARANDON · BARRY BOSTWICK · Original Musical Play, Music and Lyrics by RICHARD O'BRIEN · Screenplay by JIM SHARMAN and RICHARD O'BRIEN · Associate Producer JOHN GOLDSTONE · Executive Producer LOU ADLER · Produced by MICHAEL WHITE · Directed by JIM SHARMAN

R

8:30 PM SHOWING ONLY

U.A. Westwood Theatre

Lindbrook at Westwood Blvd. · N. of Wilshire

Thursday, October 2nd

ADMIT ONE

Dear Friend:

Here are your tickets for the performance(s) you selected for "THE ROCKY HORROR PICTURE SHOW". When you arrive at the UA Westwood Theatre you can enter by a special "ticket-holder" line which will be clearly marked.

You might have some friends who would like to see "THE ROCKY HORROR PICTURE SHOW" but were unable to order their advance tickets; the enclosed postage-paid envelopes should make it easier for them.

Sincerely,

Twentieth Century-Fox

"ROCKY HORROR PICTURE SHOW"

1. Get a small theatre, preferably no more than 500 seats. A good sound system helps.

2. House expense should be low, especially for midnight runs. The best bookings have been midnights on Fridays and Saturdays. The picture has a limited audience and this audience burns out too quickly in normal first-run continuous performance dates.

3. Trailers and posters in the theatres (and in other theatres for cross-plugging) are the single most important free publicity for the picture. They should be put to use at least one month prior to the opening date.

4. At least one month should be allowed to do pre-opening publicity before the playdate. Pre-opening publicity includes trailers and posters, handing out flyers, arranging radio station promotions, getting theatre ushers to wear T-shirts and other "free" means of promoting the picture. Opening day grosses are always larger when preceded by a strong promotional program.

5. Get an exhibitor who wants the picture and is willing to allow it to play a minimum of three weeks. The audience for this picture builds and consequently the movie should not be allowed to be pulled after one week as if it were normal product. This is why a midnight run is especially desirable; the audience lasts longer and word-of-mouth can spread while the picture is still playing. Any exhibitor willing to do the advance promotion work should ... it is in his best interest to hold the picture for a few ... to have his promotion investment pay off.

... part of the success of this ... heralds, radio station ... success. Paid ads ma...

et of admission for

E ROCKY HORROR PICTURE SHOW
s by RICHARD O'BRIEN · Screenplay by JIM SHARMAN and
uced by MICHAEL WHITE · Directed by JIM SHARMAN

Friday, February 27, 1976

One Admission $2.50

TWENTIETH CENTURY-FOX LICENSING CORPORATION

TO: John Catanzaro

CC: Ashley Boone

Inter-office correspondence

FROM: Tim Deegan

DATE: October 10, 1975

SUBJECT: ROCKY HORROR PICTURE S

Dear John:

Under separate cover I have sent you one dozen sets of materials for the ROCKY HORROR PICTURE SHOW which include the "lips" poster, t-shirt, ads, the alternate ads, and samples of the postage-paid advance sale ticket envelope. Lynn Blackburn will turn over one dozen presskits from his supply.

The plan that was used in Los Angeles was basically three-fold and worked as follows:

1. Advance Ticket Sale: the object was to try to sell enough advance tickets to sell out the 8:30 show each night for the first week, and to do this without any of the traditional forms of advertising (such as order blanks in the Los Angeles Times, etc.). As it turned out, we were able to sell over 1500 tickets by this method which allowed us to run our first ad on opening day stating that the 8:30 show was sold out for both Friday and Saturday, the first two days of the engagement.

To achieve this advance sale, a group of college students was hired who distributed 100,000 return envelopes and one-quarter million handbills for an eight week period prior to opening day. These students work through a local agency and I would suggest that if this type of sale is tried in other cities, you get so... middleman who is dependable ... as a a lot of coord... required

John Catanzaro -2- October 10, 1975

The trailers were tagged with the opening date and advance sale information. Each lobby had a 40x60 for the picture showing artwork and a message about the advance sale. Each theatre had a large supply of return envelopes. The ushers at the UA Westwood started wearing the t-shirt five weeks pre-opening. Once the picture opened, UA used the trailers as cross-plugs.

3. Radio station promotion: A station (KWST-FM) ran a five week on air promotion in which they gave away three stages of items -- the t-shirts, tickets to a screening, and a very limited number of opening night tickets. Usually a station will work for a week or ten days ... this long promotion kept the title on ... an extremely long time. ... that they rece... away ... read ... of eff... prospe... deal t...

As far as s... of "No Scree... to the theat... even the pro... his party (p... for various s...

At the moment... movie. There... recorded album... Ode Records an... is an area tha... songs - and Ode... play the album.

TWENTIETH CENTURY-FOX LICENSING CORPORATION

Inter-office correspondence

FROM: Tim Deegan

DATE: February 5, 1976

SUBJECT: ROCKY HORROR PICTURE

TO: Ashley Boone

CC: Johnny Friedkin
David Forbes

Plans for "THE ROCKY HORROR PICTURE SHOW" in the next three dates (Columbus, Madison, and St. Louis) are progressing as follows:

I. COLUMBUS: Opening date is Friday, February 27th. Advance ticket sale has been in progress for two full weeks with disappointing results. To date, seventy envelopes have been received by the theatre but only three were for ticket orders...the rest were empty.

... Friday, February 6th, there will be a radio pro... ...gh opening day. The promotion will ... (they have a tape copy ... will follow

Sharman, who had directed the London stage version of *The Rocky Horror Show,* took on the film as well. Former architect Brian Thomson and costume designer Sue Blane amended their original stage designs for the movie. Pierre Laroche, the internationally famous makeup artist whose clients include both Mick and Bianca Jagger, designed the makeup for Tim Curry, the play's original Dr. Frank-N-Furter, and the Transylvanians. The movie was on its way.

Filming of *The Rocky Horror Picture Show* was completed in the spring of 1975. That July executive producer Lou Adler arranged a preview of the film for Twentieth Century-Fox, the movie's distributor, in Santa Barbara, California. The initial reaction was not good.

"The distribution people were far from thrilled by the film," says Twentieth Century's director of advertising, Tim Deegan. "But I could tell from watching the audience there was something in the picture that people liked, and I started looking at its possibilities." Deegan, then twenty-six years old and on his way up the Twentieth Century corporate ladder, had been assigned the job of promoting *Rocky Horror*. "Nobody else wanted it," he says. "I was the token youth, and I felt there was something to it. I knew it was going to work."

Adler thinks Deegan deserves much of the credit for the movie's continuing financial success. "The preview was not successful—in the sense that the whole audience didn't go for it. But some people were so enthusiastic they'd come up to us and say, 'Thanks for making the film.' So he stayed with it."

Sept. 5th.

Johnny: What about a trade and general press screening on "Rocky Horror Picture Show"? We're running out of time.

Jet

TWENTIETH CENTURY-FOX FILM CORPORATION

ASHLEY BOONE
ASSISTANT GENERAL SALES MANAGER
SUPERVISING CENTRAL, WESTERN DIVISION & LOS ANGELES



ALL BRANCH LETTER (con't.) October 17, 1975

The Los Angeles engagement was handled as such:

1. PRE-SELL

The pre-sell consisted of handing out self-addressed envelopes at bars, discottheques, colleges, restaurants, sporting events and rock concerts. (See envelope).

This began five weeks before opening day and was handled by groups of college kids who canvassed the greater Los Angeles area.

You will note, from the attached envelopes, that we asked people to send in money order or check for $3.00 a seat, giving us their first alternate choices of ... addressed to 20th ... The envelopes were ... the studio, because as ... the theatre, but I ... theatre be the

... the exact number of ... for the 8:30 PM ... o fulfill the request. ... ween receipt of an order ... tickets to the patron. ... Again, well enough ... d checks.

... 's name and the corres- ... ere was a dispute, we

... the number of tickets ... efore each performance ... ickets enabling them to

(No date - JK
Meetings there 4/11-13 75)

For Michael White.

SOME THOUGHTS ON PROMOTION & DISTRIBUTION OF 'ROCKY HORROR PICTURE SHOW'.

It would seem from the great success of the initial undersell on the stage version which you accomplished in London and the considerably less successful attempt at oversell in New York that the question of how the work is presented to the public is critical to its finding the right audience. In view of this I would like to proffer the following thoughts on the subject for the consideration of yourself and the respective executives at Twentieth.

CINEMA

Like many so-called 'cult' movies ROCKY has always succeeded when placed in an accessible but not obviously commercial or super-trendy venue. This allows its supporters initial access and the size of the venue allows a long run to enable its audience to spread to a general public proportion. Of the possible cinemas in London the best would seem the ODEON HAYMARKET. This cinema also has the advantage of fantastic sound and as 80% of the fi... is music this is a vital factor. I am not sure if th... Dolby or not but it is a simple con... would welcome as th... projection of their... Indeed we should en... and a list from the... might save a lot of... optical being the on...

DATE

As a personal hunch I... musical of the sevent... JULY 2nd. which just... .......OH WELL- it's...

POSTERS & PUBLICITY

While eschewing over-... aspects i.e. SPOOF (we... its audience), HORROR... of publicity whic will... those (the majority)... correctly then it can... the wrong image then it... Following conversations... revelations from the pr... of the Paradise I had th... 1. The logo image used f... film as being to enigmat... far more literal in the ...

The Showmandiser, October 27, 1975
(Reprinted with permission)

BOXOFFICE Showmandiser

- ADLINES & EXPLOITIPS
- ALPHABETICAL INDEX
- EXHIBITOR HAS HIS SAY
- FEATURE RELEASE CHART
- FEATURE REVIEW DIGEST
- SHORTS RELEASE CHART
- SHORT SUBJECT REVIEWS
- REVIEWS OF FEATURES
- SHOWMANDISING IDEAS

THE GUIDE TO BETTER BOOKING AND BUSINESS-BUILDING

# Use Advance Ticket Sales, Costume Party Previews To Prime Bookings of 'Rocky Horror Picture Show'

## Six performances sell out during first three days in LA; unusual regalia helps stir Texas interest

Solid promotional campaigns, carefully planned and carried out, are meeting with great success in priming markets for engagements of "The Rocky Horror Picture Show," a Lou Adler-Michael White ... distributed by 20th Cen... the

lated one-quarter of a million flyers eight weeks ahead of the opening. They hit movie lines, concerts, clubs, beaches and many other gathering spots where Fox hoped to reach the young, potential audience. Along with the handbills, the group also passed out 100,000 postage-paid return envelopes ... opportunity to buy ad...

representative Daniel Saez, the to-do ... Austin began with posting clipped o... sheets and window cards at constructi... sites, restaurants, "head shops" and ot... spots frequented by the young, colle... age crowd. Displays were set up also ... record stores, while bartenders at var... lounges were given "Rocky" T-shirts ... wear. Augmenting the one-sheets were ... alds that were passed out at football g... and in the area surrounding the theat...

A tie-in with radio KLBJ involv... "Time Warp" dance contest one ev... with the costume contest at the ... on the next. The static ...

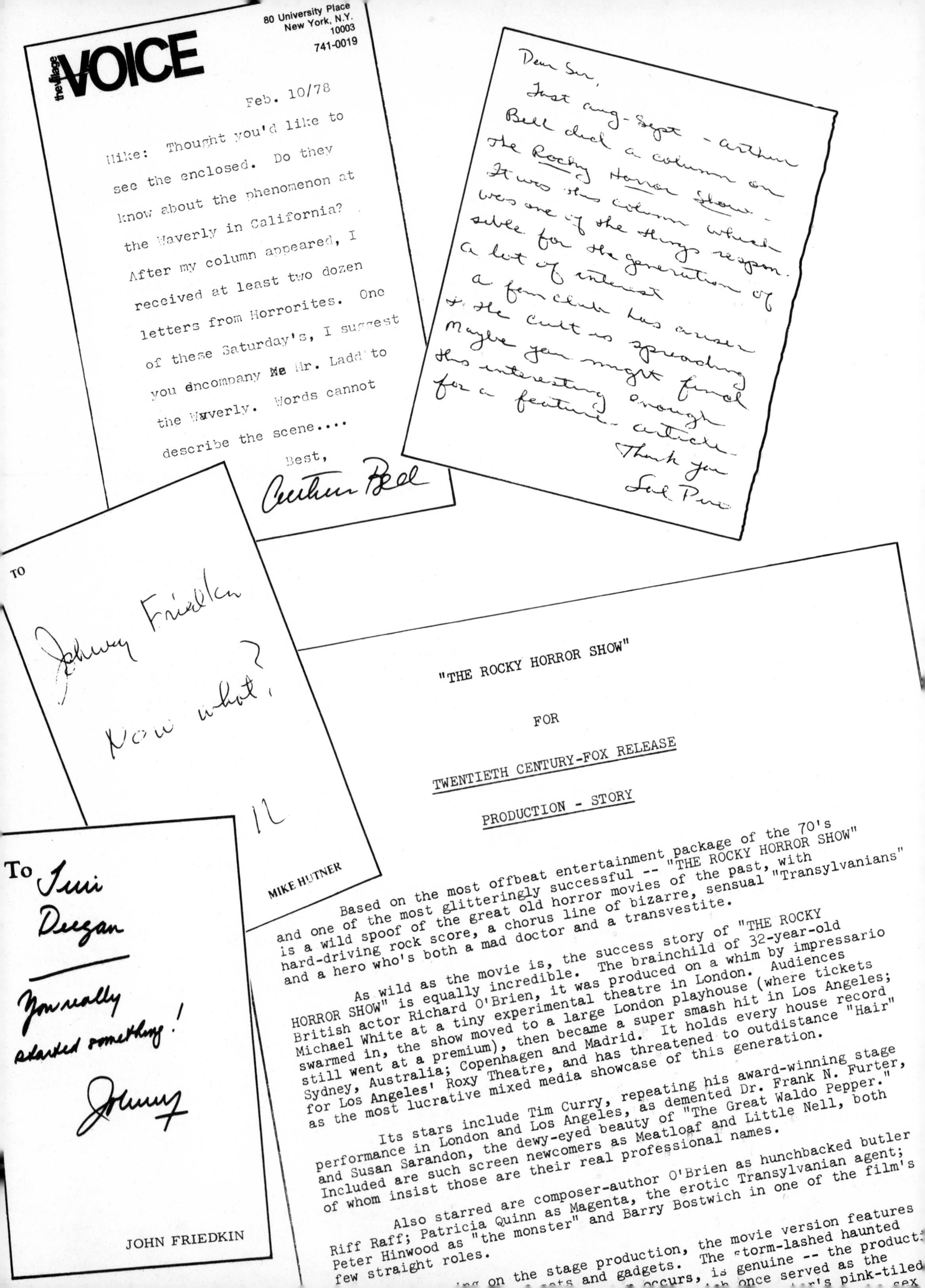

the Village VOICE

80 University Place
New York, N.Y.
10003
741-0019

Feb. 10/78

Mike: Thought you'd like to see the enclosed. Do they know about the phenomenon at the Waverly in California? After my column appeared, I received at least two dozen letters from Horrorites. One of these Saturday's, I suggest you accompany Mr. Ladd to the Waverly. Words cannot describe the scene....

Best,

Arthur Bell

---

Dear Sir,

Last Aug-Sept - Arthur Bell did a column on The Rocky Horror Show. It was this column which was one of the things responsible for the generation of a lot of interest

a fan club has arisen

& the cult is spreading

Maybe you might find this interesting enough for a feature article.

Thank you

Sal Piro

---

TO

Johnny Friedkin

Now what?

M

MIKE HUTNER

---

To Terri Deegan

You really started something!

Johnny

JOHN FRIEDKIN

---

"THE ROCKY HORROR SHOW"

FOR

TWENTIETH CENTURY-FOX RELEASE

PRODUCTION - STORY

Based on the most offbeat entertainment package of the 70's and one of the most glitteringly successful -- "THE ROCKY HORROR SHOW" is a wild spoof of the great old horror movies of the past, with hard-driving rock score, a chorus line of bizarre, sensual "Transylvanians" and a hero who's both a mad doctor and a transvestite.

As wild as the movie is, the success story of "THE ROCKY HORROR SHOW" is equally incredible. The brainchild of 32-year-old British actor Richard O'Brien, it was produced on a whim by impressario Michael White at a tiny experimental theatre in London. Audiences swarmed in, the show moved to a large London playhouse (where tickets still went at a premium), then became a super smash hit in Los Angeles; Sydney, Australia; Copenhagen and Madrid. It holds every house record for Los Angeles' Roxy Theatre, and has threatened to outdistance "Hair" as the most lucrative mixed media showcase of this generation.

Its stars include Tim Curry, repeating his award-winning stage performance in London and Los Angeles, as demented Dr. Frank N. Furter, and Susan Sarandon, the dewy-eyed beauty of "The Great Waldo Pepper." Included are such screen newcomers as Meatloaf and Little Nell, both of whom insist those are their real professional names.

Also starred are composer-author O'Brien as hunchbacked butler Riff Raff; Patricia Quinn as Magenta, the erotic Transylvanian agent; Peter Hinwood as "the monster" and Barry Bostwich in one of the film's few straight roles.

...ing on the stage production, the movie version features ... sets and gadgets. The storm-lashed haunted ... occurs, is genuine -- the producti... once served as the ...'s pink-tiled ... sex

The picture had its official opening at the United Artists Theatre in Westwood, Los Angeles, on September 26, 1975. Rated R (Restricted), it ran on a normal feature film schedule, with continuous performances through the afternoons and evenings. At the Westwood, the film sold out regularly. But when Deegan checked the returns on other openings around the country, he found that Los Angeles was the exception. In most cities, he says, "the movie bombed its first time out. It was a disaster." Adler agrees: "It wasn't a stiff, but it stiffed."

Both Deegan and Adler began to drop in at the UA Westwood almost every day after work to mingle with the crowds and find out what was responsible for the film's success there. They discovered something they had never found before in the movie business. Not only was the theater selling out every night, but many of the *same people* were returning every night. And they were singing the songs along with the characters on the screen. "I could see that the Westwood dates worked because some people were clearly identifying with the movie," Deegan says, "and I began to see a real hard-core audience developing."

The Westwood experience was being repeated on a smaller scale in a few other cities. But not even the theater owners knew what to make of their audiences. "You could go blind listening to the first exhibitors," Adler says. "They'd say, 'Nothing's happening. The theatre seats 800 and we're only getting fifty people.' What they didn't tell us was that in a lot of those cities it was the *same* fifty people who came back every week."

Meanwhile, at Twentieth Century, Deegan called Bill Quigley of the Walter Reade Theatre organization in New York. Quigley had run midnight shows at his theaters before, and when Deegan told him what was happening at Westwood, the two men started mapping out a midnight booking and special promotion for New York. "I told him I wanted a theater that would hold the film for a month or six weeks," Deegan says. "I felt that if people could discover the film on its own, without hype or ads or promo, they would be overtaken by what they had discovered, and by the fact that they had discovered it. Being the discoverers themselves, they would promote the film on their own by word-of-mouth."

This approach was totally different from the standard sort of movie hype which, Deegan says, "is all manufactured bullshit. *The Rocky Horror Picture Show* taught me that hype is not always the answer. You can sell anything with hype. Letting people discover something for themselves is far more rewarding."

Meanwhile, Adler's own staff was at work charting the promotion that *would* take place: John Beug handled graphics while Marshall Blondstein worked on radio promotion. The film was advertised somewhat in its early days, although today the budget for all of New York City, where *Rocky Horror* plays at two theaters at once, is only slightly more than $50 per week, compared with about $30,000 a week for most movies in New York. Adler had devised both famous *Rocky Horror* slogans: "A Different Set of Jaws" and "Another Kind of Rocky." At first, local exhibitors, the people who operate the theaters, used the ads to chase their audiences. They simply did not know what to do with this highly unusual film. If an exhibitor was used to *Sound of Music* audiences or John Wayne fans looking for *True Grit,* he had to think differently in order to appreciate what *Rocky Horror* meant to its small but dedicated and growing following. The exhibitors "tried to be bizarre," Adler says, "but you cannot be more bizarre than this film, and you cannot be more bizarre than its real audience. So anything they tried was lame compared to the picture. The film just had to go out and find its audience."

And find it it did. The underground grew. Adler remembers, "We'd get letters from areas where the film wasn't playing. The letter would say something like, 'My cousin told me about *The Rocky Horror Picture Show* and I went to Austin to see it and I loved it. How can we get it in Cleveland?'"

The movie officially broke into the midnight circuit at the Waverly Theater in New York City on April 1, 1976. A few weeks after that it opened at the Riverside II in Austin, Texas. One by one, as Deegan and other executives at Twentieth Century showed those theaters' box office figures to exhibitors in Philadelphia, New Brunswick, Dallas, Phoenix, Kansas City, the promoters began to catch on: It wasn't that *Rocky Horror* was doomed to the celluloid scrap heap. It was just that, as it was a

*Rocky Horror* goes over big in South Africa.

JET FORE, STUDIO PUBLICITY MANAGER • BOX 900, BEVERLY HILLS, CALIFORNIA 90213 / (213) 277-2211

TWENTIETH CENTURY-FOX
FEATURE FILM DIVISION

5/28/76

JOHANNESBURG, SOUTH AFRICA -- "The Rocky Horror Picture Show," 20th Century-Fox's madcap rock film adventure, has proven to be the most successful American film released in this country since the advent of television.

In 12 weeks at the Highpoint Theatre, Johannesburg, six weeks in Cape Town and four weeks in Durban, the picture has racked up a phenomenal boxoffice gross of $162,150.

All runs have continued and the ... now carrying over ... ers is ... r- ... and ... ry ... nal ... er

AMES DEAN CREATED A CULT.
HERE WAS 'CABARET' AND 'GATSBY'
OW FREAKY FRANK HAS BEEN
CKING JO'BURG FOR 28 WEEKS!

MISS CATHY BECK HAS SEEN IT 81 TIMES AND SAYS: "IT'S A FANTASTIC MOVIE, I SEE SOMETHING NEW IN IT EVERYTIME"
-SUNDAY EXPRESS (AUG. 8)

PHOTOGRAPH BY DANIE COETZER

E ROCKY HORROR PICTURE SHOW

YTHING YOU'VE HEARD ABOUT IT IS TRUE.

AT KINE PREMIERE JHB. & TRANSVALIA PRETORIA

NO PERSONS 4-18

KINEKOR The Entertainers

Can't you keep this out of my publicity breaks — Bob

Copyright © by The Family Circle, Inc

*9. **Shaun Cassidy**, Shaun Cassidy. Old-style rock and roll geared to kids who don't remember the original.
*10. **Foreigner**, Foreigner. Clean and driving rock.

*an especially fast-selling record

## Books (nonfiction)

(Current best sellers according to *The New York Times*)

1. **The Book of Lists**, by David Wallechinsky, Irving Wall...

...ngs Wise and Wonderful, by ...erriot (St. Martin's Press, ...e tales of a Yorkshire vet.

...nagerial Woman, by ...Hennig and Anne Jardim ...ess/Doubleday, $7.95). ...ead.

...h Between the Seas, by ...llough (Simon & Schuster, ...e Panama Canal story.

# ADVANCE NOTICE

## Off the record

Even posthumously, Elvis sells. *Moody Blue*, his last album, zipped from No. 67 to No. 5 in just one week. RCA can't keep up with demand. ... On the rise is ...a Sea, Firefall's ...eatures a soft coun... ...keting up the ...ters, whose single, ...ng the album to the ...'s new change-of- ...asy When You Lay ...s the fastest-rising ... *Before We* ...*rrupted*, the ...he original Ani... ...hat promises to ...t of noise in the ...nces are rush- ...they've heard ...g spots, ...otten airplay or ...are no ...irectly ...ince I ...the fe ...es and ...20,00 ...w York ...thm-a ...y rece ...AM sta ...The Bi ...AM, h ...Teleph ...st. An ...wave's ...Too Ho

out in early October. Diane Keaton, hailed as the next Katharine Hepburn, is powerful in the leading role. ...

Meanwhile, as 20th Century-Fox counts the take from Star Wars, another hit is quietly building for Fox. *The Rocky Horror Picture Show*, a camp comedy, has been playing to enthusiastic audiences in Greenwich Village-type areas around the country for over a year. Every large city in the United States is growing its own *Rocky Show* cult. When it's released as a regular feature in college towns, a whole new wave of *Rocky Show* freaks seems probable.

## In print

Where have all the Patty Hearst books gone? F. Lee Bailey, who parlayed his defeat in the case int...

THE ROCKY HORROR PICTURE SHOW
a different set of jaws.
THEATRE

## Around the reel

With a strong performance by Jane Fonda, Lillian Hellman's *Julia* promises to be one of the year's finest movies. Jason Robards stars as the young Dashiell Hammett. ... Singles bars may empty out, but theaters should fill up when the screen adaptation of *Looking for Mr. Goodbar* comes

US magazine, October 4, 1977.
(Copyright © by the Family Circle, Inc.
Reprinted with permission)



## 'Rocky Horror' continues to roll with $3 mil in '78

By ROGER CELS

"The Rocky Horror Picture Show" continues to defy the law of diminishing returns, earning just under $3 million in film rentals to 20th Century-Fox during 1978 while playing midnight shows on Fridays and Saturdays only.

The four-year-old film earned only around $1 million in rentals in its initial release, which was of the wide multiple variety, and was subsequently shelved by 20th-Fox.

However, a loyal following among

— continued on page 13

## 'Rocky Horror'

continued from page 1 —

the younger crowd kept the picture alive in scattered locations and 35 prints were working by the first of this year.

These engagements met with such success that 20th-Fox decided to broaden the release to the point where some 200 houses were showing the film by mid-October, all on Friday and Saturday nights only.

With the additional theatres, rentals have increased proportionately. From a total of $15,000 from 35 situations for the first week of the year, rentals peaked at $120,000 in 202 theatres during Thanksgiving Day and 20th-Fox's senior vp domestic marketing Ashley Boone noted that the picture has not dipped below the $100,000 mark for any week since the beginning of October.

Enlarging the success of "Rocky Horror" is the fact that these numbers have come from midnight shows at which the ticket price is normally lower than regular evening performances.

The Hollywood Reporter, January 24, 1979; reprinted...

**University of Pittsburgh**
DEPARTMENT OF SPEECH AND THEATRE ARTS
The University Theatre

Tim can you handle

February 22, 1979.

Mr. Leonard Kroll
Executive Supervisor
Feature Post Production
20th Century-Fox Film Corporation
Box 900
Beverly Hills, CA 90213

Dear Mr. Kroll:

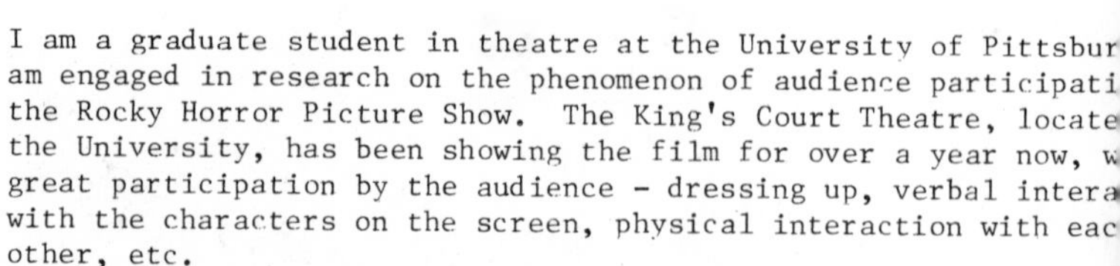

I am a graduate student in theatre at the University of Pittsbur... am engaged in research on the phenomenon of audience participati... the Rocky Horror Picture Show. The King's Court Theatre, locate... the University, has been showing the film for over a year now, w... great participation by the audience - dressing up, verbal intera... with the characters on the screen, physical interaction with eac... other, etc.

If you know of any other places where the film is being shown or... been shown, I would appreciate yorusending me as much informatio... about audience reactions and interactins as possible, including... data as times and dates of showings, length of run, estimated si... audience (plus any other audience statistics such as age, demogr... type, etc.). Also, type of location - college, community, youth... commercial, etc. and whether the audience response is spontaneou... supported by the theatre operator; what type of response it is (... the same every night? a ritual?), commentary from local news med... In short, everything you can think of!

Thank you for your help. I eagerly await your reply.

To

Tim Deegan—

Your first New Year's blessing

M

MIKE HUTNER

Dear,

Gordon Armstrong,

I am a Rocky Horror fan and am most fascinated with Tim Curry (Frank-n-furter) I have found him to be a fascinating Actor not because of his sexyness, (I guess it helps) but because he puts feeling into what he does. I am sure no matter what kind of acting he does he will always keep my interest, because of his strong will for acting and his magnificent voice that's strong and sexy. I mean this sincerely. I have seen actors and singers I have liked, but I really enjoy Tim Curry.

I don't think I'll ever be as fortunate as you to meet him, but it really doesn't matter as long as he keeps going strong I know I will.

I was a li[...] with his album "[...] There was only t[...] joyed; "Birds of a[...] tin, but I wish[...] of luck in everything an[...] sure he has inspired many people who are going for an acting career. I know he has inspired me.

I only ask one thing from you if you can, since I suppose you have met or have talked to Tim Curry if you could ask him for an autograph picture of himself and that he would send it to me. It's true I could buy one, but it's not the same. It would mean so much ~~its~~ more if it were from him. This would be deeply appreciated.

over

Sincerely—Lovingly
Yours

Jacqueline Mjurzowski

different kind of movie, it had to attract a different kind of audience. Four years after its slow start, *The Rocky Horror Picture Show* plays at well over 200 theaters across the nation and in Canada. Although the movie is a hit in the big cities such as New York, Austin, Los Angeles, Toronto, and Philadelphia, it also has run for more than a year in Nyack, New York; Kalamazoo, Michigan; Tallahassee, Florida; Petaluma, California; and Denton, Texas. It is enjoying successful midnight runs in Bozeman, Montana; Oswego, New York; Stamford, Connecticut; Hancock, Wisconsin; and Lake Charles, Louisiana. It seems that

MUSIC FAIR L BALLIN
32 EAST 57 ST
NEW YORK NY 10022

4-059658E223 08/11/78 ICS IPMMTZZ CSP LSAB
2127592810 MGM TDMT NEW YORK NY 100 08-11 0414P EST

ODE RECORDS
1416 NORTH LABREA AVE
LOS ANGELES CA 90020

WOULD LIKE TO PRESENT THE ROCKY HORROR SHOW FOR CHRISTMAS AT THE WESTBURY MUSIC FAIR AND POSSIBLY VALLEY FORGE MUSIC FAIR CAN WE OBTAIN THE RIGHTS SCRIPTS AND ORCHESTRATION FROM YOU

BILL TEUTEBERG
MUSIC FAIR

16:14 EST

MGMCOMP MGM

NOVEMBER 28, 1975

CHARGE: ROCKY HORROR PICTURE SHOW 1340-42

To: EDDIE PATMAN
CENTFOX
LONDON (ENGLAND)

UNDERSTAND YOU NOW OPENING ROCKY HORROR SYDNEY AT ASCOT FOR CHRISTMAS. PLEASE SEND CAMPAIGN DETAILS INCLUDING OPENING DATE AND SEATING CAPACITY ASCOT. THANKS.

TIM DEEGAN

*Rocky Horror* fans exist pretty much everywhere, and many more are only waiting for the film to open nearby to start doing the Time Warp in their own home towns.

Twentieth Century-Fox cultivated the midnight showings for *Rocky Horror* because four years ago that was the only way the movie could get any playdates. The company had never done anything like it before and Deegan found it hard to crack tradition, but the film's success has changed the attitudes of both exhibitors and key personnel at Twentieth Century. Now exhibitors are lined up waiting for new prints of the picture, and Twentieth Century has decided to concentrate on the idea of midnight bookings—what *Newseek* magazine called "the werewolf circuit."

"One of the things we've learned from *Rocky Horror* is not to always hurry," Deegan says. "If you're not looking for a fast buck, and you can keep costs down, and you can take a year or more, something can develop." No one could have predicted the Austin, Texas, opening, for example, when Lou Adler and Tim Curry were made honorary citizens of the city and were presented with certificates to that effect by the mayor of Austin—who was dressed in full *Rocky Horror* costume and makeup.

And, bizarre as the film may appear to some conservative members of society, no one could have predicted the little boardroom drama that ensued when Twentieth Century made a short, coming-attraction trailer to expose *Rocky Horror* to its potential audience. The trailer opened with the famous lips saying, "Twentieth Century-Fox has brought you all sorts of movies, but Twentieth Century-Fox has never brought you anything like *The Rocky Horror Picture Show*." Dennis Stanfill, president and chairman of the board at Twentieth Century, a quiet financial genius, highly regarded by his employees, but not your basic *Rocky Horror* fan, said, "Remove those lewd, lascivious lips mouthing the words 'Twentieth Century-Fox' immediately!"

"When he said that I thought the picture was dead," Deegan says. But it wasn't. Not by a long shot, because Lou Adler was about to join forces with Deegan.

See Tim Curry in perso..
Tomorrow at 8:00 P.M. at U.A. Westwood
unveiling his own larger-than-life 16 footer.
He's the hero – that's right, the hero!!
See Tim Curry as Dr. Frank N. Furter in
THE ROCKY HORROR PICTURE SHOW
20th Century-Fox Presents
A LOU ADLER · MICHAEL WHITE PRODUCTION
THE ROCKY HORROR PICTURE SHOW
Starring TIM CURRY • SUSAN SARANDON • BARRY BOSTWICK
Original Musical Play, Music and Lyrics by RICHARD O'BRIEN
Screenplay by JIM SHARMAN and RICHARD O'BRIEN • Associate Producer JOHN GOLDSTONE
Executive Producer LOU ADLER • Produced by MICHAEL WHITE
Directed by JIM SHARMAN
20th Century Fox
RESTRICTED
WESTWOOD
Blvd. 477-0575
P.M.
Fri. & Sat.
THE ROCKY HORROR PICTURE SHOW
a different set of jaws.
R
THEATRE
ROC
PIC
R
STOP PRESS!
ROCKY'S GOT A NEW HOME!
HE'S NOW AT THE KINE PREMIERE JEPPE STREET
FOR 16th JO'BURG WEEK
THE ROCKY HORROR


Cleveland . . . Brad Majors and Janet Weiss (top) of Denton, Ohio unexpectedly had their lives changed overnight when they sought help from Dr. Frank N. Furter after their car had a flat tire near Furter's castle in central Ohio. Furter, who does not drive, did not have the tools to change the flat but was able, by using his patented "Medusa Transducer" (center) to change Brad and Janet into beings who no longer needed a car. Majors and Weiss (bottom) have been signed by a Hollywood studio to play themselves in their autobiography of transformation which will be called "The Rocky Horror Picture Show".

S'wonderful, S'marvelous
A Great Big Production Over Seduction
Lucy - Mask here on all similar shots! Sandy
An Radio Pictur
HE HORROR RE SHOW
20th CENTURY FOX
Presented by JOHN MANDRACCHIA & PAUL SPIEGEL
TTENTION
ROCKY HORROR FANS!!!
Come To "THE ROCKY HORROR SHOW" Convention
Monday Night — February 20t
at the
CALDERONE CONCERT HALL
145 N. Franklin St. • Hempstead, L.I.
y to get to by
n, car, or bus.
He's the hero - that's ri
the hero!!
An Evening to Remember
A Musical Action Packed
Due to the large number of Rocky Horror Fans we suggest you buy your tickets immediately!
SEE LIVE IN PERS
RICHARD O'BRIEN (Rif
PATRICIA QUINN (Mag
LITTLE NELL (Columbi
Also in person another
name cannot b
2nd ANNUAL
MUSIC! GUESTS! FUN!
ROCKY HORROR
BIRTHDAY PARTY & COSTUME BA

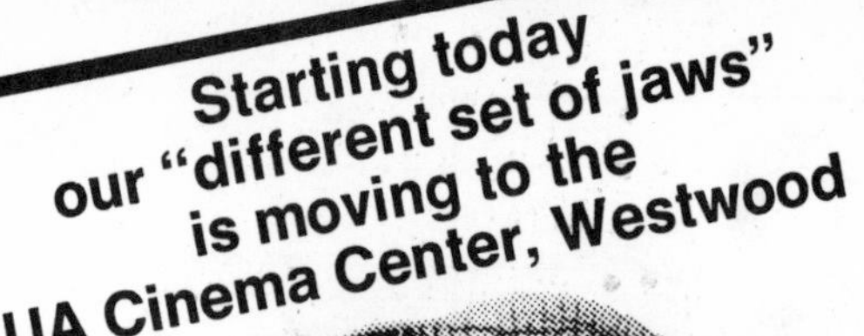

Starting today
our "different set of jaws"
is moving to the
UA Cinema Center, Westwood

THE ROCKY HORROR PICTURE SHOW

20th Century Fox

R

UA Cinema Center 474-4165
Westwood Blvd. 1 Block South of Wilshire
Daily 1:30 • 3:10 • 4:55 • 6:35 • 8:20 & 10:05

S'Wonderful! S'Marvellous!
S'Outrageous!
S'Weird!

THE ROCKY HORROR PICTURE SHOW

AA

The smash hit show is now a super musical movie.

RELEASED BY FOX-RANK DISTRIBUTORS

EXCLUSIVELY AT THE RIALTO
COVENTRY ST
437 3488
...US AND LEICESTER SQUARE

Programmes (incl. Sunday)
1.30, 3.35, 5.50, 8,15.
Late Show FRIDAY & SATURDAY 11.00

PRESIDIO ENTERPRISES, INC.

5840 BALCONES DRIVE, SUITE 100, AUSTIN, TEXAS 78731

TELEPHONE 512/454-0481

August 30, 1976

Mr. Pat Dwyer
Twentieth Century-Fox
1400 S. Griffin
Dallas, Texas 75215

Dear Pat:

Dan Saez suggested that I bring to your attention the fact that "Rocky Horror Picture Show" is going into its 15th week, doing sell-out business at midnight showin at the Riverside Twin Cinema.

Admittedly, $500 is not a monster gross for a picture but it is not bad considering we only have two shows and a 200 seat auditorium and a $1.25 ticket price, and less than $15 per week advertising the f...

The picture g...
we will...

ROCKY HORROR PICTURE SHOW

STARTING DATES FOR ANNIVERSARIES

| | |
|---|---|
| AUSTIN | 5-12-76 |
| DALLAS | 4-29-77 |
| HOUSTON | 6-11-77 |
| DENVER | 6-25-77 |
| SEATTLE | 7-29-77 |
| SAN FRANCISCO | 8-19-77 |
| BERKELEY | 9-23-77 |
| MIAMI | 7-02-77 |
| COLUMBUS | 6-10-77 |

"Working with Lou was great," Deegan says. "We could relate." At the first meeting between Lou Adler and the distribution executives at Twentieth Century, nobody recognized the lean, bearded producer when he arrived in tennis shoes and a baseball cap. Someone who was looking directly at him said, "Lou Adler is late for the meeting." Adler later asked Deegan, "How did you like the movie?"

Deegan replied, "I hate it."

"Good," Adler responded, "you can be objective about the selling of the film."

Perhaps part of the reason the two men could relate was that they both recognized from the start that *Rocky Horror* was special in a special way. Deegan admits he does not know why fans go to see the film, but he stands by them completely, and has resisted the idea of putting the film back into general release. "It's a tribute to the fans that the movie is what it is," he says. "The magic would end in thirty days if it crossed over into first run. It's too special a picture in terms of what it presents. It's too rich for regular consumption, it offers too much. It would be overpowering and intimidating to a regular audience that walked in off the street without knowing anything about it. And that makes it special to like it. If you want to see *Rocky Horror,* you've got to see it at midnight."

Adler agrees with Deegan. "There's no reason to saturate it, to take it away from the people it belongs to. I think *Rocky Horror* fans are the happiest people in the world. Every Friday and Saturday night they have some place to go where they can be with 300 people they like, and have a good time."

The movie has had a monumental effect on some of its fans: They say it has changed their lives. *Rocky Horror* is just outrageous enough so that some people who thought of themselves as outsiders could shine by association with the film. Adler notes of the movie's early fans, "They may have been outcasts in the sense that they didn't have the same joys, or seek the same outlets—sports or music or romance or whatever—as other people. They found *their* outlet in *The Rocky Horror Picture Show.* And they are the people who are writing the scripts for the audience now, creating a lot of the atmosphere. They are stars."

For Deegan, "The film was a breakthrough and a breakout. It turned out to be a lot of fun."

Although the word "cult" reportedly never came up in the preparation or early marketing of *Rocky Horror,* the phenomenal following the movie has achieved can hardly be understood in any other terms. Partly, cult overtones developed because at least to some degree the film does speak to people who see themselves as outsiders to begin with—as outré potentates like Frank, or covert henchmen like Riff Raff. But then, as Adler observes, "There are lots of Brads and Janets in the audience too."

Of course, we're all Brads and Janets when we see *Rocky Horror* for the first time. But not when we walk out after the movie; perhaps that's why some of the best audience lines are directed at Brad and Janet. A lot of *Rocky Horror* fans do *not* see themselves as outsiders. They've been straight-laced, upstanding

folk and feel it's time to step into another kind of world, another kind of life. Coming to see *Rocky Horror* is one simple, inexpensive, and safe way to take that step. It's a way to join a different kind of family. Because this phenomenon is not just a movie. For many fans, it's home.

The film's appeal may be broader than anyone outside the phenomenon realizes. The fantasy world of science fiction, do-it-yourself monsters, and the haunted house belong to all of us at some time. Richard O'Brien succeeded in writing a script, lyrics, and music that *can* be enjoyed by any ten-year-old, and yet retains an appeal for adults after multiple screenings. Kids and adults alike take pleasure in the classically stylized sets, costuming, and makeup, and the clearly defined heroes and heroines. And for that, Adler expresses great esteem for the core group that created the show: Richard O'Brien, Jim Sharman, Brian Thomson, and Sue Blane. "They created *Rocky Horror;*

they think *Rocky Horror*. If someone else had created it, I believe they still would be in the audience every Friday and Saturday night dressed up and doing the Time Warp. They created something they truly love, and they are avid *Rocky Horror* fans. They are the first four members of the cult."

In olden days people used to show their allegiances by wearing coats of arms on their shields or garments. In more recent times we hoist our flags up poles to announce which side we're on, or we wear the appropriate T-shirts. We also show the world where our hearts are by eating, drinking, wearing, carrying, reading, watching, playing with, and listening to products that reflect our devotion to our heroes and the places they have in our lives.

Conferring between scenes (*left to right*): cinematographer Peter Suschitzky; camera operator Denis Lewiston; and director Jim Sharman.

*Rocky Horror* has spawned a whole new set of heroes, and the popularity of those heroes and the movie itself have, in turn, spawned dozens of ideas for *Rocky Horror* paraphernalia. Some tie-in products are being sold in stores and on the street today; more will show up as time goes by; some will never come to market.

Because Twentieth Century is a huge corporation, and because *Rocky Horror* is—in its way—a hugely successful film, some people have assumed that only large companies can acquire tie-in merchandise licenses for products connected with the movie.

Not so, says Rand Marlis, Twentieth Century–Fox executive in charge of merchandizing. He has, in fact, been quite successful in his dealings with some of the most unlikely candidates—not

Director Jim Sharman on the set with design consultant Brian Thomson

the "big" names but rather those prospective licensees whose enthusiasm is combined with proposals for the best possible products. It seems, then, that even where big business is concerned, *Rocky Horror* very much belongs to the fans. "It's very rewarding for me to deal with people like that," says Marlis.

According to Marlis, some fans, theater owners, and manufacturers feel that they are the prime movers behind the *Rocky Horror* phenomenon, and are responsible for instigating the movement. Like many other people, places, and things that were "discovered," the movie has generated a great deal of possessiveness. Yet the success of *Rocky Horror* merchandise, like the success of the film itself, springs first from the spontaneous excitement of the fans themselves.

For that reason, licensing *Rocky Horror* merchandise requires a unique approach to marketing that reflects Tim Deegan's approach to promoting the movie. "It's unlike any other film we've ever had to deal with," Marlis notes, "because the movie was made by the fans. We can't force-feed them, so we keep in touch with them." Twentieth Century has, in fact, rejected the ideas of *Rocky Horror* rolling papers, soap, matchbook covers, video cassettes, bumper stickers, key chains, mirrors, and underwear. But they have granted licenses to some enterprising fans.

Buttons have been licensed to A & B Creations, named for Alba and Betty, two of the early *Rocky Horror* fans at New York's Waverly Theater. A & B Creations will do a first edition of six separate button designs, all two and a half inches in diameter, in full color.

Crabwalk's calendar for 1980, already on sale, is in full color, and features dripping blood indicating special *Rocky Horror* days. The calendar includes scenes from the movie with some dialogue and notes by Sal Piro, president of the National *Rocky Horror* Fan Club.

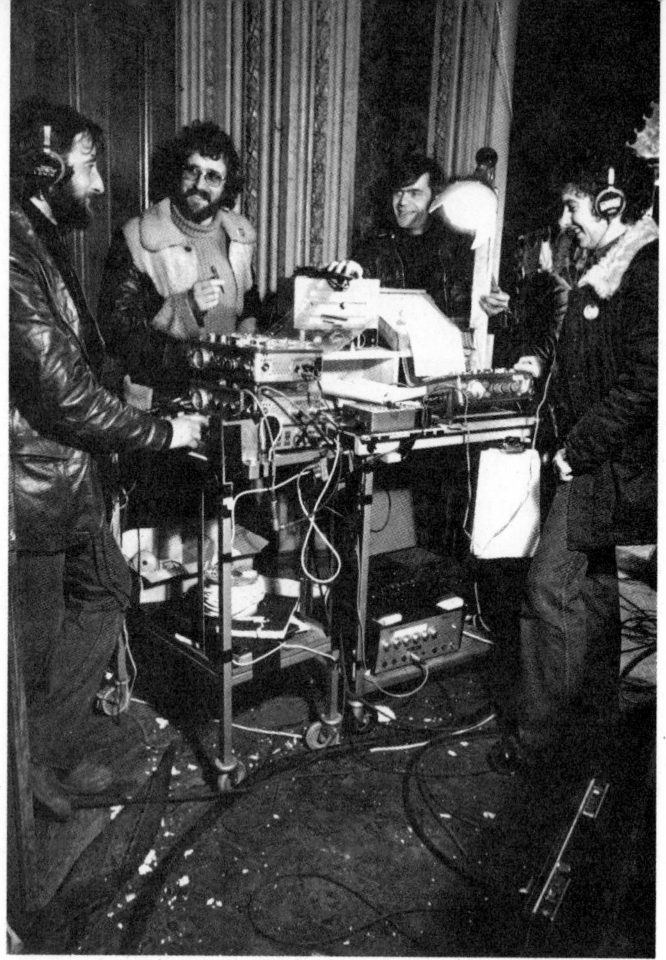

The sound crew (*left to right*): sound mixer Ron Barron; maintenance man Dougie Smith; boom operator Peter Glossop; and sound camera operator Chris Munroe.

Producer Michael White (*center*) discusses the film with Richard O'Brien and Lou Adler.

Jim Sharman directs Richard O'Brien at the control panel.

Meatloaf (*left*) with stuntman Ken Shepherd

Jim Sharman directs Peter Hinwood during Frank's death scene.

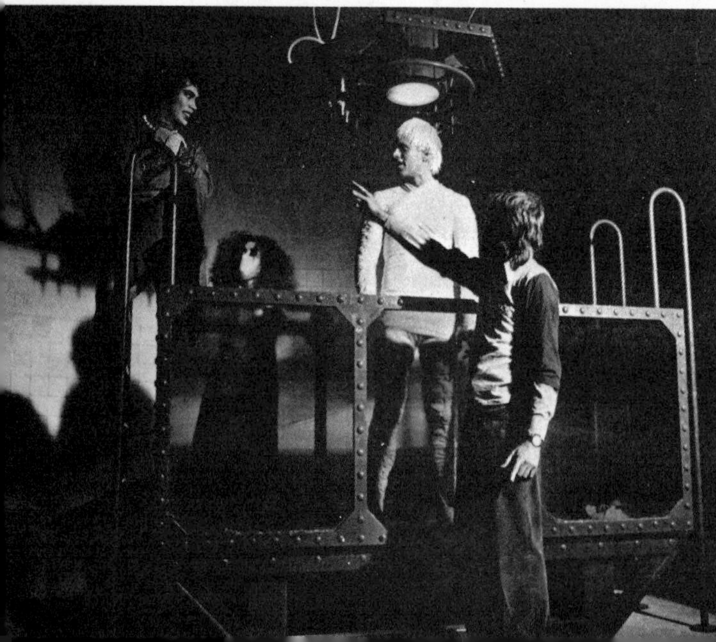
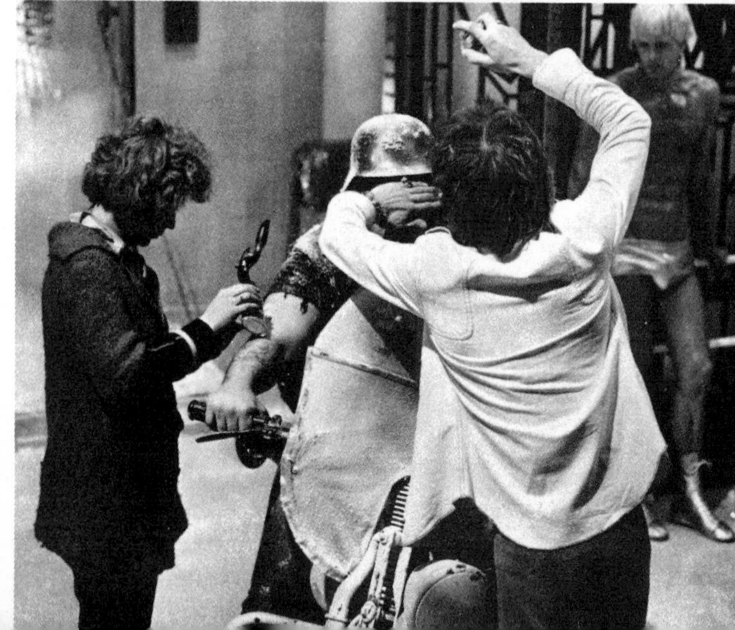

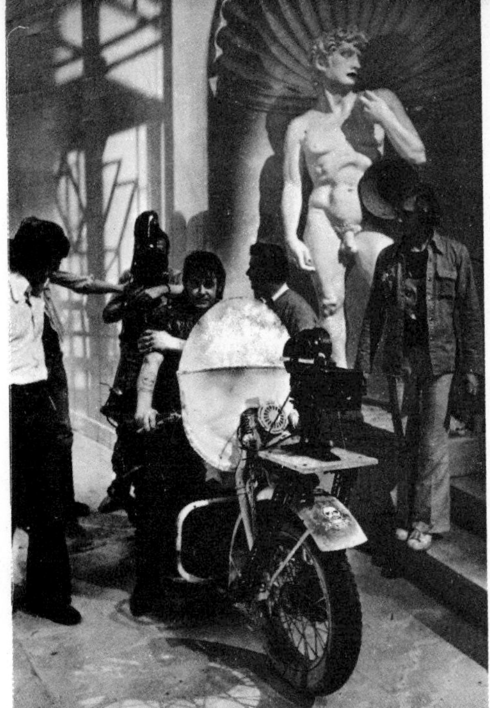

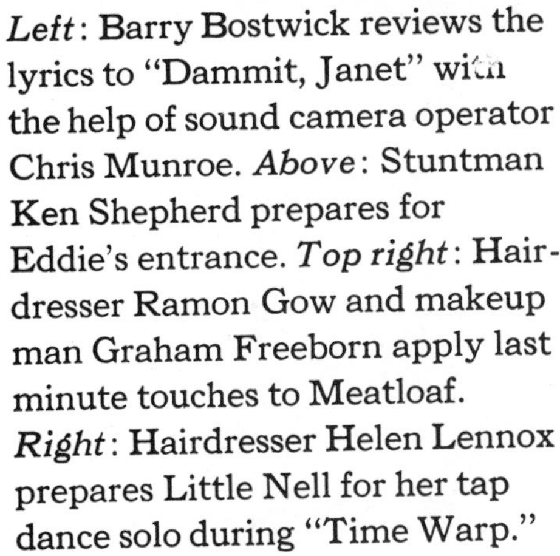

*Left*: Barry Bostwick reviews the lyrics to "Dammit, Janet" with the help of sound camera operator Chris Munroe. *Above*: Stuntman Ken Shepherd prepares for Eddie's entrance. *Top right*: Hairdresser Ramon Gow and makeup man Graham Freeborn apply last minute touches to Meatloaf. *Right*: Hairdresser Helen Lennox prepares Little Nell for her tap dance solo during "Time Warp."

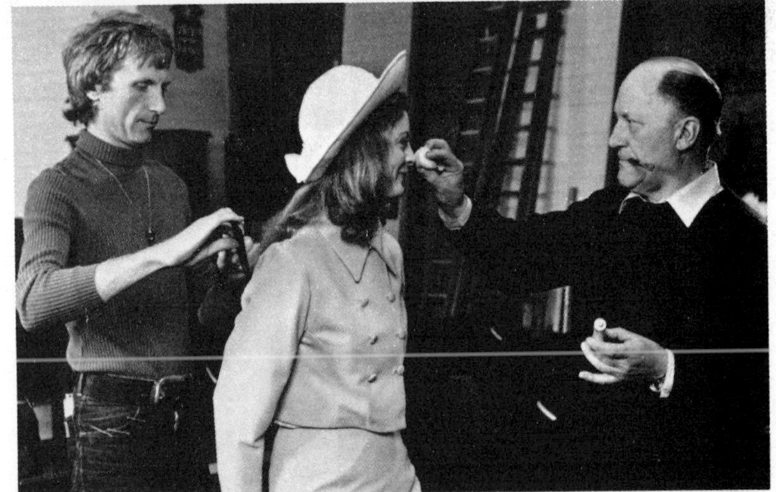

Hairdresser Ramon Gow and makeup man Ernest Gasser prepare Susan Sarandon for her entrance.

Makeup artist Michael Lockey looks on as Little Nell rehearses for the "Charles Atlas" number

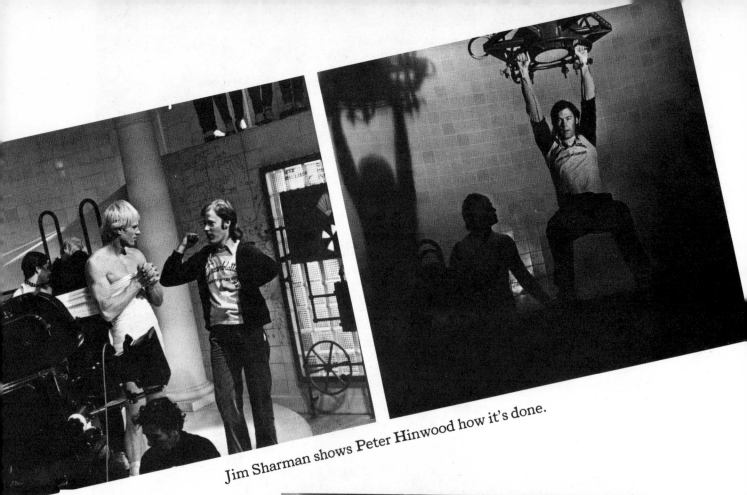

Jim Sharman shows Peter Hinwood how it's done.

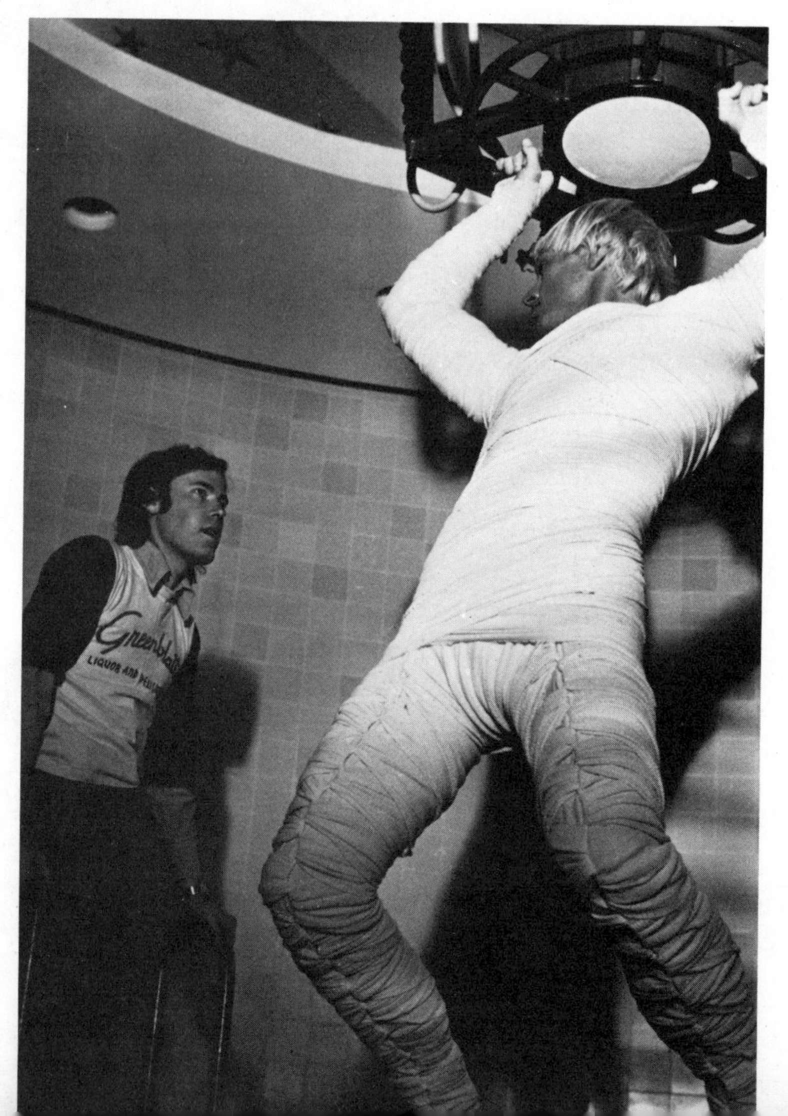

Actress Britt Ekland visits the *Rocky Horror* set.

Assistant director Mike Gowans turns clapper boy for Meatloaf's entrance into the laboratory.

The products still under consideration by Marlis's office, but which have not been licensed as of this writing, are noteworthy because, for the most part, they are imaginative follies and fripperies for the die-hard fan:

A license for *Rocky Horror* greeting cards and stationery is being evaluated.

A *Rocky Horror* participation game, somewhat akin to charades and based on flash cards, is being developed.

Beach towels, decals, and notebook covers are under consideration.

One company wants to manufacture a Transvestite Frank, similar to the Ken, Barbi, and Gay Bob dolls.

A *Rocky Horror* makeup kit may find its way to the stores.

And, of course, Twentieth Century-Fox has acknowledged the existence of the National *Rocky Horror* Fan Club, providing the club with information about the film, and permitting the use of the *Rocky Horror* typeface and lips logo. The fan club, which publishes a *Rocky Horror* magazine called *The Transylvanian,* can be contacted by writing to: The National Rocky Horror Fan Club, P.O. Box 881, Cooper Station, New York, NY 10003.

But who can say where all this licensing will lead? Will grizzly foreign men in drag pushing umbrella carts sell Frank-N-Furters in the streets? Will we see children in playgrounds aiming Riff Raff Trident Zappers? Will Columbia Tap Dance Studios punctuate the nation? When your house is a mess, will you call the Magenta Maid Service? Dammit Janet Lingerie, perhaps? Baggy Brad boxer shorts? Why not?

September 20, 1978

ntury Fox

Hills, CA 90212

evers

few weeks ago a 23-year-old crazy lady dragged me
e Varsity Theater in St. Louis for the midnight view-
f "The Rocky Horror Picture Show". I was amazed.
afternoon I had searched frantically around town for
paraphernalia this girl said we needed in order to
icipate in the experience. (She had been 13 times
viously and had never done this, but this time she said
would if I would) sooooo------for four hours I went
a Rocky Horror scavenger hunt with the St. Louis
ropolitan Area as my boundary and, lo and behold, I
nally found all the crap! And that night after sitting
rough the thing I thought there must be an easier way
get all that junk, and what about all the
here wanting to participate

Well

done for about 60¢ and could sell for 2 or 3 dollars. There
is a pile to be made!

We have this idea copywrited, so if you're interested,
give me or my partner, Dennis Haislar a call immediately
at (618) 344-7910 or (314) 436-4949.

Rick Diamond

And if you're thinking the Rocky Horror phenomenon will
fade soon, that's nonsense. While looking through the Reader's
Guide To Periodical Literature for an article on it to copy
the logo from, I found next to nothing written about it.
The new People Magazine show on t.v. just did a story on it,
and <u>now</u> the masses have been alerted. There is definitely
a market. One of our bands (did I tell you I'm a booking
agent?) is doing a Rocky Horror show and selling out every
night to a house of full regaliaed Horror crazies. So, call
me, please.

VISITOR'S PASS
17835

PLEASE
DO NOT PARK IN RED OR YELLOW ZONES.
DO NOT PARK IN NAMED PARKING SPACES.
DO NOT PARK IN FRONT OF SOUND STAGE
LOADING DOORS OR LOADING DOCKS.
DO NOT PARK IN ANY MANNER WHICH WOULD
OBSTRUCT STREET TO EMERGENCY VEHICLES.

April 4, 1979

: <u>ROCKY HORROR POSTER MAGAZINE</u>

s been brought to our attention that there is a poster magazine entitled "The Rocky Horror Official Poster Magazine," which
is being circulated nationwide. This product is not a legitimate item, the manufacturers are not Fox licensees, and the photographs are being illegally published.

Please inform all exhibitors exhibiting ROCKY HORROR PICTURE SHOW
that we expect them to refrain from carrying any illegal merchandise. Legitimate licensees distributing ROCKY HORROR PICTURE
SHOW material are:

| | |
|---|---|
| Crabwalk<br>Roach, Inc.<br>Blake Publishers | Calendars<br>T-shirt transfers<br>Rocky Horror Post Magazine<br>and a 72-page magazine |
| Hawthorn Publishers<br>Dargis<br>A & B Creations, Inc.<br>Ludlow Sales | Rocky Horror Scrapbook<br>Posters<br>Buttons<br>Stills, jewelry |

February 14, 1979

Mr. Alan Rubenstein
Box 6042 River Station
Rochester, New York 14627

Dear Alan:

Thank you for your letter regarding the ROCKY HORROR PICTURE SHOW. At this time we are not interested in licensing RHPS cigarette papers.

If we ever are interested ...
we will get in ...

... such a product,
... ect you to
... ur company's
... tribution
... the product
... om you of
... sold, and a
... numbers are
... basis of an

... luck with

February 21, 1979

Mr. Joe Leff
Franco Manufacturing Company, Inc.
Prospect & High Street
Metuchen, New Jersey 08840

Dear Joe:

As I mentioned on the telephone, we are very excited about the merchandising programs involving our film, the "ROCKY HORROR PICTURE SHOW". The "RHPS" is the most popular underground "cult" film of all-time. The picture was initially released in 1975, and has been playing to packed houses on Friday and Saturday nights only, at midnight.

The unique element about "ROCKY" is that the audience actively becomes involved with the film. It is, in fact, the first true audience participation movie. The enclosed articles from US and the New York Times relate some of the audience's fanaticism. In fact, we have been made aware of numerous people who have seen the fil... well over 100 times.

In the past six mont...
coverage - CBS's show "Si...
WPIX in New York about te...
all have upcoming article...
promotion and advertising...
of midnight shows only. W...
and 30 more on a waiting l...

Until the beginning o...
on the "RHPS". A great dea...
T-Shirts were sold. Now, ...
us and we are beginning to...
Hawthorn Publishers to do a...
series of poster magazines,...
calendar; and Roach Co. to ...
have not yet accepted, key ...
stills, photo-novels, cutout...
in obtaining licenses for a...

Mr. Joe Leff
February 21, 1979
Page II

I feel the "ROCKY" craze has just begun. In colleges, high schools, and junior highs, "ROCKY" is the hot new topic. The information is percolating out from New York and Los Angeles to the rest of the country. In fact, the "ROCKY HORROR" fan club has grown to over 10,000 due's paying members. By the way, the club is very interested in helping present new merchandise to their members. We will be working with them, and we are also working on a direct in-theater sales operation for "ROCKY" licensees.

I hope the enclosed information can give you some idea of the "RHPS". Really, the best introduction I can give you to the cult is to invite you to see the film, or tell you to ask any teenager. They'll tell you that the "ROCKY HORROR PICTURE SHOW" is terrific, its unlike anything the movies have known and everyone loves it.

Please contact me as soon as possible. I am convinced that a "RHPS" beach towel will be a huge seller for you this year.

Sincerely,

# The Cast:
# SUPERHEROES

*There are those who say that life is an illusion, that reality is simply a figment of the imagination.*

Perhaps the key to this ancient philosophical puzzle lies in answering the questions, Whose life? Which illusions? What reality? Whose imagination? For some members of the *Rocky Horror* cast and crew, life, illusion, reality, and imagination have chased each other around like a writhing orgy of snakes ever since the film first showed signs of success.

Journalists have written amazed reports about the *Rocky Horror* phenomenon. Adoring fans have prostrated their lives for the film's characters. And for the most part the principal people connected with the film have enjoyed increased renown. Not that they were amateurs when *Rocky Horror* began. The cast and crew were composed of seasoned young veterans of the stage and screen whose careers have continued to grow since the film was made.

Who are these individuals the fans know as Frank-N-Furter, Riff Raff, Brad, Janet, and the rest? My unconventional conventionists, I give you the people who made *The Rocky Horror Picture Show.*

## Tim Curry as Dr. Frank-N-Furter (A Scientist)

Like God, whose minister he portrays in the wedding of Ralph and Betty Hapschatt, Tim Curry in the role of Frank-N-Furter has the ability to create life itself. But the mad scientist has made his discovery by accident. His is the underbelly, the dark side of creation; and it should come as no surprise to us when he suffers satanic ruin.

Before he dies, however, Frank is the joy of *The Rocky Horror Picture Show.* All the film's early scenes are directed toward his entrance; every character in the movie responds to him principally; and the picture is virtually over when his life ends.

In a simple, stylized manner, Frank is a study in contrasts. He is a ruthless master who has no qualms about committing murder, whipping his supposedly "faithful handyman" for an apparently slight infraction, serving Dr. Scott's roasted nephew to him for dinner, or seducing both a male and a female virgin in a single night. Yet, it is he who engages our affections when he is triumphant, and our sympathies when he faces disaster. As a sweet transvestite with a penchant for muscle-men, he is as macho as John Wayne ever was. He is the richly charactered

magus who dies for our imagined sins, and redeems our fantasies as he lives out our hidden dreams.

Like any hero-villain of mythic proportions, Frank has his blind spot: In his monumental egotism he mistakes his true enemy. Whatever their past relationship may be—and a dire, competetive one is suggested—Frank is wrongly suspicious of Dr. Scott, while his trusted servant, Riff Raff, hovers in the background, biding time until his coup can take place. His lifestyle is "too extreme" according to Riff Raff. There is no forgiveness for Frank and his fondest illusions must come to nothing. He fails not because of his ignorance, but because he is overtaken by his own talents.

But along the way he reminds us of our possibilities and leads us in the movie's anthem, exhorting us, "Don't dream it—be it." For his willingness to live out his own dreams, we love him. And it is Frank, more than any other character, that we return to the theater again and again to see and, in our hopeful way, to be.

(photo courtesy A&M Records)

The role of Frank-N-Furter was Tim Curry's first screen performance. Born in Cheshire, England, in 1946, the son of a Methodist minister, he studied drama and English at Cambridge and at Birmingham University, from which he graduated with combined honors. His first professional success was in the London production of *Hair,* where he appeared for fifteen months, from 1968 to early 1970, followed by more study and work in the Royal Court and Glasgow Civic Repertory companies. In the course of his experience, Tim has sung opera at Sadler Wells, played in a variety of British theatrical productions, including *Galileo, Danton's Death, The Sport of My Mad Mother* and the Royal Shakespeare Company's *After Haggerty,* and appeared in a number of acclaimed British television specials, among them the BBC's 1975 Christmas show, a Victorian satire called *Three Men in a Boat.* In 1979 he appeared in a British television mini-series, the *The Life of Shakespeare* in which he played the title role. That show was originally made for America's ABC, but the network thought it too violent, and it has yet to air in this country.

In June 1973 Tim Curry landed the plum role of Dr. Frank-N-Furter in the original London production of *The Rocky Horror*

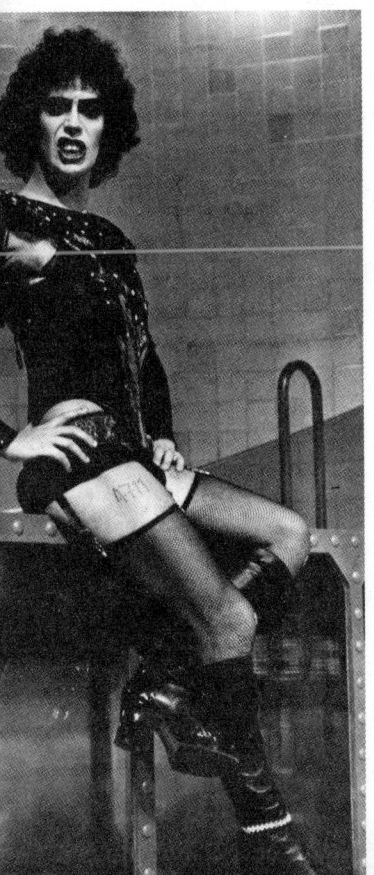

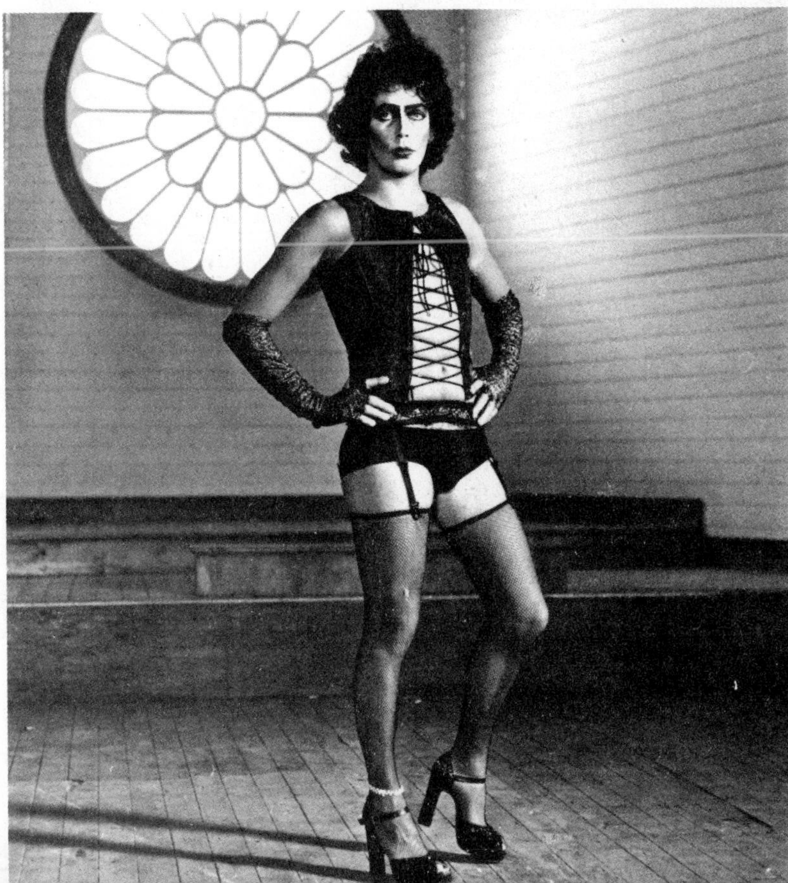

*Show,* for which he auditioned with a rousing rendition of Little Richard's "Tutti Frutti." He recreated the role of Frank in the Los Angeles and Broadway productions and, of course, in the film. He also appeared on Broadway in Tom Stoppard's play *Travesties.*

Reviews of his portrayal of Frank have always been literally "mixed." Gregg Kilday of the *Los Angeles Times* called him "half Auntie Mame, half Bela Lugosi," while Dave Berman of the Santa Monica *Outlook* described him as "a hybrid of Sophie Tucker and Mick Jagger."

As a performer, Curry says he "would like to be what they call in the business a 'triple threat'—to do movies, theater, and records, and to be as widely different in all of them as possible." He has been doing nightclub work recently in slacks, jacket, and tie and his first solo album, *Read My Lips,* was released in 1978 by A & M Records. His latest album, called *Fearless,* was released during the summer of 1979.

## Richard (Ritz) O'Brien as Riff Raff (A Handyman)

Among the outrageous characters in *The Rocky Horror Picture Show,* none is so bizarre as Riff Raff, and probably none so difficult to portray. While everyone else in the movie works from a single set of character traits and develops in a linear fashion that can be anticipated, despite occasional lapses, the hunchbacked handyman and his sister Magenta are duplicitous. They appear to be menial servants, when in fact they are powerful undercover agents waiting for the right moment to take over the Transylvanian leadership on Earth and return to their native planet of Transexual.

Riff Raff is insolent in his lack of power, cruel when he holds it, and insanely paranoiac in its exercise. It is he who works most closely with the mad scientist in charge of the Transylvanian mission; he who releases Rocky from bondage, creating pandemonium in his master's heart; and he who wields the laser gun that kills Columbia, Rocky, and Frank at the movie's end.

Richard O'Brien, who portrays Riff Raff, also wrote the script, lyrics, and music for the play. As a longtime fan of B movies, bad science fiction films, and Dr. Strange comics, it is no surprise that he wrote the part of Riff Raff for himself when writing the play that was intended to attract like-minded people to the theater. Lou Adler says, "Richard O'Brien's brain—that's where everything is. He's Riff Raff, but he's also the doctor, the monster, all the characters." It is an ideal part for the author-actor.

(*Photo credit: Richard Fendleman*)

Although *The Rocky Horror Picture Show* marks O'Brien's motion picture debut, he is no stranger to performing. Born in New Zealand and married to Kimi Wong, a Transylvanian, with whom he has recorded rock singles under the name "Kimi and Ritz," O'Brien appeared in the London productions of *Hair* with Tim Curry, and *Jesus Christ Superstar,* under the direction of Jim Sharman. He played the part of a strange creature in Sam Sheppard's *The Unseen Hand* before originating the role of Riff Raff in the London production of *The Rocky Horror Show.* He recreated that role on Broadway, and again in the movie.

After winning the *London Evening Standard*'s award for the Best Musical of 1973 with *The Rocky Horror Show,* O'Brien recently returned to writing for the theater. His play *Disaster*—featuring Patricia Quinn and Jonathan Adams, with costumes by Sue Blane—opened in London during the summer of 1978. The bizarre musical closed the same summer *(The Transylvanian* loved it; the London critics did not).

## Susan Sarandon as Janet Weiss (A Heroine)

Innocence that is not educated will surely be defiled. It is difficult to say which happens to Janet Weiss, the ingenue's ingenue in *The Rocky Horror Picture Show,* since she takes to her defilement with such enthusiasm.

Actually, Janet's is the true-life story of many American girls raised in towns much like Denton, where the story takes place. An innocent childhood and adolescence leave them ill-prepared for the horrors of the larger world, and the discovery of those horrors can only be traumatic. Instead of curling up and dying of anguish or embarrassment as some girls might, however, Janet uses her intitiation into the darker side of life as a means of educating herself.

Deflowered by a mad scientist from another planet, and finding her fiancé equally in Frank's thrall, she turns her attentions to the handsome hunk of beefcake Frank has created, taking solace in Rocky Horror's arms. As Frank has told her, it isn't all bad.

Until she comes out of her cocoon, Janet is somewhat the

person Ms. Sarandon sees herself to be. "We were very Catholic and very middle class," she says of her early years. Originally, Susan Sarandon was supposed to do some more erotic nude scenes for the movie, but she declined to go that far.

Born Susan Tomalin, in high school she studied to be a dancer. While attending Catholic University she met the actor Chris Sarandon, and accompanied him to Long Wharf, Connecticut, for a season of summer stock. An agent who was scouting Chris found Susan instead. He arranged an interview for her and her screen career was launched as Peter Boyle's daughter in *Joe*. She has appeared in nearly a dozen films since then, including *The Great Waldo Pepper, Pretty Baby, The Other Side of Midnight, King of the Gypsies, The Front Page,* and the forthcoming *Something Short of Paradise*. She has also worked extensively in television.

Reflecting her childhood and perhaps the views of the many Janets in *Rocky Horror* audiences, Susan says, "A career isn't that important to me. I'm professional about my career, but I have my life first."

## Barry Bostwick as Brad Majors (A Hero)

No matter how much we may love and adore the weird Transylvanians and their leader Frank, we Earthlings always find a certain amount of attraction for *Rocky Horror*'s romantic leads, Brad and Janet. We are attached to them at the beginning of the movie; we are greeted with them by Frank in the laboratory; we live on, as they do, after Frank has died and his castle has been beamed back to the galaxy of Transylvania. In a way, they are our inspiration on this mad journey: They get our kicks for us.

At the same time, it is difficult in our sophisticated age to see these horribly innocent kids as our representatives. It is hard, after all, to imagine a greater scion of straightness than that knight in tinfoil armor, Brad Majors.

From his first appearance at the Hapschatt wedding, it is obvious that Brad—commonly dubbed "Asshole" by most audiences—is a young fool. And every move he makes, every line he speaks, every note he sings in the entire movie makes his idiotic position more secure and more sincere. Brad is entirely laughable, but deep down we know that we are more like Brad than we are like Frank, and that is Brad's saving grace for us.

Still, as the *Rocky Horror* straight man, Brad cannot possibly escape our condemnation. He cannot even enjoy his debauchery, as Janet can. Where she discovers the desire to be touched, dirtied, and thrilled, Brad can only cry out, "Help me, Mommy!"

With an acting degree from California Western University School of the Arts, and graduate work at New York University's School of the Arts, native Californian Barry Bostwick has been trained in singing, juggling, trapeze and clown techniques, fencing, mime, and ballet.

Bostwick has appeared in leading roles with the Phoenix Repertory Company, the Huntington Hartford Theater and the San Diego Shakespeare Festival. His first Broadway production was *Cock-a-Doodle-Dandy,* followed by two off-Broadway rock musicals, *Salvation* and *House of Leather* and the first rock opera on Broadway, *Soon.* He also starred with Zoe Caldwell and Mildred Dunnock in *Collette* and costarred in the critically acclaimed American premiere of Jean Genet's *The Screens.*

In 1972 Barry received a Tony nomination as best actor in a musical for his performance in *Grease,* and won a Tony for his performance in *The Robber Bride Groom* a few seasons later. He took the national company of *Grease* to the Shubert Theater in Los Angeles and appeared in the MGM film *Slither* with James Caan, Peter Boyle, and Sally Kellerman. He appeared in the TV special, "You Can't Take It with You."

Barry Bostwick also appeared in the highly acclaimed *Movie! Movie!* and recently starred in the title role of an unscheduled TV pilot, "Young Guy Christian," a spoof (what else?) of the James Bond thrillers.

what's your favorite color?

## Patricia Quinn as Magenta (A Domestic)

Playing the role of Magenta is a severe test for any actress, because the character is so largely engaged in the art of supporting others. She helps undress Brad before he and Janet are taken to Frank's laboratory; she stands beside Frank during the delicate, final moments before Rocky is born; she announces the film's ghoulish dinner; she throws the Medusa switch at Frank's command, turning Brad, Janet, Dr. Scott, Columbia, and Rocky Horror to stone. It is wholly fitting that she is defined, both in the movie's credits and in Frank's rambunctious household, as "a domestic."

More than any other character, Magenta supports her incestuous brother-lover Riff Raff. And in their scenes together—singing and dancing the "Time Warp," and confronting Frank with his imminent doom—she is most visible and most vibrant.

Born on May 28, 1944, in Belfast, Ireland, Patricia Quinn performed in her home town theaters and in London before studying at the Drama Centre. After her course there she spent a season with the Glasgow Repertory Theatre, then returned to

London to appear in *AC/DC,* which won the Best Play of the Year award. She also played Sarah Bernhardt in *Sarah B. Divine.* She originated the role of the Usherette/Magenta in the first *Rocky Horror Show* production. She appeared in the BBC series on pre-Raphaelite painters entitled "Love School" and portrayed Christabel Pankhurst in the television series "Shoulder to Shoulder," about the British suffragette movement.

Nevertheless, she remains dauntless in terms of the characters she portrays: "From male chauvinism to women's liberation! I remember completing *The Rocky Horror Show* after the last show on a Saturday night and taking the overnight train to Halifax to give my first political speech for the television series. I was still covered from head to toe in glitter and they covered it all with my period costume."

She appeared in numerous films before *Rocky Horror,* but the four she particularly likes to remember were *Up the Chastity Belt, Rent-a-Dick, Up the Front,* and *The Garnett Saga.* On American television she had been seen in PBS's "I Claudius" and "Beauty and the Beast" with George C. Scott.

During the summer of 1978 Ms. Quinn originated the role of Martha Fortune in the London premiere of Richard O'Brien's play, *Disaster.* She lives in London with her actor-director husband, Don Hawkins, and their son, Quinn.

## Little Nell as Columbia (A Groupie)

As Frank's in-house female ex-lover, Columbia is permitted a certain latitude in her actions appropriate to her identity as "a groupie." She appears to have had time for a fling with the former delivery boy, Eddie, and she is the first member of the household to call Frank down for his selfishness. She is also the first person killed when Riff Raff seizes power in the castle, and it is her death that makes Frank understand that his danger is real.

But what Columbia will best be remembered for is her glittering Ann Miller-like tap dance across the ballroom floor during the "Time Warp," and her impossibly Betty Boopish voice.

Singing and dancing have long been a part of the life of Little Nell, born Laura Campbell, the daughter of a prominent Australian newspaper columnist for the Sydney *Telegraph* who wrote regularly about the misadventures of his four children. In her father's column, Laura was christened "Little Nell" after the Dickens character in *The Old Curiosity Shop,* and the name has stuck with her ever since. From the time she arrived in England at the age of eighteen she was a busker—a panhandling street performer. And she busked her way right into *The Rocky Horror Show.*

One day, performing her act—singing 1930s songs and tap-dancing in top hat and tails—outside the theater where *Jesus Christ Superstar* was playing, director Jim Sharman saw her and cast her immediately as Columbia in his next theatrical production, *The Rocky Horror Show.*

During the summer of 1978 she opened a one-woman play, *Stoop,* in London. She has since released a new record, "Fever" on one side and "See Ya Round like a Record" on the other, in addition to her popular "Do the Swim." Her acting credits include roles in the PBS television series "Rock Follies," and the punk rock movie, *Jubilee.*

## Peter Hinwood as Rocky Horror (A Creation)

Except that he is tall, broad-shouldered, and largely incapable of articulate speech, Rocky Horror—Frank-N-Furter's creation—bears virtually no resemblance at all to Frankenstein's classic monster with his screws loose and his brain unhinged. Though this monster has but half a brain (Eddie has the other half), he has a body straight out of an aging queen's most delirious wet dream. Blond and boyishly handsome, with his deltoids, triceps, and whatnot most engagingly in place, he is happy lifting weights, doing press-ups, and accommodating the first two sexual objects he encounters—Frank and Janet.

For his creator, Rocky Horror is unquestionably a thing, albeit a male thing, rather than a person. He is not supposed to sing, dance, or find Janet an attractive piece of adventure. Chained to Frank's bed, Rocky's job is to service his maker.

As it happens, things go wrong from the very start of Rocky's extremely short life. Fresh out of his swaddling bandages, he is hoisted up on high by an overeager Riff Raff who returns the chandelier, with Rocky clinging to its rim, to its appointed place above the operating theater. Once again on the ground, Rocky finds this bizarre man in a dress and high heels chasing him up and down a ramp full of outer-space creatures in fright wigs and

sunglasses. Dancing to the beat of a rock 'n roll sax, Rocky is imprisoned in a deco elevator. He's then waltzed off to a bed that's situated in front of a floor-to-ceiling stained-glass picture of Atlas holding up the world; presumably seduced in the night; terrified by Riff Raff bearing a candelabra with thirteen flaming tapers; chased outside in the rain by a pack of snarling Alsatian hounds; introduced to the female anatomy by Janet; dressed down by Frank for accepting the introduction; turned into a statue; forced to watch the murder of his lover; and finally zapped by a laser gun, "capable of emitting a beam of pure anti-matter," which kills him. All in the space of about eight hours.

*The Rocky Horror Picture Show* is Peter Hinwood's second stint before the movie cameras. But as a model his well-built six-foot two-inch frame has been in great demand by major magazines as a result of a photographic layout depicting "British Manhood," which appeared in the London *Daily Express*. Those photographs, which led to a role in Dino de Laurentis's film *The Odyssey,* came as a result of Hinwood's prior career as a professional photographer, which followed hard on the heels of his painting studies at St. Martin's School of Art in London. Hinwood seems to keep almost as busy as Rocky Horror; but presumably he will come to a better end.

## Meatloaf as Eddie (Ex-Delivery Boy)

Eddie is the former delivery boy greaser for whom Frank jilted Columbia. While Eddie and his motorcycle repose in a cryogenic nightmare, Frank has taken half his brain to animate Rocky Horror. But for some unexplained reason, the freezer door fails to contain Eddie, and revving his cycle, he rips through the wall of ice like a bat out of hell, sax slung back and boots kicking, just as Frank and Rocky Horror are beginning to get to know each other. In his very few minutes on camera, Eddie casts his lust-filled eyes on both Columbia, his former flame, Rocky Horror, and Janet; sings a single song, the fifties-style hot teen anthem, "Whatever Happened to Saturday Night," and gets the whole set rocking; then finally is silenced by an ice pick wielding Frank, enraged at being upstaged. Nevertheless, Eddie's nearly irrelevant and all too brief appearance is one of the high points in the movie.

Born and raised in Dallas, Texas, Mr. Loaf, as he is known in certain discreet circles, was a star football player at North Texas State University until eleven concussions, a twisted knee, and a dislocated shoulder introduced him to a two-year career of "doing nothing." For the next several years he was a singer in California and Michigan. Then he auditioned for *Hair* and was accepted on the spot. He appeared in both the Broadway and road show productions.

"For three years I had tried all I knew to get a recording contract, but nobody was interested. One week after *Hair* opened in Detroit I received four offers including Motown and Atlantic."

(*Photo credit: Robin Platzer, courtesy CBS*)

He and his leading lady from *Hair* signed with Motown; billing themselves as Stoney and Meatloaf they released "What You See Is What You Get."

As an actor and a singer, Meatloaf has appeared in a wide variety of productions, including Joseph Papp's Shakespeare in the Park, off Broadway's *Rainbow* and *Silver Queen,* and *Rock-a-Bye Hamlet* on Broadway. He played both the role of Eddie and that of Dr. Scott in the Los Angeles production of *The Rocky Horror Show,* and appeared as Eddie on Broadway. The film version was his screen debut.

Since *Rocky Horror,* he has concentrated on his singing career. His first album—it went platinum—is *Bat Out of Hell,* which contained the hit single, "Paradise by the Dashboard Light," on which he is accompanied by Ellen Foley. *Bat* is also a short film featuring Meat and Karla DeVito (who replaced Ellen Foley here and in Meatloaf's concert tour). The short is met with enthusiasm, not to mention its very own audience participation script. (*"Sing it, you fat fool!"*) His second album, *Renegade Angel,* will soon be released.

*(Photo credit: Robin Platzer, courtesy CBS)*

## Jonathan Adams as Dr. Everett V. Scott (A Rival Scientist)

Dr. Everett Scott (or *von* Scott, should I say?) is the former high school science teacher whom Brad and Janet set out to visit when the course of their journey is altered by a blowout and their subsequent search for a telephone. Miraculously, Scott turns up at Frank-N-Furter's castle the following morning.

But if Brad and Janet recognize Dr. Scott from school days, Frank recognizes him from somewhere else. He knows that Dr. Scott is employed by the government, investigating the phenomenon we call UFOs. Dr. Scott's appearance at Frank's castle comes as a surprise to everyone, but Frank refuses to believe the meeting between Scott, Brad, and Janet is accidental.

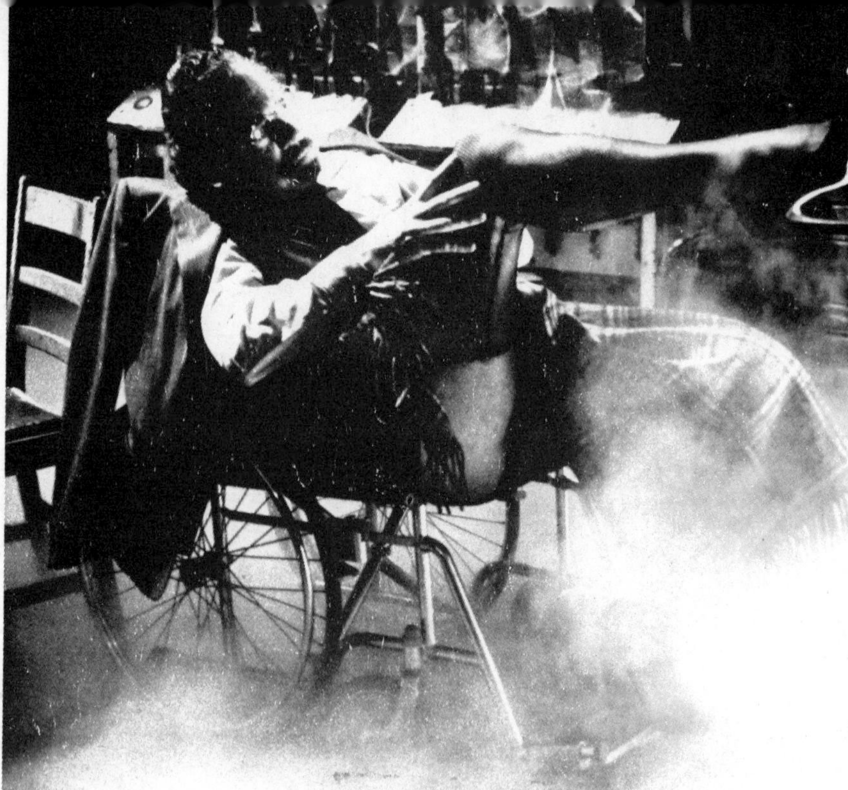

Dr. Scott's disclosure that he is looking for his nephew, Eddie, unsettles Frank still further; and though he participates sporadically in the doctor's moving rendition of "Eddie's Teddy," he concludes the song by unveiling to the assembled group the decomposing remains of what had been Dr. Scott's nephew.

Up in the lab, Frank turns all his guests to stone. When he releases them for the floor show, they are transformed. Even staid, solid, and staunch Dr. Scott turns out to be prepared to live his life "for the thrill." But Dr. Scott—known to California audiences by the affectionate nickname "Kissass"—has his finest moment when Riff Raff enters the auditorium to stage his murderous vendetta. Then, three times in less than two minutes, Dr. Scott cops out, sells out, backpeddles as best he can in his wheelchair, and makes every conceivable effort to save his own neck—which is never really endangered. What a guy. Makes you cry.

Jonathan Adams, who played the Narrator in the original London production of *The Rocky Horror Show,* is a painter, composer, and dancer, as well as an actor and singer. His interest in surrealist art was apparent in his comedic one-man show at Manhattan's Duplex Cabaret Theater in October 1978 (incidentally, *Rocky Horror* Fan Club president Sal Piro was his opening act).

Originally trained as a painter, he studied art at Chelsea Art School and London University and taught in his hometown of Northampton following a stint in the RAF Medical Corps. As an actor, Adams appeared with the Children's Theatre Company at Sadler Wells, and in various productions in London's West End, including two years in *Alibi for a Judge,* and on television in Franco Zeffirelli's *Jesus of Nazareth.* He also played the villain in Richard O'Brien's musical *Disaster,* in the summer of 1978.

Of *Rocky Horror,* Adams observes, "The show is like a comic strip come to life. It is a parody and spoof of various elements of popular culture, but done with affection. Because of the tongue-in-cheek nature of the production and the spirit of the age, no one could really be upset by the content. It is all extremely innocent."

## Charles Gray as The Criminologist (An Expert)

How much of what they witnessed would Brad and Janet willingly have shared with the world they knew? Would Brad have wished to speak of these things? Or Dr. Scott? In all probability "The Denton Affair" would never have been revealed to us had it not been for the dogged investigations of the

Criminologist, who, with his black leather-bound dossier, unfolds the matter of this case as the aristocratic, Time Warping Narrator of *Rocky Horror.*

The Criminologist is played by the veteran character actor Charles Gray. Born in Bournemouth, England, in 1928, Gray's stage successes include the leads in the London and New York productions of *The Right Honorable Gentleman* and *The Man Who Came to Dinner* in London. He has also appeared in such films as *The Seven Percent Solution* (as Mycroft Holmes), *The Secret War of Harry Frigg, The Legacy, Oliver Cromwell, Diamonds are Forever,* and *You Only Live Twice.*

According to his London agent, Angela Hepburn, when Mr. Gray was offered the role of the Criminologist, he smiled devilishly and said "Why not?"

## The Transylvanians

Just as no picnic is complete without ants, no party is complete without guests. The Annual Transylvanian Convention is no exception. In *The Rocky Horror Picture Show,* Transylvanian agents from all over this world have gathered in the castle's black and silver ballroom to boogie down. Later, they are privileged to witness the birth of Rocky Horror himself, and incidentally to perform in the rock 'n roll stomp that accompanies Eddie's "Whatever Happened to Saturday Night." Briefly, in alphabetical order, here are the Transylvanians.

PERRY BEDDEN has been involved in theater and film since he was a child. He played the Palace Theater as Kurt in *The Sound of Music* at the age of twelve. Ten years later, at the same theater, he appeared as a priest in *Jesus Christ Superstar.* His other stage credits range from *You're a Good Man, Charlie Brown* to Andy Warhol's *Pork.* Most recently he played the role of Riff Raff in the still-running London production of *The Rocky Horror Show.*

*Right*: The Transylvanians pose on the Kawasaki motorcycles used in the film.

CHRISTOPHER BIGGINS trained at the Bristol Old Vic School. In addition to playing the title role in *Winnie the Pooh,* he has appeared with both the Young Vic and the Royal Shakespeare Company as well as in numerous television and film productions.

GAYLE BROWN'S extensive stage, television, and film work includes appearances with the Royal Shakespeare Company, in *Macbird, Clockwork Orange,* and *A Touch of Class,* and on "The Merv Griffin Show." With two other actresses she is the music group Rock Bottom.

ISHAQ BUX, descended from two generations of famous Indian magicians, was educated in England, went home to India in 1938, and returned to England in 1956. Since that time he has appeared in numerous television and film productions, including *Inadmissible Evidence, Leo the Last,* and *Nine Hours to Rama.*

STEPHEN CALCUTT, six feet, seven inches tall, has worked as a fashion model promoting clothes for tall men and as a British and European photo model. His television, stage, and film work have been marked by his character roles, ranging from Toulouse-Lautrec to a giant.

HUGH CECIL has been a performing magician since 1924, and a professional actor since the end of World War II. He has

appeared in variety shows and on television, as well as in *Frankenstein and the Monster from Hell,* the musical version of *Jekyll and Hyde,* and *Henry VIII.*

IMOGEN CLAIRE studied at the Royal Ballet School before dancing with the Opera Ballet and the Royal Ballet, and appearing with the touring company of the Bolshoi Ballet. She played in Ken Russell's TV production, "Strauss," and has appeared in most of Russell's films, including *The Devils, Mahler,* and *Tommy.*

RUFUS COLLINS trained at the Actors Studio in New York, and appeared in such landmark productions as *The Brig, Paradise Now,* and *The Maids.* As an actor he has played in nearly a dozen films; as a choreographer his credits include *Hair* and *Jesus Christ Superstar.* He has been artistic director for the Robert Stigwood Organization and for Michael White Productions.

SADIE CORRE is a four-foot three-inch cabaret performer who has worked in every sphere of show business except the circus, from the pubs and clubs of London's West End to Australian television. Her films include *Chitty-Chitty Bang-Bang* and *Quilp.*

FRAN FULLENWIDER was a child stunt rider in westerns before studying at Munich University, New York University's Film School, and The Royal Academy of Dramatic Art. On her 21st birthday she gave up dieting, and now weighs in at more than 300 pounds. She has appeared on many TV comedy shows, and in such films as *The Great Gatsby* and *Mutations.*

LINDSAY INGRAM studied at the Drama Centre before touring Europe and performing in repertory theater for several years. Her films include *Butley,* David Hemmings's *The 14,* and *Adult Fun.*

PENNY LEDGER has been an opera singer, ballerina, variety entertainer, antique dealer, fiction writer, television and radio ad copy writer in Hong Kong, and movie theater owner. She has

appeared with numerous repertory companies, and in the London production of *The Dirtiest Show in Town.*

Annabelle Leventon studied at St. Anne's College, Oxford, and the London Academy of Music and Dramatic Art. She has performed with the Young Vic repertory company , in the films *Every Home Should Have One* and *The Atlantic Wall,* and as Sheila in the original cast of *Hair*. During December 1978 she directed Jonathan Adams in a musical revue at Oxford.

Anthony Milner's first film is *Rocky Horror*. He studied at the Royal Academy of Dramatic Art and has appeared in theaters throughout England, including the Royal Court's Theatre Upstairs, where *Rocky Horror* got its start.

Pamela Obermeyer joined the Glasgow production of *Hair* at the age of seventeen, transferring later to the national touring company, and then the London company of the show. She left *Hair* to become lead vocalist for the rock group Truth, and returned to London to open in *Jesus Christ Superstar*.

Tony Then, head of the jazz faculty at the Institute of Choreology, studied at the Singapore Ballet Academy and the Rambert School of Ballet. He has performed with the Western Theatre Ballet, the Bremen Ballet, and the Koln Ballet Theatre in West Germany. His films include *Dr. Frankenstein* and *Blade of Vengeance.*

Kimi Wong is married to Richard O'Brien, whom she met in the national touring company of *Hair*. They have one son, Linus, born May 1, 1972. As "Kimi and Ritz," the O'Briens have released several records in England.

Henry Woolf, who trained at Bristol Drama School, has appeared in the London productions of *Rhinoceros, Marat/Sade,* and *AC/DC,* among other plays. On television he has played in Pinter's "Monologue" and "Churchill's People." His films include *The Lion in Winter* and *Catherine the Great.*

## Lou Adler—Executive Producer

From the night he saw *The Rocky Horror Show* on the London stage, Lou Adler wanted to help bring the happily bizarre fantasy world of Frank and the Transylvanian gang across the ocean to America. It is a tribute to his abilities as a producer, and his faith in this musical—which must have seemed a little strange on first viewing—that he made his agreement with London producer Michael White in less than two days. Such negotiations often take weeks or even months to complete. It is also a reflection of his expert sense of American movies that Adler presented the live play at his own Roxy Theatre in Los Angeles in such a way that Twentieth Century-Fox could get behind the *Rocky Horror Picture Show* almost as fast as he did.

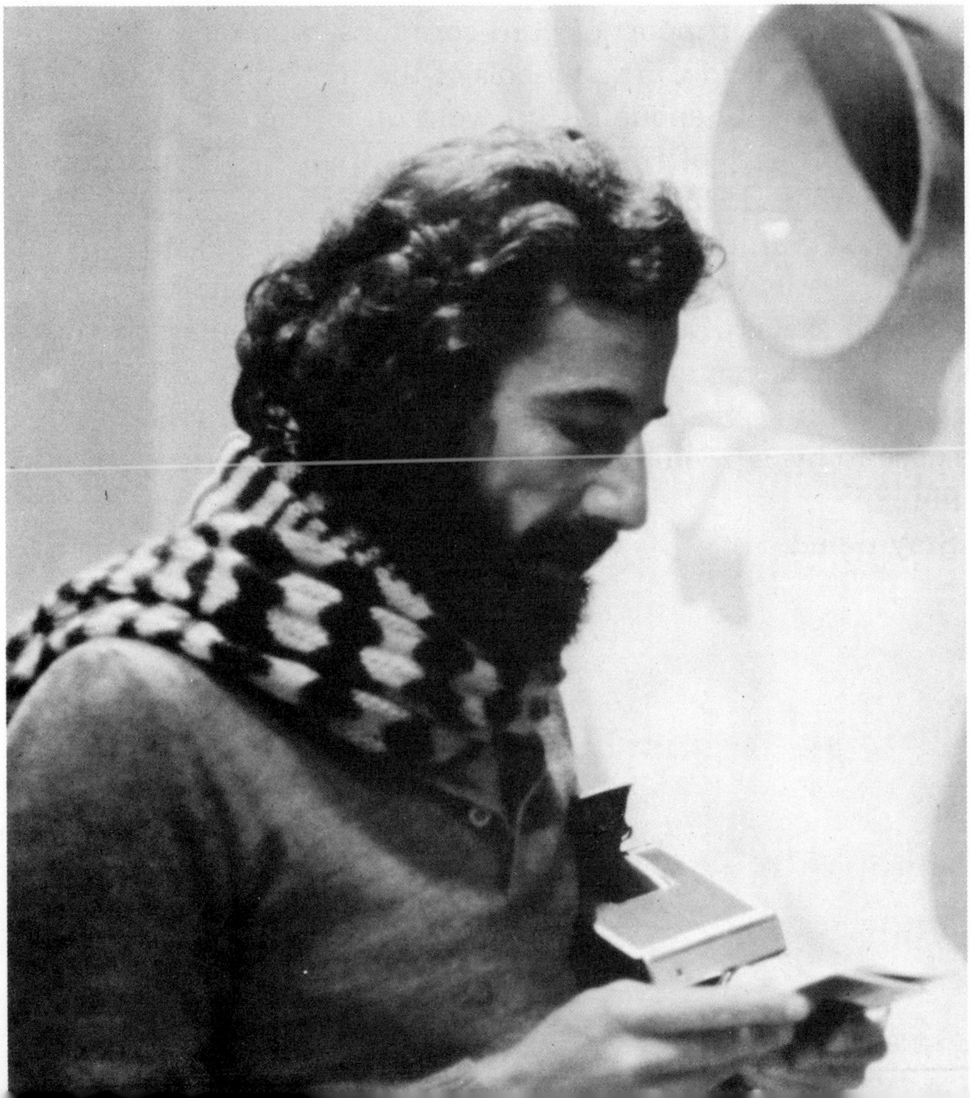

Since the fifties, Lou Adler has been a contributor to new movements in American music and film. He has been the producer for the outrageous comics Cheech and Chong since they began making records. He's been Carole King's manager and has worked with such hit-makers as Sam Cooke, Johnny Rivers, Scott McKenzie, and Spirit. As the sole owner of Ode Records, he has worked closely with some of the most important recording artists of the past twenty years, going back to the days when he used to produce records in a garage with his friend Herb Alpert.

Adler's first film was the 1967 hit documentary *Monterey Pop,* which he produced with John Phillips of the Mamas and Papas. This film, known as "the Father of Woodstock," introduced to the world Janis Joplin, Jimi Hendrix, and other of the sixties' most flamboyant popular music artists. The movie also was the first influential statement about a style of music that was to change our times.

In 1970 Adler produced *Brewster McCloud.* Although the film did not enjoy the box office success of *Rocky Horror,* it quickly gained the support of hard-core fans, who made both the film and its star, Bud Cort, symbols of the free spirit in all of our hearts. Interestingly enough, Cort went on to become the celebrated cult hero of *Harold and Maude,* playing the macabre-oriented Harold to Ruth Gordon's Maude.

Satisfied with the impact of *The Rocky Horror Picture Show,* Lou Adler continues his work with Ode Records, entertains friends such as Tim Curry when they visit Los Angeles, produces films such as Cheech and Chong's *Up in Smoke* (which he also directed), and in some mysterious way moves on through time and space to his next important contribution to American music and film.

Stay tuned.

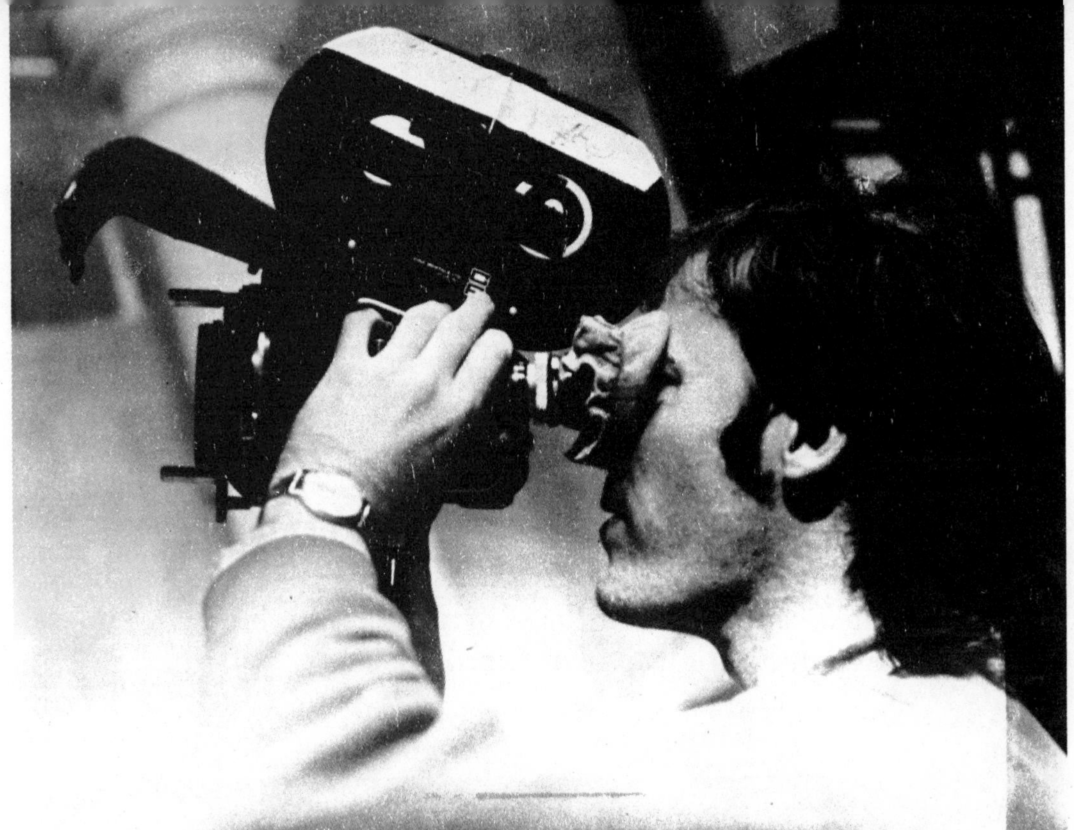

## Jim Sharman—Director

If directing a stage play that is intended to parody movies is an odd task, it can only be odder to adapt your own direction for that play back to film. As the director of both the original *Rocky Horror Show* and *The Rocky Horror Picture Show,* Jim Sharman turned the entire trick. He also wrote the screenplay for the film in collaboration with Richard O'Brien.

Before coming to *Rocky Horror,* Sharman had directed *Hair* and *Jesus Christ Superstar* in his native Australia, where he is well-known for his fondness for experimental theater. He directed a revue affiliated with the famous *OZ* magazine, a visually radical interpretation of Mozart's *Don Giovanni* for the Australian Opera Company, and a six-hour nonstop entertainment that blended disco dancing sessions with performances of Jean Genet's play *The Maids.* Sharman describes it: "People dropped to the ground with exhaustion, and financially it was a disaster. But at least it began to close the gap between theater and other forms of live entertainment."

Certainly *Rocky Horror* has helped to close the gap between movies and live entertainment, as audiences around America can attest. Sharman's first film was a 16-mm color feature called *Shirley Thompson Versus the Aliens*. "It was the first film to explore science fiction in terms of rock and roll," Sharman says. "Maybe that's why I liked *The Rocky Horror Show* so much when Richard O'Brien brought it to me."

Sharman has directed numerous plays and films in Tokyo, London, New York, and Los Angeles, as well as in Australia. In 1978 his film *The Night, The Prowler* made its American premiere at the Australian Film Festival at Lincoln Center.

# The Cult: MY FAVORITE OBSESSION

*Emotion: Agitation or disturbance of mind,*
*vehement or excited mental state.*
*It is also a powerful and irrational master.* — Look that up in your "Fuck & Wagnalls"

From what reporters, newscasters, and "virgins" have viewed in newspapers, on television, and in midnight movie lines across the nation, there seems little doubt that *Rocky Horror* fans are indeed its slaves. Every Friday and Saturday night, as the witching hour approaches, thousands of people across the United States, Canada, and the rest of the world line up to buy their tickets for *The Rocky Horror Picture Show*. Most of the people are young; many are hipsters of one sort or another; some are in costume and makeup resembling the movie's characters. Such devotional behavior has occurred in the past, but never in movie history have the proportions been so huge, the audience so devout, or the duration so long. Is this a genuine cult? Is it a new religion? Is it the end of the world?

Obviously the costumed class is most easily identified with the phenomenon. Interestingly, the costumed caperers probably

as of 3/31/79

RECEIVED
APR 16 1979
P D M'RLIS

ROCKY HORROR PICTURE SHOW

EASTERN DIVISION

| EXCHANGE | CURRENT WEEK | TOWN | THEATRE |
|---|---|---|---|
| NEW YORK | -145 | New York City | New Yorker |
| | 37 | New York City | 8th St. Playhouse |
| | 96 | Uniondale | Mini Cinema |
| | -110 | New Brunswick | Art |
| | 54 | Sunnyside | Center |
| | 51 | Bronx | Circle |
| | 23 | New Paltz | New Paltz |
| | 54 | Hackensack | Oritani |
| | 67 | New Rochelle | Proctors |
| | 45 | Union | Union |
| | 45 | Belmar | Belmar |
| | 45 | Nyack | Cinema East |
| | 45 | Westhampton | Hampton Arts |
| | 44 | Jersey City | State |
| | 41 | Rockaway | Rockaway 6 |
| | 27 | Hauppauge | Hauppauge |
| | 12 | New Dorp | Fox Plaza |
| | 11 | Little Neck | Little Neck |
| | 4 | Brooklyn | Avenue U |
| | 1 | Poughkeepsie | Hudson Plaza |
| | 1 | Verona | Verona |
| BUFFALO/ALBANY | 22 | Buffalo | Granada |
| | 10 | Greece | Cine 1 |
| | 9 | Syracuse | Studio |
| | 4 | Cortland | Plaza 1 |
| | 3 | Oswego | Oswego 1 |
| | 39 | Colonie | Cine #3 |
| PHILADELPHIA | -124 | Philadelphia | TLA Cinema |
| | 45 | Allentown | Lehigh Valley |
| | 40 | Reading | Fox North |
| | 30 | Camp Hill | Capital City Mall |
| | 30 | York | U.A. I |
| | 17 | Voorhees | Echelon Mall |
| | [illegible] | [illegible] Hill | Cinema |
| | | | [illegible] Pacific |

Happiness

ANSYLVANIAN
SELECTIONS

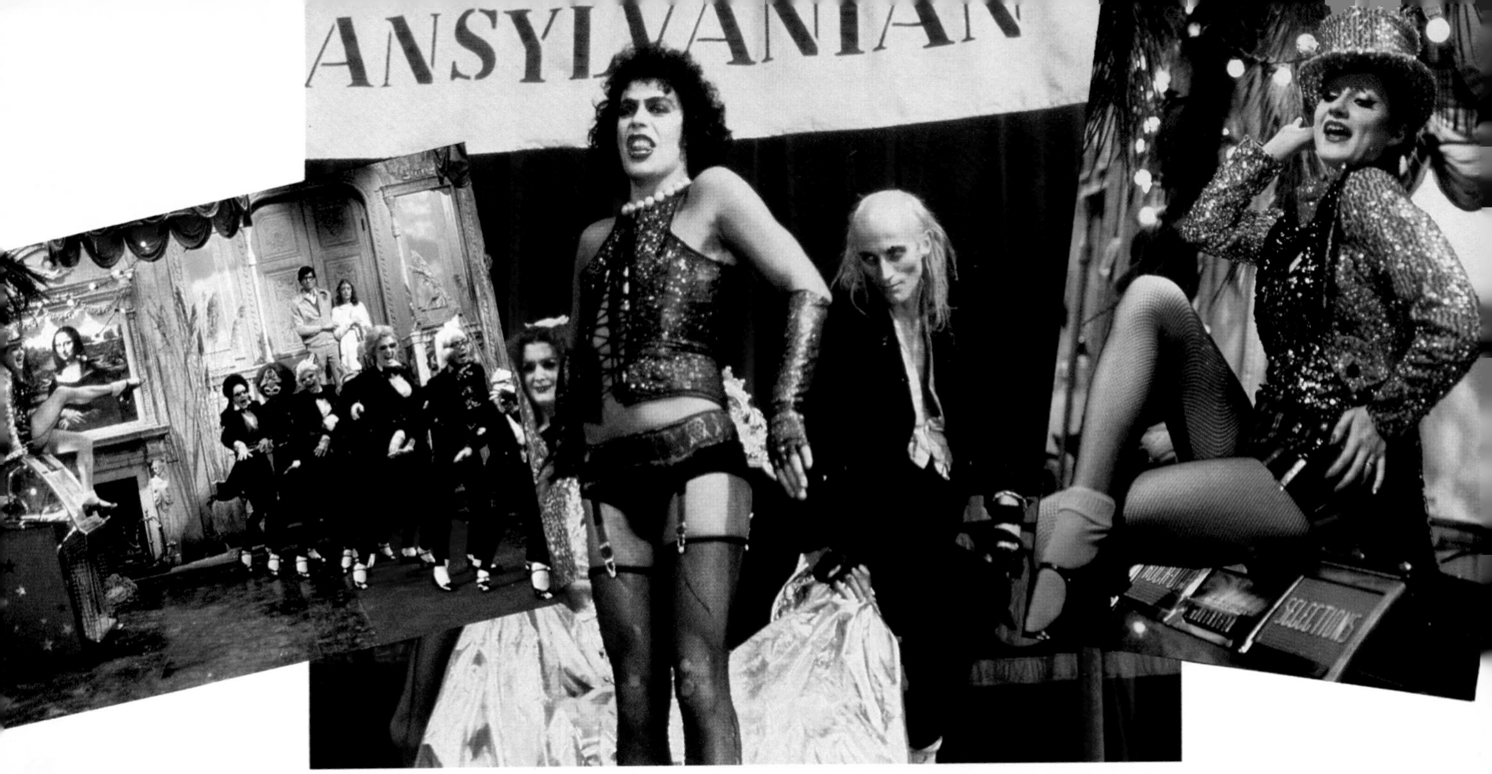

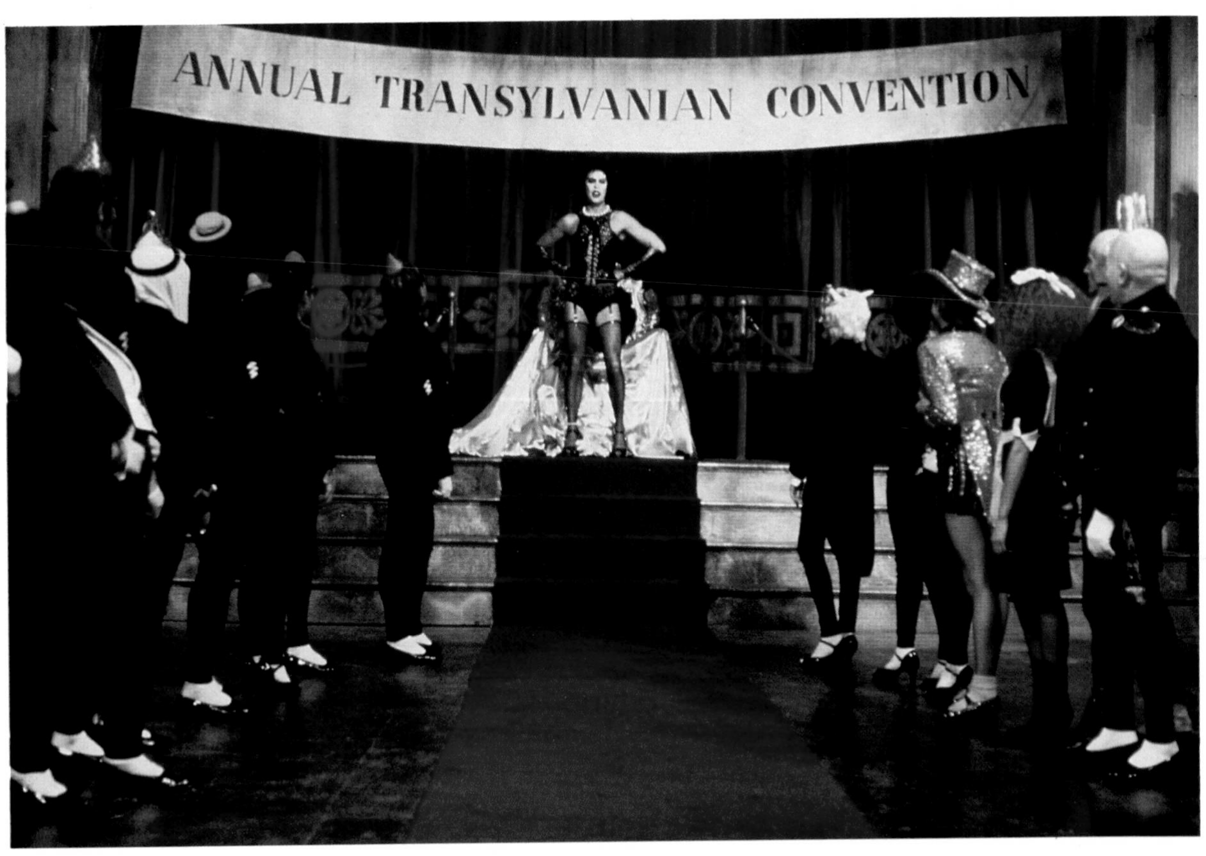

ANNUAL TRANSYLVANIAN CONVENTION

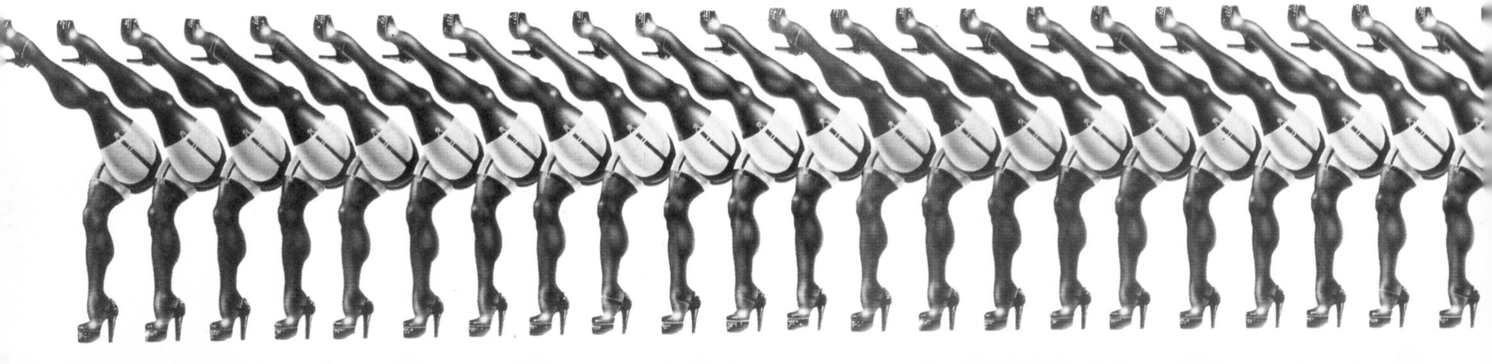

ANNUAL TRANSYLVANIAN CONVENTION

REACTOR
POWER
INPUT
SONIC
TRANSDUCER

DEEP FREEZE
DEEP FREEZE
IM OUT OF
MY HED.
O HURRY
I MAY BE
DEAD
EY MUSTNT
ARRY OUT THEIR
EVIL DEEDS
LOVE
EDDIE

Members of the National Rocky Horror Fan Club, based at the 8th Street Playhouse in New York City, pose for some post-midnight madness around Dori Hartley's portrayal of Frank-N-Furter. Kneeling in forefront *(left to right):* Sami Jae and unidentified Transylvanian. Back row *(left to right):* Greg Cline, David Hahn, Robin Lipner, Freddie Frick, Jule Klanit, Lillias Piro, Cissy Urami, Nora Controne, and Ed Bordenka. *(Photo by P. Pouridas/ K. Kuchaver; courtesy National Rocky Horror Fan Club)*

Fans in costume at San Francisco's Strand Theatre. Left: Transylvanians *(from left to right)* Tammy Foltz, Alana Rogers, and Kathy Sorensen. Right: Marni Scofidio poses as Frank to Mishell Erikson's portrayal of Columbia and Denise Erikson (Mishell's twin sister) as Magenta. *Photos copyright © 1978 George Post, Berkeley, California)*

contribute less to box office coffers than other fans because they often get in to see the flick for free. When a full-fledged cast shows up to perform the movie in some sort of déjà-vu simulcast beside or before the screen, part of their expenses may even be picked up by the theater's management.

It's easy to see why. Not only are some of these shock troupes good, they actually may generate revenues for the theaters at which they perform by furthering the development of the ticket-buying cult.

A few of the live cast performers who are good, determined, and lucky end up with movie careers of their own. But whether *Rocky Horror* street theater will propel its participants into a genuine limelight or not, their presence on the scene is a powerful force. The appearance of a live cast renews the film's reality for the viewer. Yet this live theater has begun to edge the movie off to the side—not out, however, because without the film the whole sideshow would go *pffft*! But it is legitimate to ask, at least, whose show the whole show really is.

The most perceptive assessment of the *Rocky Horror* phenomenon published so far was written by D. Keith Mano, and appeared in the *National Review* (November 24, 1978). Mano found, as we all have, that the audience is half the show. As he observed, *Rocky Horror* is a place where forces meet, and one is given a brighter definition of the relationship between audience and performer. It began with the one word: "groupie." "Groupie" suggests an intimateness that the older word "fan" never had: I-am-of-these-people. Groupies make a hard commitment: almost familial. They assume imitative lifestyles: clothing, make-up, morality, you-name-it. But this, after all, is a thankless aphid-dependent connection. And stars—film or TV stars especially—are distant, vainglorious (though they, in turn, have inescapable symbiotic dependence). The *Rocky Horror* Cult foretells a new art coming; or a renegotiation of terms anyhow. Public access TV and call-in radio have already conceded it. Audiences want more credit, imput; equal billing at least. Or else they'll go into open competition: a corporate mass cult star.

Competition? No. At least not yet.

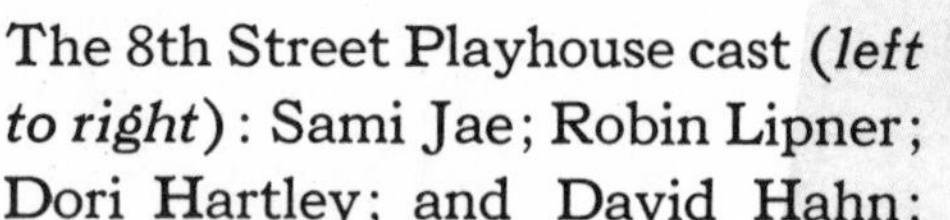

The 8th Street Playhouse cast (*left to right*): Sami Jae; Robin Lipner; Dori Hartley; and David Hahn; (*photo*: *Fredda Tone*)

The 8th Street Playhouse cast (*left to right*): David Hahn; Dori Hartley; and Robin Lipner; with Julie Klanit as Dr. Scott (*photo*: *Fredda Tone*) *Right*: Sal Piro as Janet (*photo*: *Fredda Tone*)

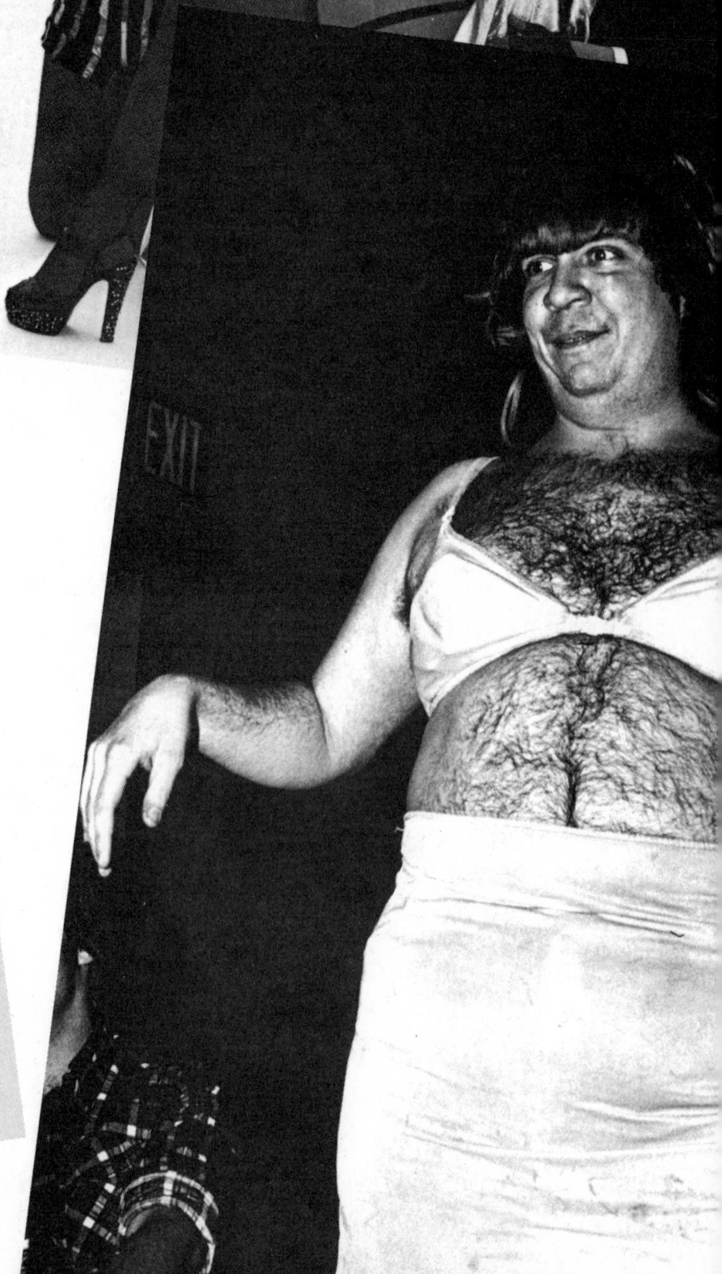

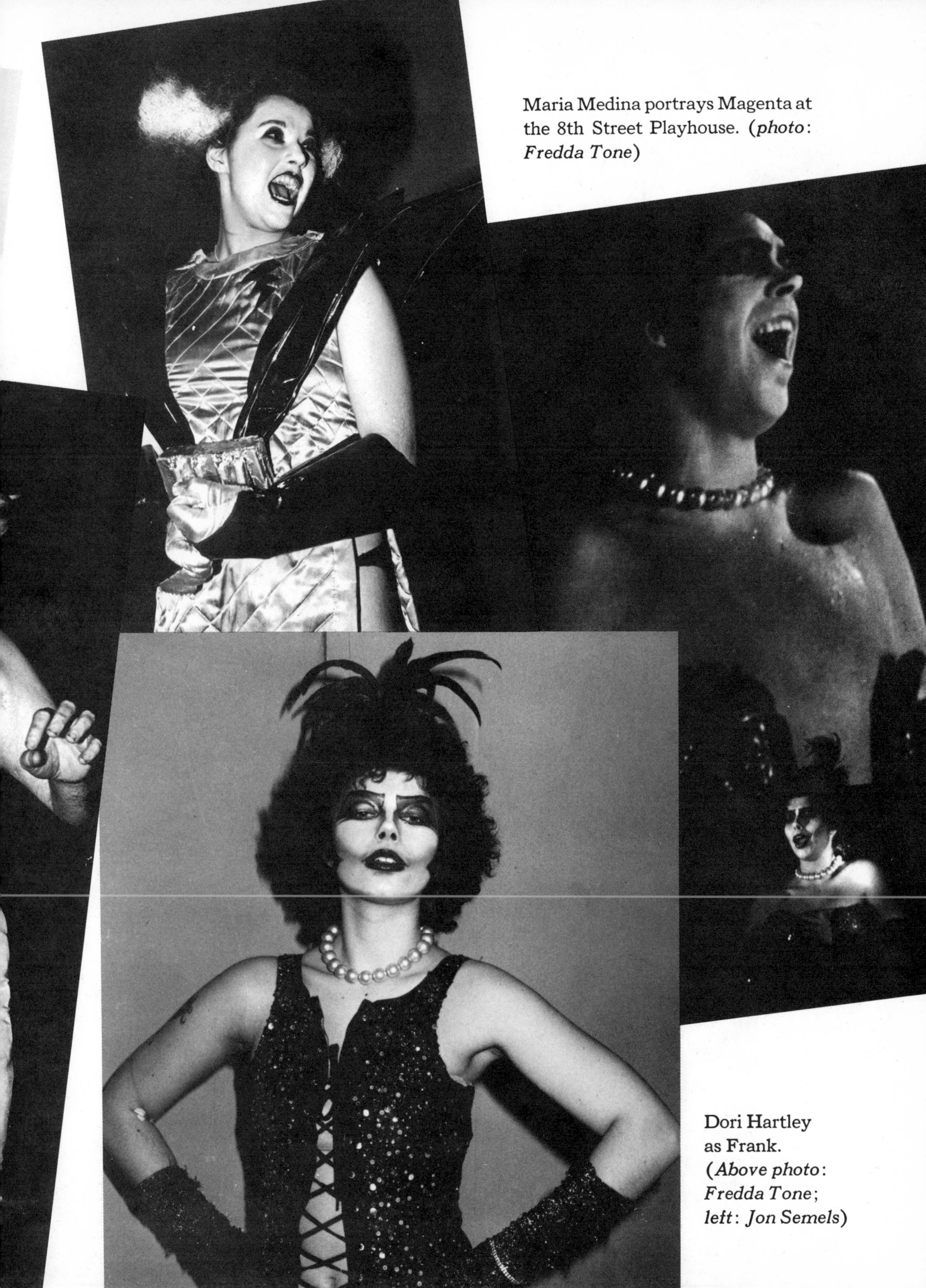

Maria Medina portrays Magenta at the 8th Street Playhouse. (*photo*: *Fredda Tone*)

Dori Hartley as Frank. (*Above photo*: *Fredda Tone*; *left*: *Jon Semels*)

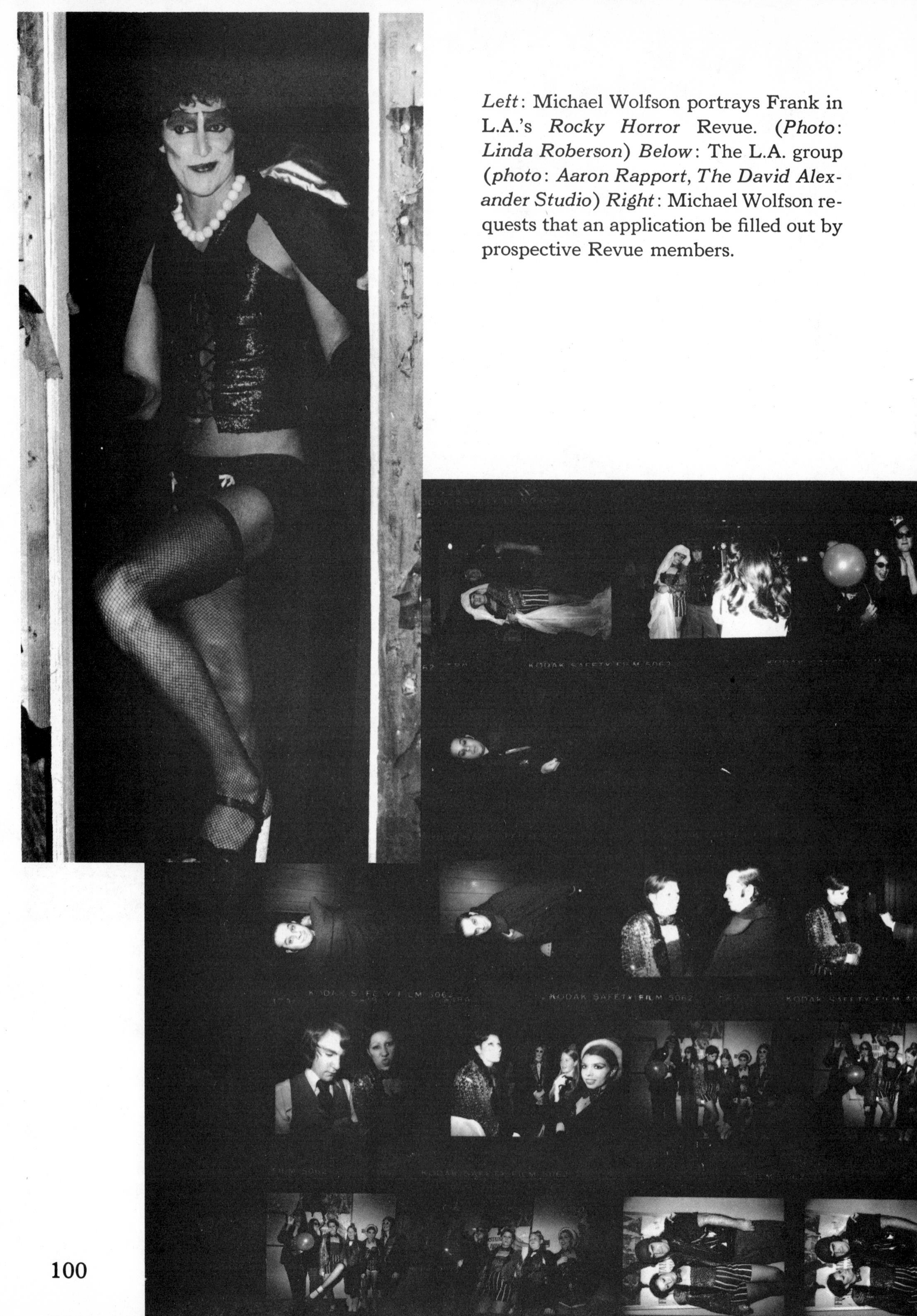


*Left*: Michael Wolfson portrays Frank in L.A.'s *Rocky Horror* Revue. (*Photo*: *Linda Roberson*) *Below*: The L.A. group (*photo*: *Aaron Rapport*, *The David Alexander Studio*) *Right*: Michael Wolfson requests that an application be filled out by prospective Revue members.

The Rocky Horror Picture Show started more than a cult for Cheryl Mathison and Bill Spears, the resident Columbia and Eddie at the Tiffany theater in Los Angeles. Following a midnight show in October 1977, they were married. Michael Wolfson (the *Rocky Horror* Revue's Frank) served as best man. (*Photo credit*: *Leigh Charlton*)

ROCKY HORROR REVUE

°RENT
°PARENTS
°OTHER

:

RESS:

SEX

AGE

ONE: ( )

ESCRIPTION OF YOURSELF:

TALENTS, INTERESTS:

DO YOU HAVE A COSTUME? . WHICH CHARACTER(S):

COULD YOU PERFORM FRIDAY & SATURDAY MIDNITES?

DO YOU HAVE YOUR OWN TRANSPORTATION? . OR ACCESS TO?

WHY ARE YOU INTERESTED IN BEING IN THE REVUE?

PLEASE SEND THIS PAPER WITH A SASE TO: THE ROCKY HORROR REVUE c/o 3758 INGLEWOOD BLVD. #4 LOS ANGELES, CALIF. 90066

THANK YOU FOR YOUR ENTHUSIASM!!



(Credit: Casey Dan)

The dictionary defines the word *cult* as “a system of religious worship or ritual; devoted attachment to, or extravagant admiration for, a person, principle, etc., especially when regarded as a fad; *followers; sect.*”

Cults, like religions, are founded on beliefs, and members take themselves *seriously.* But not the *Rocky Horror* brigades. The movie’s a place to have fun, to celebrate, to shout what must be the most delightful obscenities in the land. And although members of the inner circle have seen the film an incredible number of times, membership requires no more than three or four bucks and midnight attendance. *Rocky Horror* is more like a Sunday afternoon barbecue or a church picnic for the night people.

As Mano observed, these night folk surely do want some credit, input, and billing, and to acquire it they’ve taken one of the most creative steps live theater has seen in years. Audience response to the movie is widespread and often spontaneous. Although certain elements of the audience script remain identical from one location to another, other elements are unique to specific regions, theaters, and even performances. No one knows for certain how talking to the screen developed, although people in New York, Los Angeles, Columbus, and other early *Rocky Horror* cities lay claim to the original practice. It may have started in several different places independently, and then merged into a single phenomenon. Who knows? And who really cares? The point is, when Frank says “antici—” and we say, “Say it!” *we are there.* We have our own cues, our own lines, and our own stage (audience) presence. (“pation!”)

| | | | |
|---|---|---|---|
| BOSTON/NEW HAVEN | 48 | Boston | Exeter |
| | 10 | Providence | Cinerama |
| | 52 | Bridgeport | Merritt |
| | 8 | Hartford | Cinema City |
| | 1 | Stamford | Ridgeway |
| CLEVELAND | 81 | Cleveland | Heights Art |
| | 59 | Toledo | Westwood Art |
| | 33 | Cleveland | Westwood Art |
| | 29 | Kent | Kent Cinema 1 |
| | 14 | Cuyahoga Falls | New Falls |
| | 10 | Youngstown | Newport |

| | |
|---|---|
| PITTSBURGH | 48 |
| | 82 |
| | 6 |
| WASHINGTON | 27 |
| | 36 |
| | 40 |
| | 64 |
| | 26 |
| | 21 |
| | 3 |

the village
# CHOICE
MARCH-APRIL, 1978
THE BI-MONTHLY FILM SCHEDULE OF THE GROVE CINEMA
©1978 VOL. 2, NO. 3

# ROCKY HORROR ON FRIDAY, TOO

Saturdays have been wierd and now we're spreading the insanity to Ridays as well. Yes folks, the cult film of the '70s, *The Rocky Horror Picture Show* (1975) is manifesting itself on Fridays at midnight as well as its now legendary Saturday midnight showing. So tell all your strange friends that they can now join in on the musical science fiction madness and visit with Brad, Janet, Frank N Furter, Rocky, Columbia, Riff Raff, Magenta, Dr. Scott, and Eddie on Friday nights as well. *Rocky Horror* is moving into its second half a year of continuous run at the Grove Cinema, and we thought that it was time to start spreading it around. Do the Time Warrrrrrppppppp!!!!!!

He's the hero–that's right, the hero!!

3199 Grand Ave., Coconut Grove

## Madness Takes Its Toll on Wednesday Too

You asked for it and you got it. No, it's not a Toyota, but *The Rocky Horror Picture Show*, which is now going to delight and enlighten on Wednesdays at 10:00 as well as its usual unreeling at midnights Friday and Saturday.

All your favorite wierdos are on hand (both on the screen and sitting next to you) as Brad and Janet spend the night with Dr. Frank n Furter, Rocky, Riff Raff, Magenta, Columbia, Eddie and the crew from Transexual (in the Transylvanian galaxy). Kinky and outrageous, this rocking musical spoof on just about everything has been selling out for nearly a year and there is no end in sight. The pleasure of your company is requested about an hour before showtime in order to insure that you will get tickets.

FLASH FLASH FLASH

Save those ticket stubs! The Grove Cinema, in cooperation with 4 Way Street, is going to hold a weekly drawing for free pairs of jeans. Each week, some lucky *Rocky Horror* fan will have

urgh
College
aysburg

k
e
ond
ngton
ge Park
more
rd

Kings Court
Movies
Blair Cinema

Pembroke 1
Valley Cin. 1
Biograph 1
Key
Key College Park
Playhouse
Radford

SOUTHERN DIVISION

| EXCHANGE | CURRENT WEEK | TOWN | THEATRE |
|---|---|---|---|
| ATLANTA | 44 | Knoxville | Kingston 1 |
| | 44 | Nashville | South 4 #1 |
| | 2 | Dothan | Circle West 2 |
| | 25 | Birmingham | Vestavia |
| | 71 | Atlanta | Cinema Gallery |
| CHARLOTTE | 58 | Charlotte | Southpark |
| | 9 | Charleston | Fox 2 |
| | 49 | Columbia | Bush River |
| | 13 | Fayetteville | King I |
| | 5 | Greensboro | Janus Wings |
| | 34 | Greenville | Tower |
| | 7 | Myrtle Beach | Dunes I |
| | 4 | Wilmington | Manor |
| | 44 | Chapel Hill | Varsity |
| | 1 | Orangeburg | Camelot 2 |

DALLAS

OKLAHOMA

While audiences were heard singing along with the movie in *Rocky Horror*'s first general run in Westwood, California, fan consensus indicates that talk-back participation began with the first midnight booking at the Waverly Theater in New York City. Certainly the groups of fans who perform before, during, and after the film in dozens of *Rocky Horror* theaters owe their prominence to the New York cast led by Dori Hartley as Frank-N-Furter, and Sal Piro, their producer, director, counselor, emcee, performer extraordinaire, and general all-around den mother.

Piro, twenty-nine, is a former high school religion, algebra, and drama teacher who works as a stand-up comic in Manhattan clubs like the Duplex when he isn't busy with his chores as president of the National Rocky Horror Fan Club. He first saw the movie in January, 1977 and has missed just three available screenings since that time. By his own calculation he is one of four members of the national fan club group now based at Manhattan's Eighth Street Playhouse who have seen the movie more than 300 times.

While some audience groups around the country have set performers with clearly delineated roles, the Hartley-Piro cast

| | | |
|---|---|---|
| -150 | Austin | Riverside II |
| 82 | Austin | Riverside I |
| 101 | Dallas | Village |
| 48 | El Paso | Northgate |
| 59 | Houston | Alabama |
| 57 | Denton | Plitt |
| 61 | Ft. Worth | 7th Street |
| 50 | Ft. Worth | Ridglea |
| 50 | College Station | Campus |
| 33 | Abilene | Paramount |
| 22 | Abilene | Westwood |
| 34 | Wichita Falls | Wichita |
| 22 | Amarillo | Plitt |
| 19 | Corpus Christi | Movies |
| 83 | San Antonio | Northwest |
| 1 | Portales | Tower |
| | | |
| 42 | Oklahoma City | May |
| 31 | Norman | Satellite |

maintains a sort of organized flexibility. For instance, they have five Frank-N-Furters; Dori does not perform every night. They also have five Magentas, two Columbias, and two Eddies. Piro says he is "more or less the main Janet, but I have two back-ups—real girls—because I never show up as a specific character. I'm known for having a big bag. I have slips, bras, wigs, Riff Raff wigs, tail coats, wedding hats—you name it and I've had it in that bag. I play Janet, I play Riff Raff, and when the theater screens Meatloaf's short, *Bat Out of Hell,* sometimes I play Meatloaf.

"It's all very repertory. We have a schoolteacher in her thirties who is a Transylvanian and our second Eddie; if I can play Janet, she can play Eddie. (But not always.) We have a ten-year-old girl who sometimes does Columbia. Actually, we have a *nine*-year-old girl who played Frank-N-Furter when we had our Munchkin night last February. One of the original Brads at the Waverly is a forty-two-year-old woman named Alba. (She and Betty have the button license from Twentieth Century-Fox and also run the Tim Curry fan club.) After I got into the movie I took my younger sister Lillias to see it at the Waverly and she got scared of the girl playing Magenta. Now she's seen it almost 200 times and she's our number one Magenta."

Around Halloween 1976, an anonymous group of people, largely unknown to each other, began to dress up when they went to see *Rocky Horror* at the Waverly Theater in New York. Spontaneously they started to lip-synch the sound track, just as the Westwood audiences had in the movie's first Los Angeles run. About the time the group was beginning to form some loose association, problems with kids in the neighborhood of the theater and problems with the theater's management (who were not entirely happy with this influx of costumed and made-up freaks) intruded on their style, and they stopped dressing in costume. For several months there was little or no participation from the New York crowd at the movie.

Then, around March 1977, as spring broke in Manhattan, the true hard-core *Rocky Horror* fans in New York came out of the closet. Dori Hartley was the first person to return to the theater in complete costume. She looked like Frank-N-Furter, she sounded like Frank-N-Furter, and now she was dressed like Frank-N-Furter. People began to rise to their feet when she walked down the theater aisle, and the first audience cult hero of the *Rocky Horror* age was born. Within a couple of weeks the New York group was working with a full cast. In one form or another, they have been dressing and performing continually, every weekend, since then.

At the end of January 1978, disturbances caused by the proverbial outside agitators forced the Waverly Theater to close its Greenwich Village doors on the movie. *Rocky Horror* had opened a midnight run at the New Yorker in the spring of 1976, but its uptown clientele did not provide the participation that Dori, Sal and the rest of the group needed to support their activities. And despite the fact that *Rocky Horror* was now also showing at New York's Festival Theater, the group went out on tour. For several months they searched the outlying areas surrounding Manhattan looking for a home. They performed in Brooklyn, Queens, Long Island, and New Jersey, but conditions were never quite right. In July 1978 *Rocky Horror* opened at the Eighth Street Playhouse.

The group approached the theater management and explained that they wanted to return to the Village. They were

SOUTHERN DIVISION

| EXCHANGE | CURRENT WEEK | TOWN | THEATRE |
|---|---|---|---|
| JACKSONVILLE | 92 | Miami | Grove |
| | 44 | Palm Springs | Dolphin |
| | 59 | Orlando | Interstate |
| | 52 | Jacksonville | San Marco |
| | 52 | Gainesville | Royal Park |
| | 9 | Hollywood | Florida |
| | 50 | Tampa | University |
| | 39 | Tallahassee | Capitol Cinema |
| | 1 | Clearwater | Sunshine 2 |
| | 2 | Daytona | Daytona Mall |
| | 22 | Sarasota | Plaza I |
| | 22 | Ft. Myers | Plaza |
| | 16 | Key West | Picture Show |
| NEW ORLEANS/ MEMPHIS | 3 | Ft. Smith | Mall Trio |
| | 13 | Little Rock | Heights |
| | 13 | Memphis | Movie House Poplar |
| | -86 | Baton Rouge | University |
| | 47 | Jackson | Deville |
| | 47 | Lafayette | Plaza |
| | 40 | New Orleans | Plaza Lake Forest |
| | 10 | Biloxi | Surfside |
| | 40 | New Orleans | Sena Mall |
| | 2 | Lake Charles | Lake Prien |
| KANSAS CITY | -00 | Kansas City | Bijou |
| | 27 | Columbia | Missouri |
| | 9 | Wichita | Pawnee |
| | 6 | Warrensburg | Campus 2 |
| | 4 | Maryville | Missouri |
| ST. LOUIS | 25 | Carbondale | University #1 |
| | 57 | St. Louis | Varsity |



able to point out that their appearances seemed to improve attendance wherever they went. During the six months they had not been performing, *Rocky Horror* had received no New York media attention, but the night they returned reporters from several publications were present. On their tour, theaters which had been playing the film to half-empty houses found they were selling out within three weeks of the group's first appearance. The Eighth Street management agreed to let them in, and they have been based there ever since.

Unlike several other performance groups, the national fan club cast never acts out the complete movie. Instead, they do selected parts, such as "Dammit, Janet" and "Time Warp." If Dori does not do "Sweet Transvestite" before the film begins, she will probably do it during the movie. Piro retains some measure of control over the evening's proceedings and selects the cast so that it varies from night to night—as does the quality of the performance. There have been some nights when Piro says he would have been embarrassed to have reporters or members of the movie cast, who do show up from time to time, watching.

Although other *Rocky Horror* theaters do as well with the film as Eighth Street (such as the Biograph in Chicago, where the Anticipation Players' "regulars" perform most Saturday nights, and the "irregulars" perform on Friday nights as well as those Saturdays when the "regulars" do not), it is hard to imagine the New York crew being upstaged in the evolution of the phenomenon surrounding the movie. In addition to their outings at the Eighth Street Playhouse, they have appeared *at Rocky Horror* theme parties, on New York television, at the first *Rocky Horror* convention, and, during the summer of 1979, on national television on "Prime Time Sunday" with Tom Snyder.

What the group will do if and when the *Rocky Horror* cult fades away is anybody's guess. Some members, like Dori Hartley, have set their eyes on professional performing careers. Others have no desire for such a life. Piro himself is aware that his

CENTRAL DIVISION

| EXCHANGE | CURRENT WEEK | TOWN | THEATRE |
|---|---|---|---|
| CHICAGO | -57 | Chicago | Biograph |
| | 17 | Gary | Ridge Plaza 1 |
| | 10 | Bloomington | Eastland 1 |
| | 13 | De Kalb | Campus 2 |
| | 27 | Champaign | Coed 2 |
| DES MOINES/OMAHA | 8 | Lincoln | Plaza 2 |
| | 25 | Bettendorf | Duck Creek #1 |
| | 1 | Waterloo | Waterloo |
| MILWAUKEE | 4 | Hancock | Pic |
| | 44 | Madison | Majestic |
| | 65 | Milwaukee | Oriental |

participation in the *Rocky Horror* phenomenon cannot hurt his own career. "I was acting and doing stand-up comedy before I got into *Rocky Horror,* and I really don't plan on giving it up after *Rocky Horror.*" He is also writing a book about his experiences with the cult, called *Creatures of the Night.*

Among all the major performance groups, the one Piro claims to know least about is the one based in San Francisco. In part, the reason is that the San Francisco performance group, known as Double Feature, is one of the newest big city groups on the scene. Perhaps it's just difficult to be visible in a city that has such a long tradition of outlandish and bizarre behavior. A few people wandering around downtown San Francisco at midnight in high-camp drag excite rather less comment than they do in New Brunswick, New Jersey, or Dallas, Texas, or Kansas City, Missouri, where, as it has in New York, San Francisco, and another dozen towns, *Rocky Horror* has played for more than 100 weeks.

According to Marni Scofidio, the San Francisco group's rousing Frank-N-Furter, Double Feature came together by a set of karmic accidents: "phone calls that really shouldn't have been made, but were. People talking to each other when there was every reason they shouldn't. Everybody just kind of found everybody else."

By the summer of 1978, a small performance cast was working at the University Theater in Berkeley, across the Bay

| | | | |
|---|---|---|---|
| CINCINNATI | -96 | Columbus | Graceland |
| | 44 | Dayton | Art |
| | 26 | Cincinnati | Skywalk |
| | 1 | Cynthiana | Studio |
| DETROIT | 54 | Grosse Pointe | Punch & Judy |
| | 33 | Southfield | Movies Prudential |
| | 31 | Ann Arbor | Movies 3 |
| | 29 | Grand Rapids | Movies 3 |
| | 29 | Kalamazoo | West Main |
| | 22 | Midland | Cinema 2 |
| INDIANAPOLIS | 28 | Greenwood | Greenwood #3 |
| | 23 | Ft. Wayne | Northwood Pk. #2 |
| | 7 | Bloomington | College Mall #1 |
| | 7 | Muncie | Movies #1 |
| | 17 | Louisville | Vogue |
| MINNEAPOLIS | 46 | Minneapolis | Uptown |
| | 6 | LaCrosse | King #1 |
| | 6 | Moorhead | Safari #1 |

From *The Transylvanian* (*copyright © 1978, 1979; courtesy The Rocky Horror National Fan Club; used by permission*)
*Inlay photo credit*: *Fredda Tone from Bayonne*

50¢

# The Transylvanian



VOL. 1 No. 1

ROCKY HORROR NEWS

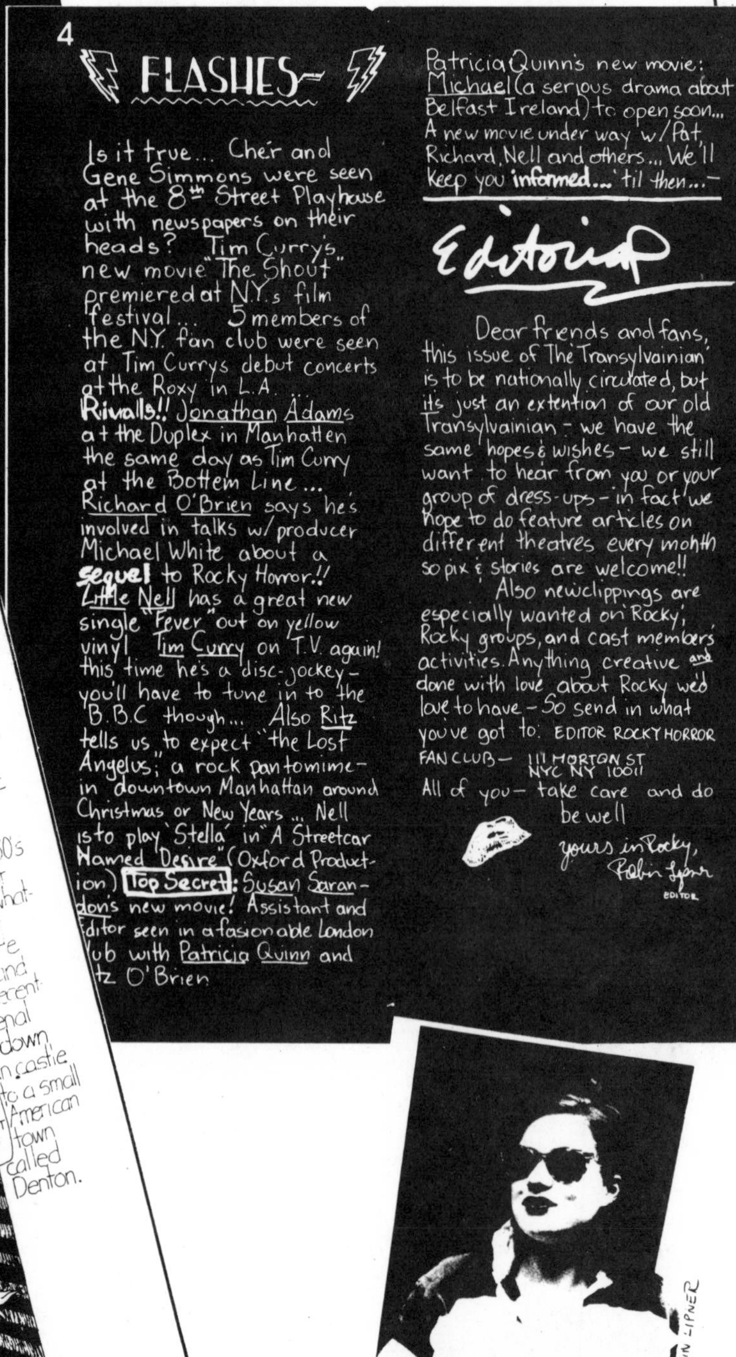

4

## FLASHES—

Is it true... Cher and Gene Simmons were seen at the 8th Street Playhouse with newspapers on their heads? Tim Curry's new movie "The Shout" premiered at N.Y.'s film festival... 5 members of the N.Y. fan club were seen at Tim Currys debut concerts at the Roxy in L.A. ... **Rivalls!!** Jonathan Adams at the Duplex in Manhatten the same day as Tim Curry at the Bottem Line... Richard O'Brien says he's involved in talks w/ producer Michael White about a **sequel** to Rocky Horror!! Little Nell has a great new single "Fever" out on yellow vinyl. Tim Curry on T.V. again! this time he's a disc-jockey— you'll have to tune in to the B.B.C though... Also Ritz tells us to expect "the Lost Angelus," a rock pantomime— in downtown Manhattan around Christmas or New Years... Nell is to play "Stella" in "A Streetcar Named Desire" (Oxford Production) **Top Secret**: Susan Sarandon's new movie! Assistant and Editor seen in a fasionable London club with Patricia Quinn and Ritz O'Brien. Patricia Quinn's new movie: Michael (a serious drama about Belfast Ireland) to open soon... A new movie under way w/ Pat, Richard, Nell and others... We'll keep you **informed...** 'til then...—

## Editorial

Dear friends and fans,
this issue of The Transylvainian is to be nationally circulated, but its just an extention of our old Transylvainian— we have the same hopes & wishes— we still want to hear from you or your group of dress-ups— in fact we hope to do feature articles on different theatres every month so pix & stories are welcome!!

Also newclippings are especially wanted on Rocky, Rocky groups, and cast members' activities. Anything creative and done with love about Rocky we'd love to have— So send in what you've got to: EDITOR ROCKY HORROR FAN CLUB— 111 MORTON ST NYC NY 10011

All of you— take care and do be well

yours in Rocky,
Robin Lipner
EDITOR

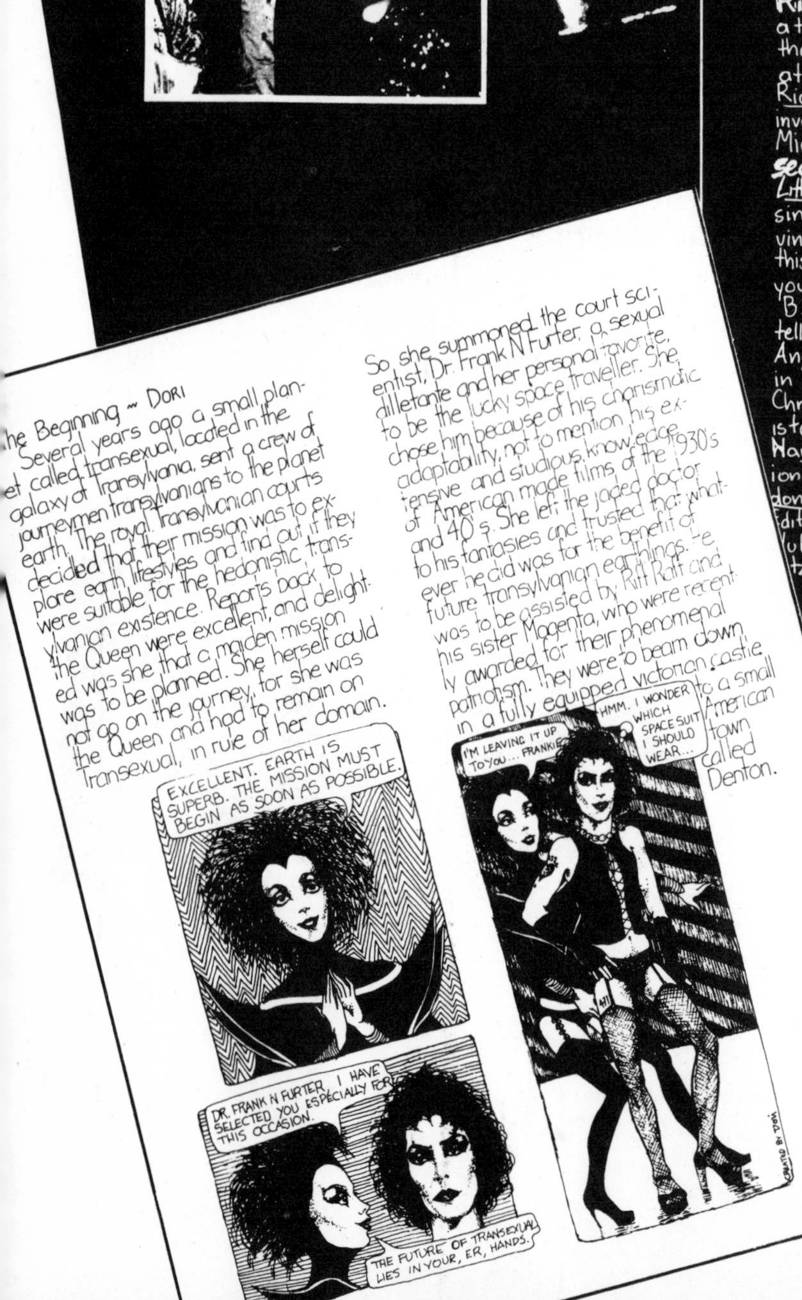

## The Beginning ~ Dori

Several years ago a small planet called transexual, located in the galaxy of Transylvania, sent a crew of journeymen transylvanians to the planet earth. The royal Transylvanian courts decided that their mission was to explore earth lifestyles and find out if they were suitable for the hedonistic transylvanian existence. Reports back to the Queen were excellent, and delighted was she that a maiden mission was to be planned. She herself could not go on the journey, for she was the Queen and had to remain on Transexual, in rule of her domain.

So she summoned the court scientist, Dr. Frank N Furter, a sexual dilletante and her personal favorite, to be the lucky space traveller. She chose him because of his charismatic adaptability, not to mention his extensive and studious knowledge of American made films of the 1930's and 40's. She left the jaded doctor to his fantasies and trusted that whatever he did was for the benefit of future transylvanian earthlings. He was to be assisted by Riff Raff and his sister Magenta, who were recently awarded for their phenomenal patriotism. They were to beam down in a fully equipped victorian castle to a small American town called Denton.

EXCELLENT. EARTH IS SUPERB. THE MISSION MUST BEGIN AS SOON AS POSSIBLE.

I'M LEAVING IT UP TO YOU... FRANKIE

HMM. I WONDER WHICH SPACE SUIT I SHOULD WEAR...

DR. FRANK N FURTER. I HAVE SELECTED YOU ESPECIALLY FOR THIS OCCASION.

THE FUTURE OF TRANSEXUAL LIES IN YOUR, ER, HANDS.

CREATED BY DORI

NELL STRIKES A CASUAL

*for a chapter on trivia*

...or Fan Club, this fan ...ence since January ...ng stages for 3 months ...n that it has taken us ...point is simply that we ...at we're doing and ...ans with the best pos- ...formation we can. As ...have also chartered ...ters (Brooklyn, Queens, ... Louis).

...attention that there are ...dvertising, whose purposes ...e your money rather than ...with other "Rocky" fans ...u with information about the ...and the cult. All we can say ...ot confuse our organization ...

Larry Forer and Robin Lipner
Editors

# The Home of Happiness?

**by Marc Perton (Bronx, N.Y.)**

Take your pick! According to **Hammonds World Atlas** there is Denton, Georgia (pop. 255); Denton, Kansas (pop. 161); Denton, Kentucky (pop. unlisted); Denton, Maryland (pop. 1,938); Denton, Missouri (pop. 97); Denton, Montana (pop. 410); Denton, North Carolina (pop. 852); Denton, Nebraska (pop. 99); Denton, Texas (pop. 26,844). My personal guess is Denton Kansas, with Frank-N-Furter's castle on a side road somewhere off Route 116. Of course, Denton, Nebraska fits the description pretty well, as do the ones in Missouri, Kentucky and Montana. But it's up to you to decide which one is **your** home of happiness. (Of course you can go and check a few of them out by questioning the natives and the employees of the local church!)

Right after receiving Marc Perton's article about the location of all the Dentons in the U.S.A. we got this article from Dana Whitehurst of Treasure Island, Florida. Just a coincidence . . . or maybe Rocky "people" have the same things on their minds!

"What state is Denton supposed to be in? After pulling out my atlas and doing a little research I have found several Dentons, the most interesting being in Kentucky (editor's note: the same conclusion reached by others. Our opinion is that it is in Ohio but not found on an atlas because . . . perhaps it is just a figment of the imagination!). In Kentucky not only is there a Denton but also towns of **Frank**fort, **Columbia, Eddie**ville, **Brad**fordsville, and that great town of **Scotts**ville

Think about it!

5

# 'Rocky' Reflections

**Carmen Rivera**

Shortly before my 29th birthday I went to see the Rocky Horror Show. Prior to that I had ...ever **experienced** a movie, seen one, yes. ...t experienced one, never. I came away ...h the feeling that I must as quickly as pos- ...e return. There were times when I clap- ...l, sighed and totally lost myself in what ...happening on the screen.

...wish I had heard of Frank sooner. What I ...issed!

...ng doesn't diminish the more you ...nly grows. Fantasy, true. But more ...e fantasy. Light, revelation and ...t an understanding of what I knew ...be true. That I have completely ...e with a man who wears more ...an I do is strange, but that I was ...beyond that is marvelous.

...have never seen it, run to your ...ake your reservation NOW and ...It is difficult to explain why one ...ne does.

...an exaggeration but does ...ere is both female and ...n are an integral part. To ...at in the past has been ...male component and ...nale is to be whole.

...nd see the Rocky Horror Show, enjoy, and let the light shine through.

**Sal Piro**

*Good Stuff — Credit Sal*

There is no other movie that I love as much as Rocky Horror and yet I'll be the first person to admit that there are some mistakes in the film! The mistakes are not serious ones that would be noticed by new viewers. Rather, they are the type which are picked up by those people who have seen the movie many times. Let's see how many you've noticed.

1. The father of the bride in the white jacket at the wedding walks up the church stairs twice (once in the close-up and then again in the long shot) –bad editing!!
2. In the "Wedding Song" when Brad is showing the ring to Janet her pocketbook is laying behind her–when they go to pick up the ring, it is in front of her –poor continuity!!
3. Nixon resigned in August–not late November. (Nixon's speech is being played in the car–and the criminologist has already told us that it takes place in late November)
4. During the Time Warp–the large male Transylvanian (Christopher Biggins) gives away the pastry tray then immediately has it back in his hand –poor editing!!
5. Also in the Time Warp right before Columbia jumps off the juke box you can see her hat on the floor, and yet she has it on her head as she jumps down–poor continuity!!

MORE MISTAKES ••••••SEE THE NEXT ISSUE

7

## CONNECT THE DOTS

THREE FACES OF O'BRIEN

from San Francisco. The cast was incomplete and their shows sketchy, but enthusiastic. On Halloween, Marni, dressed as Frank, was walking on Polk Street, San Francisco's major gay drag strip, when she suddenly heard, *"It's the master!"* "I turned around and I had all these strange people jumping on me. It was Riff Raff and Columbia and Magenta. From that moment there was never any question about who should do what. Everybody *was.*" With her costumed companions, Marni went over to Berkeley. She had not realized her new acquaintances were part of a performance group and was embarrassed the first time a flashlight found her. Soon, though, she began to get into her role in and around the theater.

The manager of the University Theater did not encourage the group, however. And, surprisingly, in the town that gave us People's Park, the Free Speech Movement, and other politically radical causes, they were harassed on the street. Having eggs and tomatoes thrown at them was a common experience. Once, one of the Transylvanians was nearly beaned by a bottle thrown from a passing car. On New Year's Eve, the cast married two of the regulars in front of the theater in the middle of University Avenue. But after that, things fell apart. The hassle was a bit too much, and Marni took three months off from her weekend role.

In March 1979 Marni dropped in at the Strand in San Francisco. Although she was out of costume, people recognized her immediately as a Frank-N-Furter. Someone told her wistfully about a *Rocky Horror* group in Berkeley that performed no longer, and she realized he was talking about *her* group. "I called them all up and said we had to have a Strand party."

Double Feature, not yet named, began to perform at the Strand on March 24, 1979. The group was still seriously incomplete without a Brad, Janet, or Rocky Horror, but their reception was far better than it had been in Berkeley. After the show one of the cashiers offered to talk to the manager about having the group perform regularly for the promotional benefits. Everyone in the group wrote his or her name down on a list so that the manager could call them all.

Marni remembers, "This guy in a pink suit and a huge blond wig approached us. Because of our Berkeley experiences we

WESTERN DIVISION

| EXCHANGE | CURRENT WEEK | TOWN | THEATRE |
|---|---|---|---|
| LOS ANGELES | 114 | Ocean Beach | Strand |
| | 86 | Hermosa Beach | Cove #1 |
| | - 106 | Phoenix | Sombrero |
| | 67 | Covina | Covina |
| | 73 | Tucson | Loft |
| | 71 | So. Pasadena | Rialto |
| | 30 | Sherman Oaks | Sherman |
| | 18 | Tempe | Valley Art |
| | 13 | Venice | Fox |
| | 81 | Balboa | Balboa |
| | 30 | Glendale | Sands |
| | 21 | San Bernardino | Central City |
| | 1 | Downey | Avenue |
| | 38 | Long Beach | U.A. #1 |
| | 9 | Riverside | U.A. Cinema #1 |
| | -100 | Los Angeles | Tiffany |
| | 6 | Orange | Wilshire |
| | 17 | Honolulu | T.H. Royal |
| | 11 | Keaau | Mountain View |

preferred not to have much to do with strangers, and we told him to go away. But he added his name to the list and tried to talk with us some more. He seemed nice, so we invited him to a party.

"His name was Bob, and he came over with Kathi Dolan. We started to go over some numbers like 'Planet Shmanet Janet' and she knew everything, did everything perfectly. Bob turned out to be a perfect Rocky Horror. Two weeks later I was in a garter belt and fishnet stockings for the first time since October.

"We pulled Brad out of the line. He had only seen the movie twice, but we needed a Brad. He came in looking like the lead singer in DEVO, but when he walked out to get his credits at the beginning of the film, he *was* Brad. Now when he walks by the line people call him 'Asshole.' He loves the recognition."

Marni finds portraying a man portraying a woman to be a challenge. "The one thing I wanted was to get to the point where people would not be sure which I was. I am intrigued by the fact that there is a masculine element in me, and I enjoy being able to bring it out. Women's lib aside, we still believe femininity is soft and passive. As Frank, I have a chance to be on top of things, to be a faggot Clint Eastwood. Frank-N-Furter may wear Joan Crawford makeup and high heels, but he's still so masculine there's no way you could mistake him for a woman."

Unlike the New York performance group, Double Feature does act out almost the entire film. Their mime is nearly letter perfect and still improving thanks to the Strand's manager, who agreed to run the film for them on an occasional Saturday morning so they could work out their timing more exactly. The group has performed at two major science fiction conventions, one in San Francisco and one in Los Angeles. They have filmed "Time Warp" for Argentine children's television. And they were offered a regular gig at San Francisco's major punk club, The Mabuhay, after doing a benefit performance there.

The members of Double Feature range in age from fifteen to twenty-nine. As with their New York counterparts, some—such as Marni—have ambitions of doing professional theater, or as in the case of their Janet, Kathi Dolan, would like to pursue modeling careers. Others, such as the group's Riff Raff, Linda Woods, have concentrated their attentions on *Rocky Horror,* at least for the time being. And still others are in the game just for the kicks. Or the absolute pleasure of it, as the case might be.

In the spring of 1979, when fan club president Sal Piro went to Los Angeles to meet with Rand Marlis and other executives at Twentieth Century-Fox, he also met with members of the Los Angeles performance group known as the *Rocky Horror* Revue.

The Revue dates back to the summer of 1977, when the Fox Theater, in the Los Angeles community of Venice, staged a look-alike contest. The Frank-N-Furter winner was then-twenty-five-year-old Michael Wolfson. In what he calls his "daylight life," Wolfson is a customer service representative in a local bank. "I enjoy it immensely. I like talking with people. Even better, I like listening to people. I'm a good adjuster. Of course, that's different from what I do at night. I'm like Dr. Jekyll and Mr. Hyde." It all seems all right, by the light of the night, eh?

Since Wolfson sees his life in terms of one classic science fiction/monster character, and liked to play Dracula "when I was a kid—actually, I did it up through four years at UCLA," it should come as no surprise that he revels in his Frank-N-Furter role. "I like the dressing up, letting the alter ego have its time, its coming out."

LET'S DO THE

# TIME WARP

BASIC STEPS

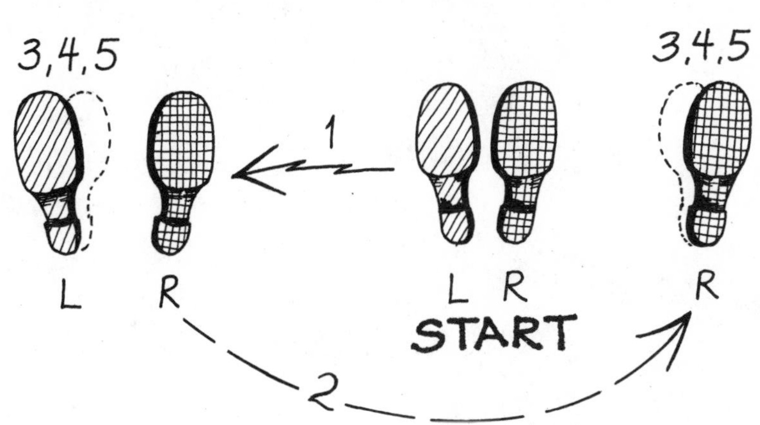


1 (ITS JUST A) **JUMP TO THE LEFT,** WITH HANDS **UP**
2 **A STEP TO THE RIGHT** (TIME-WARPER **ANNETTE FUNICELLO** SUGGESTS A VERY **WIDE** STEP)
3* (WITH YOUR HANDS ON YOUR **HIPS)** **YOU BRING YOUR KNEES IN TIGHT**
4 (THEN) **THE PELVIC THRUST** (IF REPEATED **FIVE** TIMES, IT NEARLY DRIVES YOU INSA-A-ANE)
5 **HIPSWIVEL** (IF NOT DRIVEN INSA-A-ANE BY STEP FOUR)
6 **LET'S DO THE TIME WARP AGAIN!!**

* THOSE WITH **LIMB DISABILITIES** MAY FIND IT NECESSARY TO **ALTER** OR **DELETE** THIS ACTION, BUT **NO EXCUSES** FOR ALTERATIONS TO STEPS FOUR AND FIVE

# From The Denton Affair

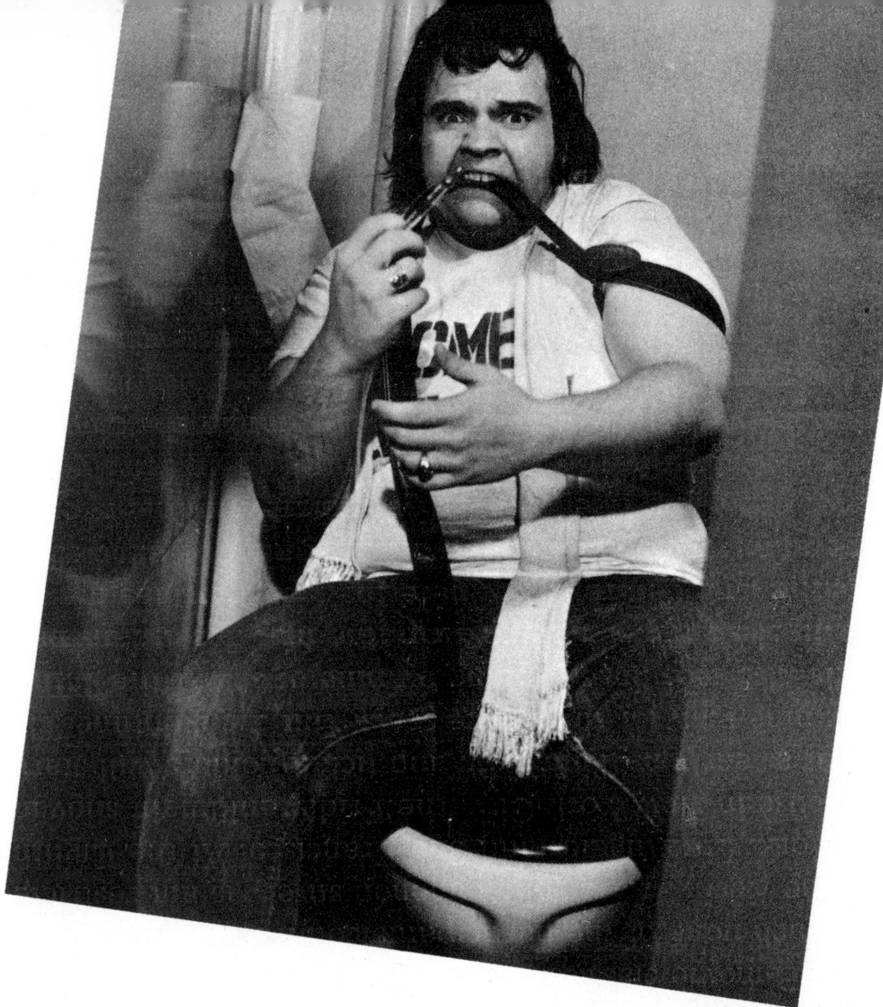

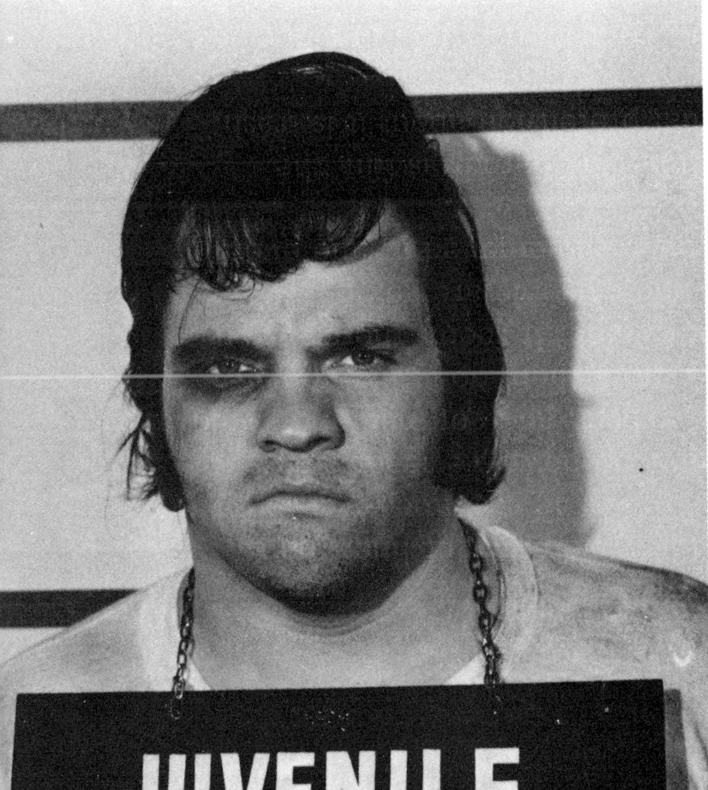
JUVENILE
DELINQUENT

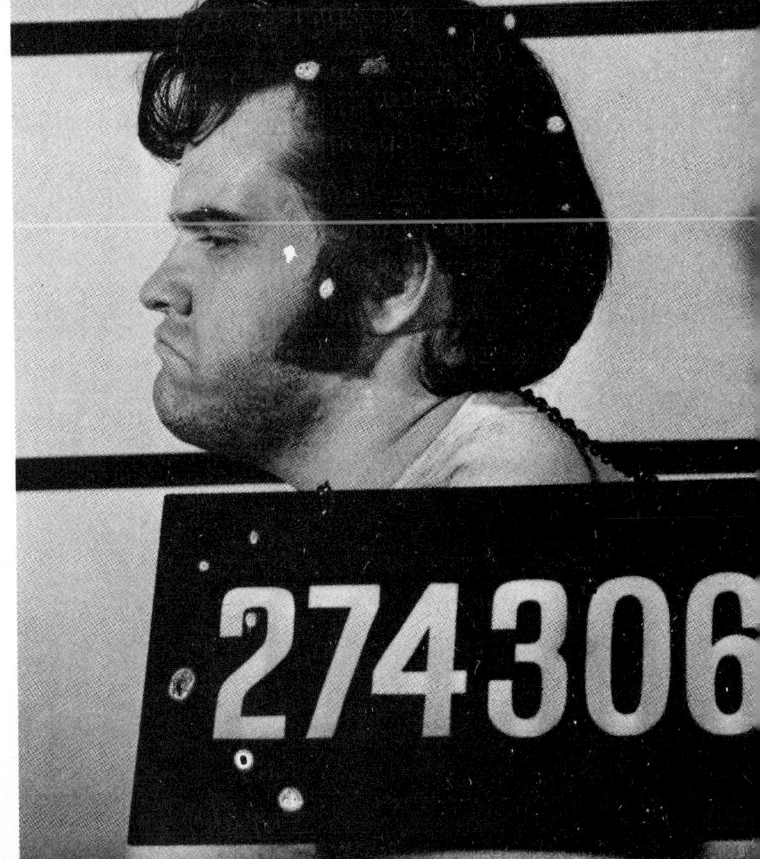
274306

| | | | |
|---|---|---|---|
| DENVER | 91 | Denver | Ogden |
| | 61 | Albuquerque | Don Pancho |
| | 31 | Colorado Springs | U.A. 150 |
| | 5 | Greeley | Cooper #1 |
| | 4 | Ft. Collins | Campus West |
| SALT LAKE CITY | 33 | Salt Lake City | Blue Mouse |
| | 1 | Idaho Falls | Paramount |
| | 2 | Bozeman | Rialto |

Wolfson had been into the movie for a year or so before the Fox/Venice contest, and had already seen it some fifty times. Something had been gnawing away in his mind for much of that time, and the whole revue concept came to him during the contest. He went to another look-alike contest the following week at the Tiffany, on Sunset Boulevard, and won again. But as important as winning the contest was, it was no less important than connecting with the people who made his plans possible.

Sandy Thomson, Shannon Wade, and Kristy Talm, all about seventeen, are residents of Hollywood. They had been at the Fox when Wolfson won the contest, and when they saw him on the street outside the Tiffany they shouted, "There he is! There's Frank!"

Was it merely coincidence that Sandy was dressed as Columbia, Shannon as Magenta, and Kristy as Janet? Coincidence or not, Wolfson suddenly had the first three critical members of his revue all at once. In the course of the next week or so, he got in touch with the Riff Raff of the Fox's contest, an independent movie cameraman named Corky Quakenbush, and enrolled him into the troupe. With the addition of a few hot-to-trot Transylvanians, the *Rocky Horror* Revue was on its way. "I found the rest just by going to theaters that had look-alike contests," Wolfson says. "I'd hand out flyers there, telling people about the Revue and inviting them to apply." Within a few weeks he had his entire cast together.

Perhaps because all of Los Angeles wears at least the faintest trace of the Hollywood tinsel, Wolfson's revue met with a happy reception from the local theaters almost at once. To begin with, the Fox asked him to perform a live stage show in between their two late-night screenings of *Rocky Horror*. The theater advertised the Revue's thirty-minute floor show, and made it a special part of the evening's festivities. Other theaters in the Los Angeles area got wind of what was happening, and asked the Revue to perform for them as well.

By now, the *Rocky Horror* Revue has turned in command performances in Fullerton, at the Balboa Theater in Balboa, at the Cove in Hermosa Beach, and at the Sands in Glendale. In June 1977 the management at the Sombrero Theater in Scottsdale, Arizona, invited the Revue east for that theater's first anniversary celebration of *Rocky Horror* madness, and the group did two shows of half-a-dozen numbers each, including "Sweet Transvestite," "Whatever Happened to Saturday Night," and "Over at the Frankenstein Place."

The theater Wolfson likes to work at best, though, is still the Fox, which is the Revue's home base. "It's a very *Rocky Horror* sort of place," Wolfson says. "They have a big balloon ceiling covered in red velvet, and a guy sits up there with strobe lights and flashes them when there's thunder and lightning on the screen." But the special feature show he remembers best was the July 4, 1978 performance in Hermosa Beach. The theater sent for him in a chauffeur-driven 1952 Silver Streak limousine, complete with champagne. When he arrived at the theater and stepped out of the car, "Sweet Transvestite" burst from the nearby loudspeakers, and Wolfson strode and strutted his way into the theater, leaving a trail of gasping fans in his wake. He recalls, "That's the first time I ever saw *men* reaching out to me, trying to shake my hand. Frank-N-Furter has this feminine side that many males don't want to cope with. For instance, I've seen one very macho Frank—and there's nothing wrong with that, but I don't think it's as true as the Frank in the movie. And I have yet to see a male performance group Frank last as long as I have."

Wolfson calls the *Rocky Horror* fans "enthusiasts." He says, "If you're an enthusiast, you can relate to the characters. I feel quite comfortable relating to Frank on a one-to-one basis. The movie is a takeoff on all the monster and rock 'n' roll and science fiction films. Every type of fantasy personality is in the movie. So it appeals to a wide range of people. Then there's the sheer fun of dressing up and going to the theater."

The *Rocky Horror* Revue is well set up by now, with a variety of props, including a transducer, and special lighting. But Wolfson envisions greater things to come. "I'm trying to organize all of L.A. and get groups going at all the theaters," he says.

If his first couple of years at the forefront of California's *Rocky Horror* movement are any indication, the whole of southern California may soon be dancing the Time Warp down Wilshire Boulevard.

While some parts of the *Rocky Horror* phenomenon are the same all over, it's also true that every city, every audience, and even every performance has its own special character. In New Orleans, says Ann Milligan, manager of the Sena Mall Theater, the audience is ". . . wild. They scream everything they can think of. Everybody just loves *The Rocky Horror Picture Show*."

For a while the New Orleans live performers had a motorcycle that tore through the auditorium with the local Eddie aboard. And during "Over at the Frankenstein Place," Ms. Milligan says, "You can't even see the screen, it's so light in the theater. People really have a good time. It's wonderful. We have two security guards here. One of them hates the movie, but I do the Time Warp with the other one—not in front of the audience, though."

On the first anniversary of the movie at the Sena Mall, she bought pink champagne and an enormous, tiered wedding cake for the fans. The cake said *Rocky Horror Picture Show* in black, and had a huge pair of red lips on it, as well as a bouquet of red roses. The party napkins were also *Rocky Horror* red, with *Rocky Horror Picture Show* in black. Ms. Milligan wore a black corsage, and joined in singing "Happy Birthday" to the movie.

The New Orleans theater did have to make some house rules a while back. Ms. Milligan stopped letting people bring in twenty-pound bags of rice, and stopped the audience from throwing toilet paper—"it used to wrap up the whole theater." She also placed a ban on squirt guns after someone ruined the theater's screen by squirting it full of Coca-Cola. And confetti has been her biggest problem, because when it gets wet it sticks to the floor and the seats. But even with the management headaches, she's delighted to have the movie at her theater. If she had it to do all over again, would she? "Oh, *yes!*"

Jonathan Weinberg, assistant manager of the Biograph Theater in Chicago (where John Dillinger was gunned down by the FBI years ago) says that the Chicago fans also had a big cake—in the shape of lips—for the first anniversary showing of *Rocky Horror* there in March 1979. They had contests and prizes and an all around good time. The Chicago live cast—The Anticipation Players—performed on stage to the movie sound track for twenty or thirty minutes before the film, and did some numbers during the film. At the end of the movie the Players and other *Rocky Horror* fans climbed up on the stage for some final dancing.

As happens at many *Rocky Horror* theaters, things get a little messy in the Biograph auditorium. "We have a man and his wife and their two kids come in to clean up after every show. They get here about four or five in the morning, and don't leave until afternoon. But we don't get a rowdy crowd," Weinberg says. "They can act wild, and that's okay. But they're not hard to control by and large. We try to keep cans and bottles out of the theater because the screen got damaged in the early days. Also, we try to keep eggs, tomatoes, and hot dogs out. We never have to buy toilet paper for the theater, that's one good thing. And the members of the audience actually help us out themselves. There's one guy dressed as a Transylvanian who goes up and down the line for me every week collecting garbage before the show. He walks around out there with a trash bag I supply, singing out, 'Cans and bottles against Disco! Cans and bottles for Leprosy!'

WESTERN DIVISION

| [illegible] | CURRENT WEEK | TOWN | THEATRE | A |
|---|---|---|---|---|
| SAN FRANCISCO | 86 | San Francisco | Strand | |
| | 79 | Berkeley | U.C. Cinema | |
| | 64 | Sacramento | Cinema J | |
| | 67 | Fresno | U.A. Cinema | |
| | 12 | Reno | Granada A | |
| | 12 | Santa Clara | Cinema 150 | |
| | 63 | Mt. View | Old Mill Cinema | |
| | 31 | Walnut Creek | 812 Cinema | |
| | 39 | Monterey | Sash Mill | |
| | 8 | Santa Cruz | Cinema 2 | |
| | 18 | Davis | Plaza | |
| | 40 | Petaluma | UA Cinema | |
| | 11 | Merced | Stateline | |
| | 3 | So. Lake Tahoe | Valley | |
| | 21 | Stockton | Covell | |
| | 10 | Modesto | Cinema II | |
| | 19 | Novato | Coast | |
| | 1 | Fort Bragg | | |

"The crowd is very loud and vocal. When people first come to the show they're exhilirated by what they see, and by what seems to be the spontaneity of the audience. It's a real treat to see people bring their friends the next week—watching them share their big secret. And for a lot of them it's social: They've made friends among the other members of the audience."

One of the few theaters in the country to dispense with the problems of sweeping up rice, confetti, toast, toilet paper, cards, hot dogs, and water is the Riverside II in Austin, Texas—since *Rocky Horror* closed at the Waverly in New York, the longest running *Rocky Horror* theater in the world. Bobby Little, assistant manager there, notes that after the screen got cut a couple of times, the Riverside simply decided to ban the audience props. Still, "We have a lot of audience participation, lots of dress-up. We have an annual *Rocky Horror* birthday party. Tim Curry came to the first one. At the third we had a live stage performance, live music, dance contests, look-alike contests, and so on. We gave prizes. It's just a good time."

At the Plaza Theater in Petaluma, California, Michael Goudeau works security for *Rocky Horror* screenings. As a professional juggler—one-fourth of the Fly-By-Night Juggling Company—he is a fairly well-known local performer himself, and he has become part of the show.

"I liked the film the first three times I saw it, and I didn't like it the next five times. It comes and it goes. I'm enjoying it a lot right now. By any ordinary standards it's a bizarre movie. Disney wouldn't have made a film like that. I would find it bizarre to see Bambi nibbling his way through Janet. But I like the people in the audience. I've gotten to know a lot of them, since they come back every week. My job is to check bags, make sure they haven't got any alcohol or eggs or stuff. What I do now is I hassle the people I know—not because they'd *have* alcohol or anything to throw at the screen that would hurt it, but just because we're friends. I push them around and open their bags and dig through them because we both think it's funny.

| | | | |
|---|---|---|---|
| SEATTLE/PORTLAND | - 86 | Seattle | Neptune |
| | 16 | Tacoma | Tacoma Mall #1 |
| | 8 | Spokane | Garland |
| | 7 | Seattle | Lewis Clark #1 |
| | 51 | Portland | Clinton Street |
| | 17 | Eugene | Mayflower |
| | 1 | Corvallis | 9th Ave. Cinema #1 |

ROCKY HORROR

RHPS is now well established as America's number one cult film. Once established in a particular market the picture is capable of running every weekend for years.

Like all late shows, the key to RHPS is its appeal to an entirely different movie-going audience. Generally, this audience consists of people between the ages of 17 and 35 who are seeking off beat, unusual and imaginative entertainment. RH provides just this in a participatory party-like atmosphere that is capable of attracting people week after week.

Our experience indicates there are several very effective means of promoting and establishing the picture in a particular market. Promotion should be relatively subtle. The audience should feel they are discovering something rather than being hyped or sold.

This is best accomplished with several very small pre opening ads in the local "underground" paper using just the title treatment and the opening date. Additionally, the same notation in a regular directory ad and a similar posting at the bottom of the marquee seem to help.

If possible, a tie-in with the local fm-album oriented radio station is very effective. For a relatively small number of passes and the purchase of several spots, a few "mentions" can go a long way. If a tie-in is not possible a few well placed radio spots on a station of this format can provide the needed awareness.

The following is roughly indicative of the kind of copy that has proved most effective on radio. (This voice over is accompanied by music from the picture's soundtrack):

> "Into every life a little 'horror' must fall."
> "America's number one cult movie, THE ROCKY HORROR PICTURE SHOW. This Friday and Saturday at the ____________ theatre. At midnight only. Because it's special."
> "Try it, you'll like it."
> "Only at midnight, Friday and Saturday at the ____________ theatre."

Other catch phrases are "Take a walk on the Wild Side" and "The hero wears heels!" These spots are most effective when run late afternoon and early evening Thursday, Friday and Saturday during the opening week.

With these basic concepts and a little effort you should be very pleasantly surprised with the quality of opening business. From then on word of mouth will take over.

There is simply no other late show picture capable of sustaining the size and loyalty of the audience for THE ROCKY HORROR PICTURE SHOW when it is properly promoted.

"When I first saw the movie there were longer lines than there were for *Star Wars.* Everybody was in costume, everybody was young, a lot of people were gay. By now I've seen some parents who did not know what to expect, and got mad and asked me to ask people to quiet down. A lot of them don't like to get wet. You wonder, though, why they came. It seems there's been enough publicity that they would know people are going to scream. I've also seen a lot of parents who enjoyed it, and even returned."

He shrugs. "*Rocky Horror* is fun. The parody is fun, the audience is fun, and any intellectual pretension about it is trash."

And so, by some extraordinary coincidence, fate had decided that *The Rocky Horror Picture Show* should keep its appointment with destiny and earn its unique spot in the pantheon of science fiction, B-movie classics. But it was to accomplish this feat in a way which none of the participants could possibly have foreseen.

The *Rocky Horror* phenomenon surely is not restricted to New York, Los Angeles and San Francisco. At the Eighth Street Playhouse in New York City, the Friday midnight showing may sell out as early as Thursday, and ticket holders will start to line up by nine P.M. for the choice seats. But the Neptune Theater in Seattle also sees lines forming by nine or so. At the Tiffany, on Los Angeles's upper Sunset Strip, the first dozen fans have settled in long before ten. Where the local cast has the theater's cooperation, the cosmetic/sci-fi/drag set may be allowed into the theater early and free. The early-bird crew in line is often a mixture of other hard-core fans catching up on family news, and a few wide-eyed thirteen-year-olds out painting the town with bubble gum, kid sisters in tow. *They've* been told the audience is half the show. And while they may not be sure whether they're there to dare or be square, they usually seem certain that there is *where* they should be.

At some theaters, such as the King's Court in Pittsburgh, Pennsylvania, all costumed fans used to be able to get into the movie free. There were Time Warp contests, and prizes for the best costume. At the University Theater in Berkeley, coming attractions regularly feature previews of such films as *Flash Gordon, Invaders from Mars,* and *Woodstock.* At the Strand, in San Francisco, the theater's daytime offerings include *THX 1138, A Clockwork Orange,* and *When Dinosaurs Rule the Earth.* The marquee of the theater next door sometimes promises "Free Burial for Patrons who Die from Fright."

Wherever *Rocky Horror* plays, the street in front of the theater is littered with Transylvanians long before eleven P.M. virgins (Rocky Horror first-timers) drop uneasy glances over their shoulders and huddle against the walls of nearby buildings. For the moment the scene is beyond them. Tonight, in San Francisco, one virgin is dressed like Brad. Behind his black horn-rimmed glasses his eyes glitter in the sodium-vapor-arc lights like Pop Rocks bursting on the tongue. He takes in the comic book scenario his Magenta-haired girl friend has brought him to. He's wearing his costume because she wanted him to. She's wearing hers because fantasy frees her.

Inside the theater there's noise pounding from the auditorium already. I've been here before—lots. I can tell by the whistles, stamps, and cheers that the crowd is getting behind the Betty Boop cartoon, *Snow White.* In some theaters the management runs Meatloaf's short film, *Bat Out of Hell.* Some places run cultish previews. It doesn't matter, in a way. The audience has taken to participatory cinema with a vengeance. Nothing escapes our commentary.

Of course, it's all practice—part of the party. In a few minutes the real thing will start. We know what's coming.

"*Rocky Horror* is a style," Sal Piro told me. "It preaches freedom as a way of life."

He explains, "When people were into Elvis they started to look like him. When the Beatles were popular, the Carnaby Street look came in. *Rocky Horror* is different because it's a movie. But after multiple viewings you develop a need to participate in it, and live out your celluloid fantasies."

I always enjoy myself thoroughly when I come to see *Rocky Horror*. There's always something going on. The first time I saw it I missed a lot—dialogue drowned in the raging seas of yelling, picture obscured by rice, toast, confetti, toilet paper, hot dogs. . . . It took three viewings to realize what Eddie was doing in that deep freeze. The screaming and yelling is part of having a good time, which is what this game's about. Sure, it's escapist. Sure, it's something to do on a boring Saturday night. Sure, it's a kind of cloistered group experience. But *any* film can be those things. If it's a midnight special, that's an extra. And the energy. . . .

Tonight the audience is especially hot. Forty or fifty kids are practicing the Time Warp in the aisles (it's not *just* a jump to the left), applauded and egged on by the seated house. Coleman lanterns pick them out in a preview of the show to follow: There's Riff Raff, there's Rocky, there's Columbia.

"*Rocky Horror* spawns new life." Sal Piro again. "Some people decide they're not into it anymore, and they leave. Others join. We all think of being movie stars from time to time. Why not? Any cult is made up of outsiders looking for a group to belong to: the PTA, the disco scene, *Rocky Horror*. Ours is a family affr. Going to see *Rocky Horror* is like going to a party every weekend where everybody knows everybody else."

There's an odd kind of camaraderie practiced here, just perfect for the seventies. Fast-food intimacy: a burger jack and a small order of *whoopie, I'm wearing a garter belt!* A large coke and an apple pie filled with *look ma! I'm yelling and throwing stuff!* Fun? You bet. *I think I'll be a girl tonight. Hey, that's great! I'll be a guy!* Tee hee. Take a walk on the wild side.

Sal says, "The film has eroded some sexual prejudice. While Tim Curry is raw sex to most fans, he transcends sexuality in the film."

Lou Adler: "The film is not erotic. Tim Curry is erotic."

Indeed. The gay, straight, bi, and incestuous sexuality is so totally parodied that any "message" of sexual liberation is incidental. The film is much more a hybrid fantasy of social decadence plugged straight into the brainstem of an extroverted culture. Even cannibalism slides by as part of the package. And since the show is by no means confined to the screen, our responses are pure catharsis. I have heard that one Frankie fan underwent a sex

*(Credit: Aaron Rapport, The David Alexander Studio)*

change operation, the better to conform to the mad Transexual's transvestite role. (Whether he became a she, or she became a he, my informant could not say.)

Lois Dolan, fifty, is the director of the Sexual Trauma Center in San Francisco and San Mateo. In the early days of Double Feature she acted as guide, counselor, and protector of the group. From her observations, *Rocky Horror* provides an outlet for its fans that may not be available elsewhere in society. "No matter how confused you are, *Rocky Horror* says it's okay. It's okay if you wear a corset and garters, and prance around and sing. Enjoy—you're not terrible. That's why the movie's going to last ten years. For two hours you're *okay*.

"Many of the people here live in a world that never was, and probably never will be. It has imagination, and it's unreal, and they are proud of that.

"I've looked at the lines outside the theater and they've been different every night. I was disturbed when I saw the straight, middle-class, quiet, watching-everything first-timers. This was not designed to be a couth show, it was not supposed to be acceptable in our suburbs. What are all these people doing here?"

The cartoon ends, and the audience applauds as if Betty and her wicked stepmother, the Queen, could hear. They part the curtain for a curtsy. This pattern remains during *Rocky Horror* too. More so, in fact. The audience cheers and boos as if the characters were there, and we can do so without the usually intimidating problems such adoration entails. While we can afford to be cruel to our celluloid heroes—pointing out that Columbia's breasts are "lopsided"; that Janet has "chicken legs"; that Brad is an "asshole"; that the Criminologist has "no neck"—there is never any doubt that the audience *loves* the characters without reserve. They are known quantities, and they are on our side—or we are on theirs. And, in a peculiar sort of cinematic turnabout, it almost seems as if the actors turn in better performances when the audience gets really wiggy. The movie cast are performers in the most wonderful sense, willing to let their hair down and kick out the jams. Several of the performances—Tim Curry's in particular—are masterpieces that will, no doubt, go down in the annals of kitsch and camp drama long after the cult is but a memory.

The Twentiety Century-Fox fanfare begins, and its logo lights up the screen. How is it possible to cheer a movie studio? Yet we do—and if you'd been asleep that cheer would drop your socks. Then as the titles appear, the house settles in for some serious noise. You can gauge by the chaos that nothing succeeds like excess.

笑いと恐怖とSEXが1950年のロッカ・バラードに彩られて爆発する異色ミュージカル大作！

# ロッキー・ホラー・ショー

〈カラー作品〉

HE ROCKY HORROR PICTURE SHOW
LECTED SELECTIONS FROM
SIDE 2 OSV 21653
HE ORIGINAL SOUNDTRACK FROM THE ORIGINAL MOVIE
TOUCH-A, TOUCH-A, TOUCH ME 2:27
SWEET TRANSVESTITE 3:21
MANUFACTURED AND DISTRIBUTED BY ODE SOUNDS AND VISUALS


――――ロンドンで生れ
スペイン、ドイツ、オーストラリア、デンマーク、パリ
更にロサンゼルス、ブロードウェイで
大ヒットのミュージカル劇完全映画化！

ティム・カリー
スーザン・サランドン
バリー・ボストウィック

原作ミュージカル劇■作曲・作詞リチャード・オブライエン
主題歌〈サントラ盤＝ODEレコード〉
脚本ジム・シャーマン／リチャード・オブライエン
製作補佐ジョン・ゴールドストーン
製作総指揮ルー・アドラー
製作マイケル・ホワイト
監督ジム・シャーマン

ルー・アドラー＝マイケル・ホワイト作品
FOX映画

THE ROCKY HORROR PICTURE SHOW

20th Century-Fox Presents
A LOU ADLER-MICHAEL WHITE PRODUCTION

映倫

UAL TRA SYLVAN

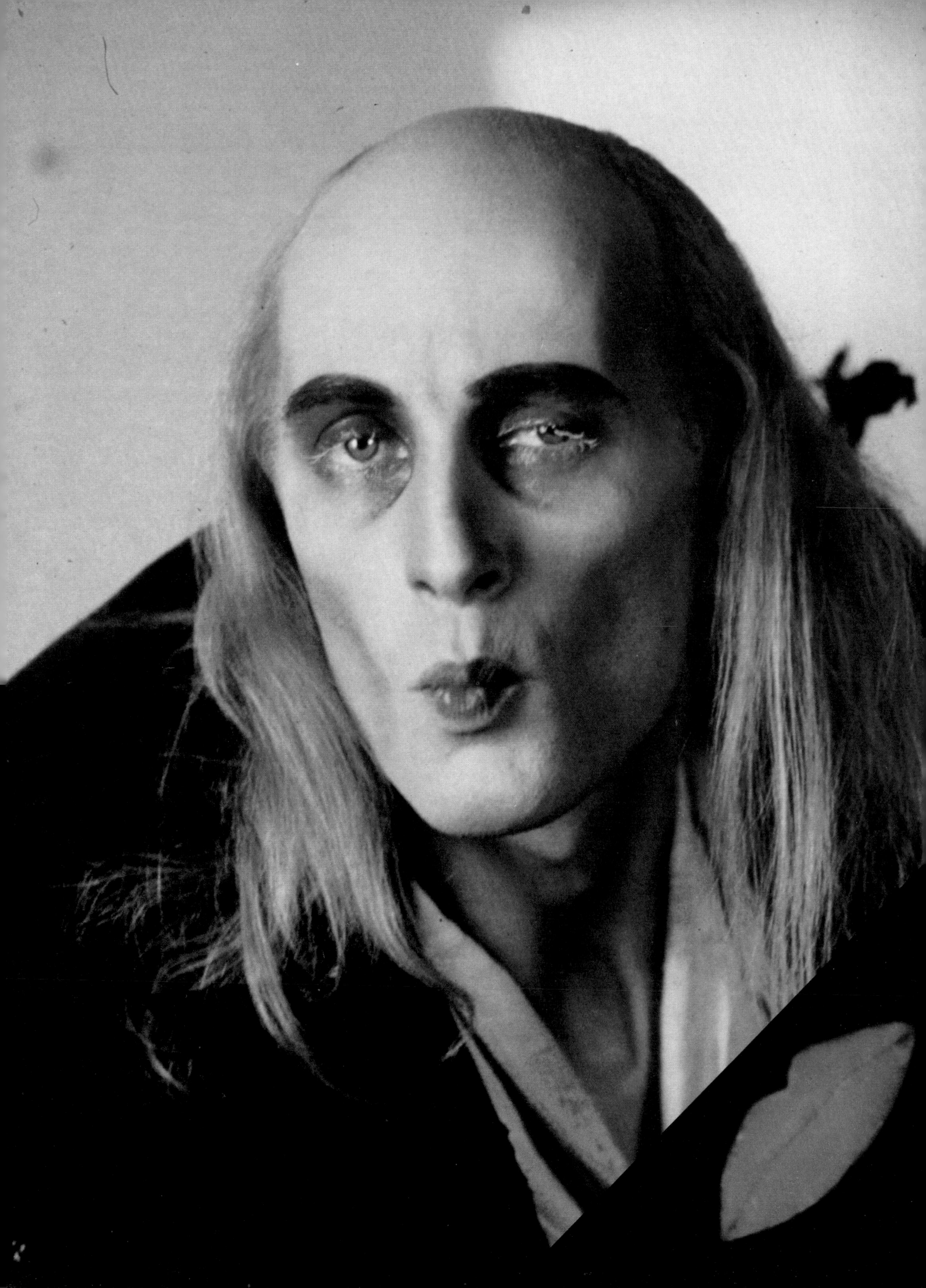

SONIC OSCILLATOR
REACTOR POWER INPUT
SONIC TRANSDUCER
MONITOR

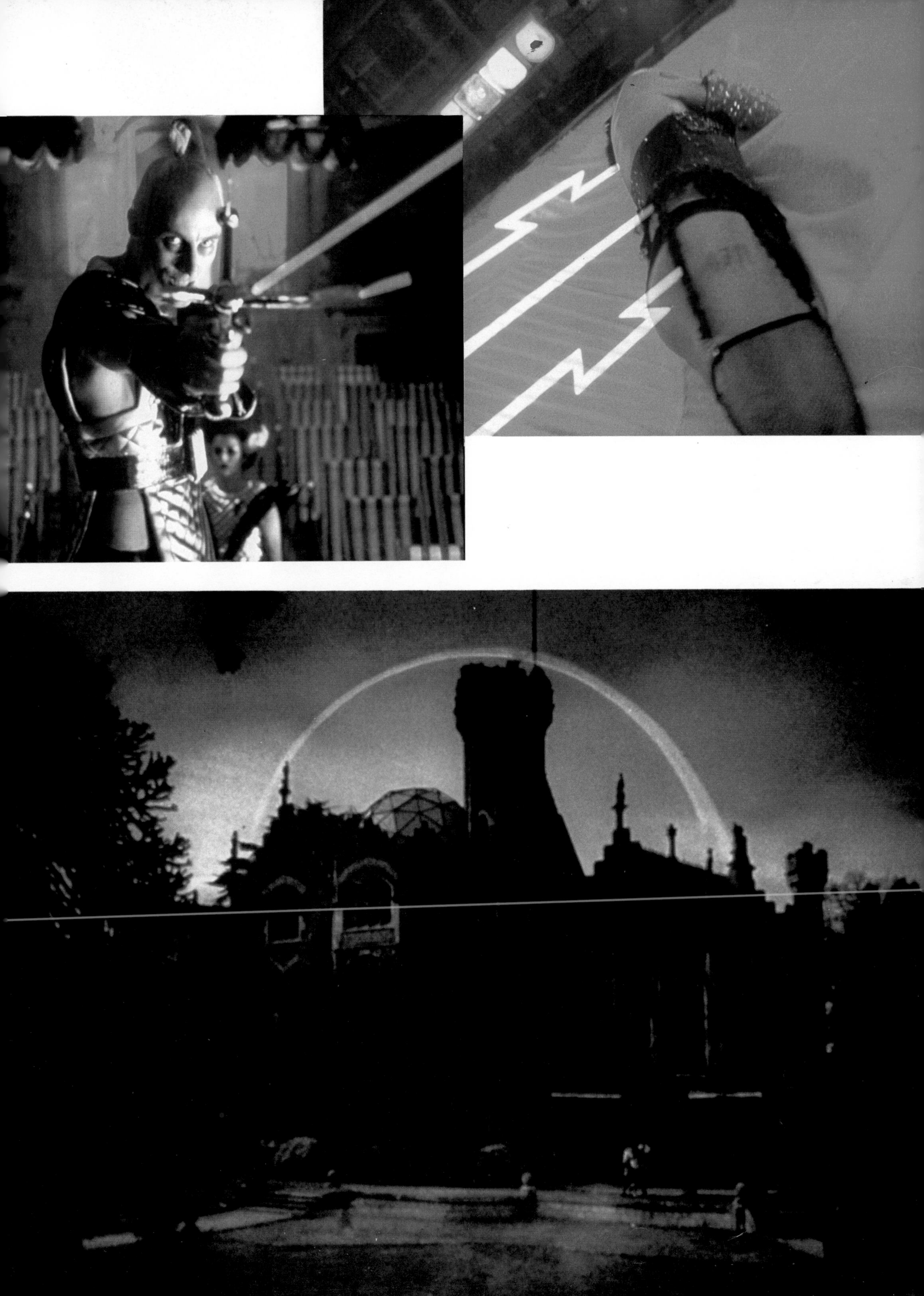

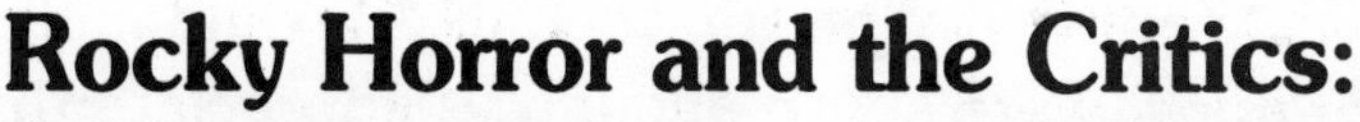

# Rocky Horror and the Critics: I DIDN'T MAKE HIM FOR YOU

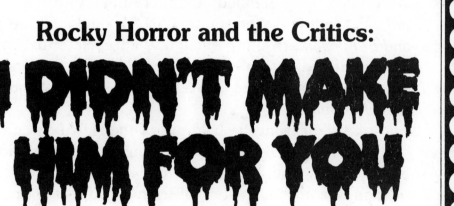

*And crawling on the planet's face, some insects, called the human race, lost in time, lost in space and meaning.*

What's your favorite TV Science Fiction Show?

Not only did *The Rocky Horror Picture Show* fare poorly with the public in its premier engagements, it also fared poorly with the press. Most local reviews ranged from indifferent notices to pans. *Variety* thought the movie's "campy hijinks . . . only [seem] labored." The San Francisco *Chronicle's* John Wasserman, who had liked the stage play in London, found the film "lacking both charm and dramatic impact." Tony Rayns, writing in the *Monthly Film Bulletin* of the British Film Institute, called it a "general failure . . . ill-conceived." As late as July 17, 1978, reporters from *Newsweek,* who could not even quote the dialogue accurately, thought the movie "tasteless, plotless, and pointless," and were totally bewildered by the phenomenon.

These responses were typical. It was easy to see *Rocky Horror* as crude, heavy-handed, and more than a little bit deranged. Only a few reviewers, such as Alexander Stuart in *Films and Filming,* were sharp enough to appreciate that the movie was a shrewd, informed attempt to "parody the cinema itself, in much the same vein as Mel Brooks' *Blazing Saddles* and *Young Frankenstein.*"

It *must* be clear from the bald use of the ridiculous, such as having Rocky Horror, the homemade monster, climb a mini RKO tower with a dead ersatz Fay Wray on his back, that sophistication was not the goal of O'Brien and director Jim Sharman. Nor have they endeavored to fit the film neatly into any single genre. Rather, O'Brien, who makes it a habit to collect old comic books and who often drops in on the B-movie revivals, has taken the whole broad scope of pop features from his childhood days and blended their highlights into a script that both participates in and comments upon several major movie traditions.

Thus, while *Frankenstein, Dracula,* and *King Kong* are obvious resonances for anyone lightly schooled in film, you have to like to *go to the movies* to pick up the Edgar Lustgarten thrillers, Sam Katzman rock 'n' roll exploitation flicks, Nelson Eddy-Jeannette MacDonald operettas, *Freaks* or *The Fearless Vampire Killers.* If you're young enough to have a fondness for Freak Rock, you may legitimately read in overtones of *Phantom of the Paradise, Lisztomania, Tommy, Hair,* and *Jesus Christ Superstar* from a more recent era.

This movie is intended to be fun, says Lou Adler. And its overtones can be fun even for the uneducated film goer because they are common denominators of our movie heritage. You need

*The Star*, Johannesburg, South Africa, August 12, 1976 ***(reprinted with permission)***

not have seen *King Kong* to recognize the ape in Rocky Horror's final climb. You need not have heard of Mary Wollstonecraft Shelley or seen Boris Karloff's monster to know the legend of Frankenstein. Certain themes and cinematic images have become part of us. They are easily recognizable.

Need we point out that the oddly made-up antihero of *A Clockwork Orange*—Frank-N-Furter's distant antecedent—describes his pleasures as "real horrorshow?" While several critics have noted that Tim Curry's classic performance as the transvestite scientist bears some similarity to the multisexual ravings of rock 'n' roll's satanic majesty, Mick Jagger, none have attached it to Jagger's most important film, *Performance*.* There, as a decadent former rock star given to dramatic entrances, he presides over a different castle and another bi-straight-gay menagerie of outcasts, entertains unexpected company, and dies at the hand of a man leading a double life. And the Time Warp dance itself never fails to remind me of the gangsters' exhausting strip-down during Jagger's "Memo from T."

Not that *The Rocky Horror Picture Show* is as clean, slick, and pointed as either Kubrick's or Roeg's masterpieces. But neither *Clockwork Orange* nor *Performance* intentionally set out to be B movies or parodies, while *Rocky Horror* set out to be both and succeeded. For the fun of it, this movie can even offer such gratuitous cinematic touches as the Esther Williams extravaganza

Johannesburg, South Africa

# Freaky Frank rocks

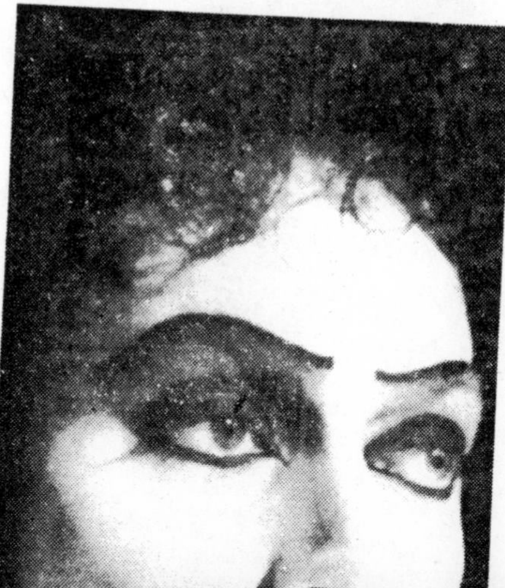

He wears a lace-up corset, fishnet stockings, suspender belt, star-studded platform shoes and long evening gloves.

His face is made up: heavy mascara, eyeliner, eyeshadow, face powder and purple lipstick.

He swaggers and wiggles. Pouts his sensuous lips and oozes sex.

Revolting?

Sick?

Maybe, to the straight-laced.

But Tim Curry, alias Frank N Furter, chief pervert of the freaky Rocky Horror movie, has caught the imagination of South Africa and fuelled the Rocky Horror cult among the under 30s.

Since the movie began its run 22 weeks ago, box

**James Dean created a cult. Then there was the Gatsby. Now the Rocky Horror cult has caugh cans in its clutches. ANNABELLE WARD phenomena.**

film because it was so "different"

Inside the cinemas, the young audiences tune into the movie. They know when to react. They've seen it all before.

## "I'm not much of a man...

Frank N Furter's arrival on the screen is preceded by a build up of anticipation.

Gasps of "Isn't he beautiful!" greet him as he steps out of the elevator.

Words from the songs ripple through the cinema

sayings from the film text or music.

Discos blast out "The Time Warp".

Advertisers use Rocky Horror themes to promote their wares.

What's the attraction?

Tom, a 21-year-old Johannesburg student who had seen the film three times, said he enjoyed its "colour".

## ...by the light of day...

"It involves concepts so close to youth today, people can

# 'Rocky Horror' Delightful, Innovative

## Campy Musical Humorously Challenges Traditional Se

The Transylvanians do the 'Time Warp'

**By CHICO COLEMAN**
**Texan Staff Writer**

**"The Rocky Horror Picture Show;" directed by Jim Sharman; starring Tim Curry, Richard O'Brien, Meatloaf; at the Varsity.**

"The Rocky Horror Show" began as a six-week project in London's experimental Theatre Upstairs and burgeoned into a smash musical at London's King's Road Theatre and at the Roxy in Los Angeles, both relatively small theaters.

The show was a flop on Broadway, however, because the scope of the production was incapable of carrying a large-size theater; this rather eclectic musical, a campy combination of '70s decadence, rock'n'roll and the Frankenstein story, was essentially a goof, and the ideal atmosphere for its presentation was a club environment. There was a danger, then, that the film version of "The Rocky Horror Show" would suffer from the same difficulties that the Broadway version did.

Fortunately, this is not so. "The Rocky Horror Picture Show" is a hit.

Although the film is slightly flawed by its removal from its natural environment, this is more than offset by the film's slick production and utilization of the intrinsic advantages of film, notably crosscutting and fluid camera work. Backed by Lou Adler's production, director Jim Sharman does a commendable job transferring the musical to the screen and enjoyably creates the "time-warped" atmosphere that the Broadway production lacked.

**THE PLOT IS** very funny. Because of car trouble, a young, middle-American couple, Brad and Ja to seek help at tle, unaware tha beamed to ear galaxy Transylv tle belongs to Furter, a trans the planet Tran in the process piece of beef Rocky Horror.

"Normal" se are blurred in ment and Brad their own sexua ed; as the narr was a night th remember."

For all its hu "The Rocky H Show" has a se takes the quite that the human more than ins through space. the guilt and sti to sex and dif tastes is nonse

## Folk Group To Bri... n Song to Au

Columbus MONTHLY July, 1978 Volume 4; Number 7

The Movies

# The Rocky Horror Picture Show

*It's the longest-running movie in the city, a campy, culty rock-music movie about a transvestite mad doctor . . . and the hard-core fans are into audience participation.*

**By John Maher**

"I knew it was different when it opened. We had about 220 people the first night and the same number the second night. But they were the same 220 people," says Graceland Cinema manager Jim Pearce.

"I've seen the movie 61 times," says Linda McCown, a former Columbus Business University student who works for Royal Graphics Inc. "Sometimes I just watch the movie and other times we get rowdy, throw the rice, dance and put spaghetti in our hair."

Both are talking about Columbus's longest-running movie and all-around late-night weekend event, the *Rocky Horror Picture Show.* The cult film, where the wild crowd is more than half the show, is normally shown at Graceland only at 11:15 pm on Fridays and Saturdays. But it has already been seen by more than 50,000 young Columbusites. Attendance is almost certain to hit 100,000 sometime in October or November. That's just about the time that the *RHPS* will begin the third year of its continuous run at Graceland.

If you can guess the exact time that the film will pass that magic mark, you could win a private screening for yourself and your friends. But in case you aren't very good at contests or if you aren't sure whether you want to spend a night getting pelted with assorted foodstuffs, here's what it's like:

Fierce, throaty complaints issue from the parking lot as family economy and second-hand cars are given one last theatrical overdose of gasoline before they are turned off.

Under the theatre's misspelled marquee (one "r" too few), the massing of casually dressed teen-agers and college-age kids looks more like an elongated party than an organized line.

Up front, a blue-jeaned girl gives a start of semi-recognition, elbows her companion and then excitedly confides, "Look, there's what's-his-name."

Seconds later, a beaming what's-his-name bounds over, dispensing hellos without mentioning any names.

Further down the line, a young male is yelling at Bob.

"You've got a bottle under your tire."

"I know," Bob coolly replies, "I put it there."

The questioner turns his attention elsewhere, apparently satisfied that Bob has good reasons for sticking a beer bottle beneath the left rear wheel of his own car.

To the rear, one of a group of guys is exclaiming, "Wow, that stuff just hit me. What was it. PCT? TPC? CPP? Huh?"

Others in the crowd are quieter and straighter. A few expectantly handle the rice, playing cards or beans they have brought to throw at the screen and at others in the audience. Some have taken the precaution of buying their tickets when the box office opened at 7 pm. They were sure not to be among the 150 novices who will be turned away after all 670 seats in both sides of the twin theatre have been sold. The *RHPS* always sells out. There are fans who see it every weekend without fail, and the most ardent are reputed to have seen it 100 times.

They are hooked on what the film's own press booklet describes as "an outrageous assemblage of the most stereotyped science fiction movies, Marvel comics, Frankie Avalon-Annette Funicello outings and rock'n'roll of every vintage. Running through the story is the sexual content of two middle-American 'Ike





The morn

## 'Ro

Gene Ger

If I were to tell you that "The Ro Horror Picture Show" is currently longest running movie in town, w you believe me? Well, of course wouldn't!

Actually, on a seven-day-per basis, "Star Wars" has been sh longer than any other film in C bus. But "The Rocky Horror Show" is now in its second yea

There's a catch, howeve bizarre grabber at the Gr Cinema is shown only at the hour on Friday and Saturday "Star Wars" is in its 38th continuous showings, both at and in the evening.

10 THE OHIO STA

**By Roger Addleman**

The third year of "ur adulterated insanity began Sunday evening dedicated fans of th

1975 (*reprinted with permission*)

# ntertainme

## Boundaries

altogether original idea, but one that is effectively presented within the framework of the film.

**UNQESTIONABLY, THE** music is the strongpoint of the show. The songs are integrated within the story line rather than being distinct from it (as in "Cabaret"), which allows for some hilarious lines, the most printable of these being "You're a hot dog, but you better not hurt her, Frank Furter."

All the songs are good, the arrangements and singing infectious and far superior to those on "The Rocky Horror Show" album. Four songs, "Time Warp," "Sweet Transvestite," "What Ever Happened to Saturday Night?" and "Rosetint My World," are knockouts.

The film is bu fine cast, many c in the origin Upstairs prod Curry is exceller Furter; aided b voice, an extr face and a cam masculinity an he steals the s core of the O'Brien, who w music and lyric as Riff Raff, favorite is Mea the anachroni punk from enough, "The

Because of Rocky Horro may be unpop Moreover, th not perfect, much new g much fun to

Tim Curry ...

"...half Auntie Mame, half Bela Lugosi."
--Gregg Kilday, Los Angeles TIMES 3/17/74

"...a cross between Greer Garson and Steve Reeves."
--Dan Sullivan, Los Angeles TIMES

"...a hybrid of Sophie Tucker and Mick Jagger."
--Dave Berman, Santa Monica Outlook 3/20/74

"...a combination of early Joan Crawford, Francis Lederer and Carmen Miranda."
--Emory Lewis, Boston Record 3/11/75

"...Little Richard meets Elsie Tanner."
--Melody Maker 10/20/73

"...part David Bowie, part Joan Crawford, part Basil Rathbone."
--

"Imagine Liza Minnelli in 'Cabaret,' Alice Cooper at his most demonic, Jagger at his most sensual. Then throw in Vincent Price and Bowie's drive for a neuter sex."
--Daily Mail 8/16/73

"...brings to mind the young Milton Berle."
--Douglas West, New York Daily News 3/11/75

"...Charles Laughton, doing Captain Bligh, and Nita Naldi at the same time."
--William A. Raidy, Long Island Press 3/11/75

###

Sat., March 11, 1978 ★★★★

...

# Horror' continue

FUSED? I don't blame you. It's sing business.
e Rocky Horror Picture Show" is known in the trade as a "cult What is a cult film? Well, it's any that possesses an apparently nable quality which keeps audi- coming back for more — time time — over a period of years. Harold and Maude" is a cult film. "King of Hearts." Both movies been playing in some cities for as as five years.

From an experimental production a small London theater to a smash ernational stage hit to a major otion picture, all in the space of 18 onths! That's the cinderella history one of the most outrageously offbeat ctures ever made.

American by the co morality c in the p Frank N. the planet Transexual Transylvania.

Originally created by Richard O'-Brien — who wrote the book, music and lyrics — this homage to the horror film genre opened in London at the Royal Court's experimental theater.

**IT ALL BEGAN IN** the Theatre Upstairs as a six-week workshop project in June 1973. The show received such wildly enthusiastic acclaim at this 60-seat theater that it was quickly moved to larger quarters in a converted cinema in Chelsea.

Following the demolition of the movie house, "Rocky Horror" found a ... at the 500-seat King's

creative forces ... industry, Lou Adler, ... saw "Rocky London at the time, saw "Rocky Horror" and promptly sewed up the American theatrical rights to the show within 36 hours.

Filming of the work began in October, 1974, at Bray Studios, England's famous "House of Horror," and at a 19th Century chateau which served once as the war-time refuge of General Charles DeGaulle. The rest is history, and "Rocky Horror" continues to make history right here in staid old Columbus.

*The Ohio State Lantern*, November 3, 1978 (*reprinted with permission*)

riday, Nov. 3, 1978

# ppy birthday 'Rocky Horror Picture'

nning movie in elebrated the econd anniver-

vie is "The Rocky Picture Show" (RHPS), and it has played every Friday and Saturday evening for the past two years at the Graceland Cinema, 230 Graceland Blvd.

The "birthday party" was celebrating the fact that the movie is not only the longest running film in Ohio, but also the longest running national engagement of the RHPS, said Jim Pearce, manager of the Graceland Cinema.

"We're very proud of the fact that we took a picture that was nothing to start out with and made something of it," Pearce said. For the past several months we have sold out both sides of the theater — 670 seats — every weekend and turned away about 200 people each night, he said.

"We are close to having 100,000 viewers," said Pearce.

"Some of the people have seen the movie 300 times and come dressed in costume; rice, popcorn and confetti are thrown during the movies each weekend," said Dave Howson, one of two Columbus Police officers assisting at the theater each weekend.

Although the crowd does not get out of hand, the officers make sure that no bottles or cans are thrown inside the theater, Howson said.

***'Give yourself to absolute pleasure'***

Pearce warns people viewing the film for the first time about the audience participation. A lot of "first-timers" are unaware of the content of the film

ation, Rocky Horror, and has a party, during which the couple tries to escape.

"The whole meaning of the film is to give yourself over to absolute pleasure, which I believe in very much," said Tim Williams, a Worthington High School student, who was dressed in full costume.

"The movie has every type of sexual perversion there is. It's really an experience. A person hasn't lived until they have seen it. I really love it," said Rob Bainter from Lancaster.

Amy Dawson, a high school student from Columbus, who has seen the film 45 times said, "It is a release from school and everyday stuff. I look forward to the weekend and 'Rocky.'"

in the swimming pool signed by Michelangelo; or the lifebuoy from the S.S. *Titanic;* the *Mona Lisa* on the ballroom wall; and *Whistler's Mother* (portrayed, if you examine the photograph in the Criminologist's dossier, by Meatloaf).

Such heavy-handed parody invests the movie with the genres and references it satirizes. It is immaterial whether or not the *Rocky Horror* fan knows *American Gothic.* The film is riddled with references to that painting, as we see the pitchfork in Riff Raff's hand during the wedding scene turn into his triune laser gun in the closing sequence. Yet it requires no effort at all to absorb the whole mythic context of the *American Gothic* theme.

Similarly, the film combines the salient elements of the science fiction, horror, monster, fantasy, surrealist, underground, and operetta genres. That one scene does not always lead convincingly to the next; that Frank's killing rage is utterly out of character; that, while the movie prepares us for Riff Raff's treason, it does not in any sense prepare us for his puerile, psychopathic motive—these holes and contradictions are part of the movie and do not detract from the movie's primary goal of parody and satire.

*Rocky Horror* is designed to move from one thrill to another with a minimum of imposition. If we've suspended our disbelief enough to accept that fatuous virgin as our ingenue and her turkey of a boyfriend as our hero; and if we've bought the fortuitous circumstances of a dead-end road on a rainy night with a spare tire in want of air and an eerie gothic castle whose "Enter At Your Own Risk" sign becomes illuminated with a highly effective, highly unsophisticated bolt of special effects lightning; why should we balk if we are not carried along on eddies of cinematic and literary perfection? No one said this was *The Seventh Seal.* Finding fault with the structure of *Rocky Horror* is a little like objecting to the Classic Comics version of *Hamlet.* It is not germane that we've lost the King's English; it is only germane that we can follow the story line.

Does this beg the value of criticism all together? No. It asks only that criticism remain appropriate. Thank heaven for writers like Chico Coleman, whose review in the October 6, 1975 (remember how new the cult was back then) issue of the *Daily Texan* reflected that writer's ability to give himself over to

*The Columbus Dispatch, October 31, 1978 (reprinted with permission)*

# Happy Riceturns On 'RHPS' 2nd Birthd

TUES., OCT. 31, 1978 cCol

f Raff, Dr. Frank-N-Furter And Magenta

By Shirley McNeely
Of The Dispatch Staff

When birthdays roll around, most persons think in terms of cake and candles.

But for the second birthday of the *Rocky Horror Picture Show*, rice is nice.

Did you say rice? Pelt, pelt pelt.

The cult film is entering its third year of play at the Graceland Cinemas. The event was ushered in (as in *Fall of the House of?*) Sunday night with *Rocky* survival kits, costumes, plenty of howling, audience participation — and rice.

Rice? Pelt, pelt, pelt.

**THE MOVIE, YOU** see, is a bizarre mix of the Frankenstein build-your-own-monster plot, complete with an Igor-type hunchback; some KISS-like rock 'n' roll characters; transvestitism and transsexualism; and movie cliches at their best.

But the most important element of the *Rocky Horror Picture Show* — known as *RHPS* to aficianados — are those bodies in front of the screen, not the ones on it.

Before the film rolls, the audience stomps and chants, "Lips! Lips! Lips!" Lips — much like the Rolling Stones' logo — appear and sing the intro. The first scene is that of a wedding and mushy love. The audience members throw rice — on the screen and on each other. The rice-throwing continues spontaneously throughout the film, sometimes to the pockmarked flinch of faces.

Pelt, pelt, pelt.

**THE AUDIENCE** members mouth the dialogue; they stand up and dance the Time Warp in the aisles; they sing and they talk back.

The anticipation of dialogue and the gimmicks fans have brought along are the most entertaining parts of the evening. The fi

When it rains in *RHPS*, people pull out newspapers and cover their heads. Some had squirt bottles of water to make the rain authentic. When Dr. Frank-N-Furter proposed a toast, slices of toasted bread were thrown in the air.

**AND WHEN HEROINE** Janet Weiss is mentioned, the reaction is "Weiss?" Pelt, pelt, pelt.

Graceland manager Jim Pierce says the *Rocky Horror Picture Show*, released in 1975, is one of the three longest runs in the country at Graceland.

He also says the audience — generally under 30, mostly under 21 — knows there are limits. He said the worst thing that can happen to a kid is to get thrown out of *Rocky*.

**AT ONE IN**
acter, Eddie (pla
Loaf), has been
have little wond
whom — is being
The theater ran
Eddie." "Eddie Sp
Again?" "Eddie H

Some may view
*Picture Show* as or
with utterly no
values. It does ha
total, off-the-wall f

The movie is s
Fridays and Satu
Graceland's twin th

For those who f
bizarre, it's worth t

Price? Pelt, pelt.

*The Hollywood Reporter, September 24, 1975 (reprinted with permission)*

## The Rocky Horror Picture Show

The same team that was responsible for the delightfully camp science fiction satire, "The Rocky Horror Show," have now turned the rock musical into a rather heavy-handed, unimaginative motion picture for 20th Century-Fox.

**THE ROCKY HORROR PICTURE SHOW**
**20th Century-Fox**

Executive producer .................... Lou Adler
Producer ........................ Michael White
Director .......................... Jim Sharman
Associate producer ............... John Goldstone
Screenplay .......... Jim Sharman/Richard O'Brien
(Based on the original book, music and lyrics by O'Brien)
Musical direction/Arrangements .. Richard Hartley
Photography .................. Peter Suschitzky
Film/Music editor .............. Graeme Clifford
Design ........................ Brian Thomson
Original costume design ............. Sue Blane
Cast: Tim Curry, Susan Sarandon, Barry Bostwick, Richard O'Brien, Patricia Quinn, Little Nell, Jonathan Adams, Peter Hinwood, Meatloaf, Charles Gray.
Running time—98 minutes
**MPAA Rating — R**

On stage, the piece was a glittery, tongue-in-cheek sendup of a long line of horror films, with the unknown alien elements of these films representing the sexual revolution of the last decade in the form of the flamboyant Dr. Frank N. Furter, a transvestite from Transexual, Transylvania. It was an exciting, highly theatrical piece.

The screenplay by Jim Sharman and Richard O'Brien, based on O'Brien's original book, music and lyrics, retains the same basic story line. But, as directed by Sharman (who also staged the original) and photographed by Peter Suschitzky, the film lacks the excitement and theatricality of the stage version.

Some portions of the film, which was designed by Brian Thomson, work very well, most notably the climactic finale, which is done as a Busby Berkeley parody on a set duplicating the old RKO Radio Pictures logo. Most of the time, however, Sharman has not been able to re-create the excitement and theatricality of the original, and what was once camp and glitter has now become almost grotesque and perverse.

Not helping matters are the musical direction and arrangements by Richard Hartley, which

*Rocky Mountain News, January 6, 1978 (reprinted with permission)*

# Movies' Saturday Night H w r

By WILLIAM GALLO
News Film Critic

For the 200 or so faithful who catch their own brand of Saturday Night Fever each week at the Ogden Theater, "Rocky" is not a romantic pug from Philadelphia. He's a mad doctor's stitched-together monster-boy, who springs from the customary tank of electrolyte as a gorgeous blonde Adonis singing and dancing in gold bikini briefs.

He is the star of a kinky bit of heavy-decibel Grand Guignol called "The Rocky Horror Picture Show," itself reconstructed and brought back from the dead by a charge of electricity.

A failure at the box office when first released by 20th Century-Fox in late 1976 (at Denver's Flick it grossed a paltry $3,200 in two weeks), "Rocky Horror" has now attracted a cult. In Denver and 26 other cities — there are only 27 prints in existence — the faithful come to cheer the villains and hiss the good guys, to go crazy over one of the oddest movies ever.

**SINCE LAST JUNE 25**, Denver's Ogden Theater contingent has gathered each Saturday at midnight. Many are repeaters who have seen the film six, 10 or two dozen times and are so enthralled by its pop carnality and raging rock n' roll that they happily plunk down $2 once again, then streak for the choice balcony seats.

What happens then varies
manager Terry Thoren has seen
"Sometimes people come
"simulating members of the ca
either. The "Rocky Horror"
scientist in sequined high hee
glowering hunchback named I
Magenta; a tap-dancing group
quined top hat and pencil strol
The villains include a pair of c
Janet, who just might drop the
this lurid Transylvanian depra

**"THERE'S A SORT OF**
Thoren says, an audience whi
gay. When Brad and Janet g
throws rice. When Riff Raff
Warp Dance, the faithful resp
of their own, in the aisles and

The horrorphiles let fly
Furter is called a hot dog, tl
anticipation of the madman
hoot and dance and ring bells

Don Reynolds, a 35-year

The Rocky H
e called the c
Vhat's the app
pokes at a lot
ovies. The pict
tharine Hepbu
ner' and Willia
There's a parc
ose Judy Garl
It's a movie bu

**FOR THE GAY**
or" provides a
"Two kinds of
ety there's a lo
ld I say the pse
t for the satire
y it gives to sex

The repeat aud
t of the average
ror" cult.

"At one time it
ds says. "There'

absolute pleasure—and the reality of the situation. He says, "This rather campy combination of 70's decadence, rock 'n roll, and the Frankenstein story was essentially a goof."

Thank you.

Moreover, Coleman seems to be one of the few reviewers who were able to drop their own insecurities long enough to even note two hitherto unsung elements in the film: the music (unsung is the wrong word!) and the performances of the actors. Of the former, Coleman reports:

"All the songs are good, the arrangements and singing infectious. . . . Four songs, 'Time Warp,' 'Sweet Transvestite,' 'What Ever Happened to Saturday Night?' and 'Rosetint My World,' are knockouts."

And of the latter:

"The film is buttressed by a fine cast. . . . Tim Curry is excellent as Frank N. Furter; aided by a powerful voice, an extremely mobile face, and a campy mixture of masculinity and femininity, he steals the show and is the core of the film. Richard O'Brien, who wrote the play, music, and lyrics, is also facile as Riff Raff, and a personal favorite is Meatloaf as Eddie, the anarchistic rock 'n roll punk."

Lest Coleman is accused of overzealousness above and beyond the call of his film review duties, he assures us of his sanity at the close of his article: "The film is surely not perfect, but it breaks too much ground and is too much fun to worry about."

Ain't it the truth.

*The Rocky Horror Picture Show* may or may not succeed according to some theory of absolutes, but does it succeed on its own terms and accomplish the purpose of its makers? Critics who have been horrified by some of the movie's absurdities have been inclined to see its thematic perversions as horrible too. But there are lots of people who have found those perversions—at least as presented here—to be entertaining, and who do not require stringent coherence between theory and form in order to enjoy a laff. These are the people for whom *Rocky Horror* was made, and this is the audience the film has found.

Music and Lyrics:
THE
ROCKY HORROR
PICTURE SHOW

# Sweet Transvestite

FRANK:
How d' you do
I see you've met my faithful handyman
He's a little brought down
Because when you knocked
He thought you were the candyman
Don't get strung out by the way I look.
Don't judge a book by its cover
I'm not much of a man
By the light of day
But by night I'm one hell of a lover
I'm just a sweet transvestite
From Transexual
Transylvania.
Ah, ha.
Let me show you around, maybe play
you a sound
You look like you're both pretty groovy
Or if you want something visual that's
not too abysmal
We could take in an old Steve Reeves
movie.

BRAD:
I'm glad we caught you at home.
Could we use your phone?
We're both in a bit of a hurry.

JANET:
Right!

BRAD:
We'll just say where we are,
Then go back to the car,
We don't want to be any worry.

FRANK:
Well, you got caught with a flat
Well how about that
Well babies don't you panic
By the light of the night

It'll all seem alright
I'll get you a satanic mechanic.
I'm just a sweet transvestite
From Transexual Transylvania.
Ha ha.
Why don'tcha stay for the night?

RIFF RAFF:

Night

FRANK:

Or maybe a bite

COLUMBIA:

Bite

FRANK:

I could show you my favorite obsession — SEX!
I've been making a man
With blond hair and a tan
And he's good for relieving my tension.
I'm just a sweet transvestite
From Transexual Transylvania.
I'm just a sweet transvestite

GUESTS:

Sweet transvestite.

FRANK:

From Transexual

ALL:

Transylvania . . . Ha ha.

FRANK:

So come up to the lab
And see what's on the slab
I see you shiver with antici . . . . pation — SAY IT!!
But maybe the rain.
Is really to blame
So I'll remove the cause—
But not the symptom.

But what about the symptom?

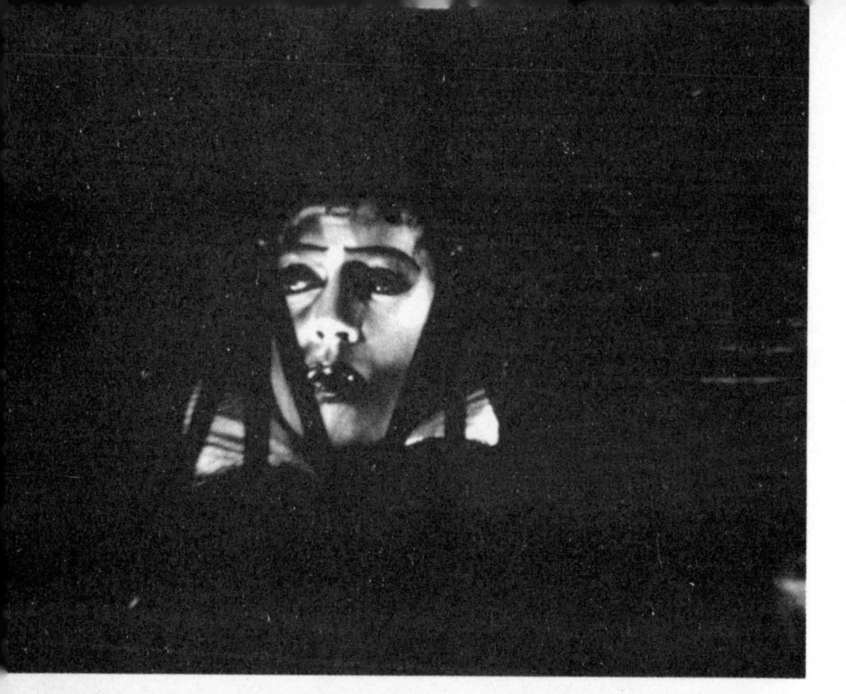

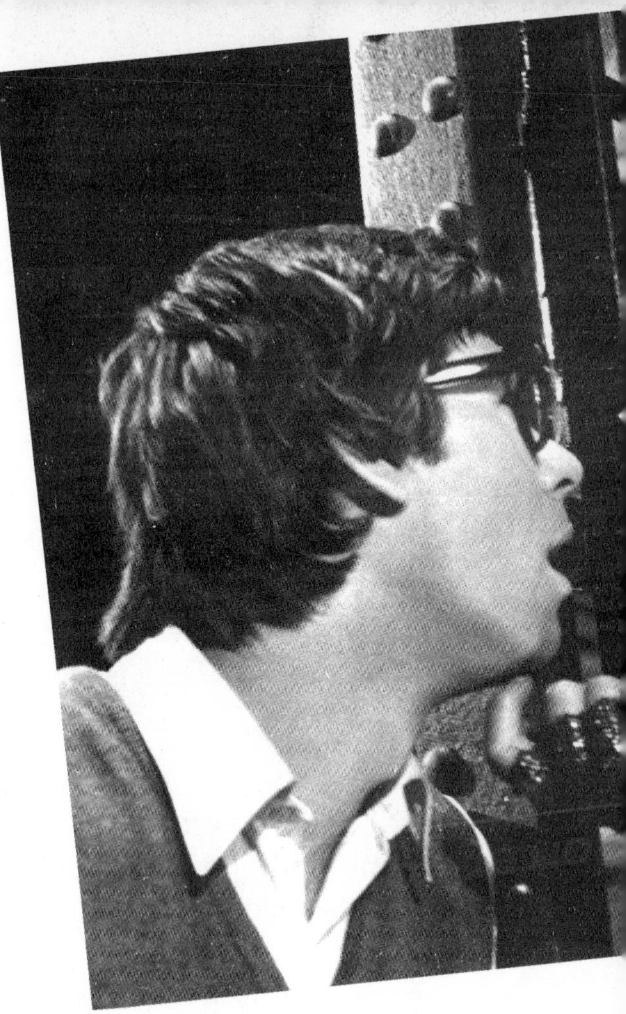

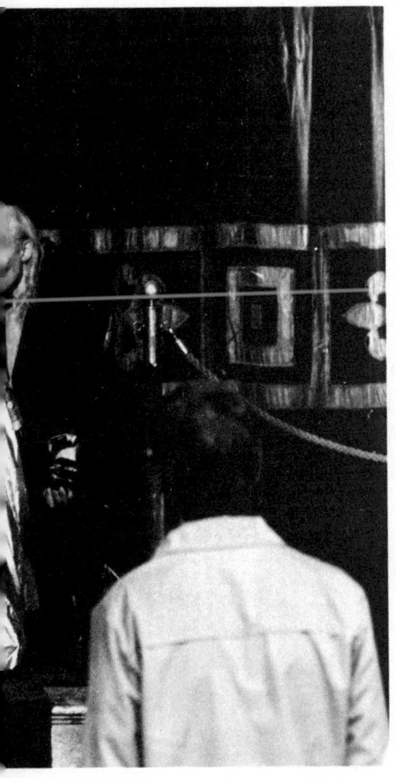

ANNUAL TRANSYLVANIAN CONVENTIO

Throw it!!

ROCKY HORROR PICTURE SHOW MICHAEL WHITE PRODUCTIONS LIMITED 24.9.74

SHOOTING SCHEDULE

WEEK ONE

**MONDAY 21st Oct.**

SET: EXT. DENTON CHURCH
SCENE NOS: 15 DAY
64 DAY (subliminal flash)
LOCATION Studio Lot
(Weather Standby: INT. DENTON CHURCH 17 DAY

ACTION PROPS
American cars $20 Bill
Bouquet Cameras
Confetti Pitchfork
Tin cans on car etc.

CAST AND CROWD
BRAD
JANET
RALPH
BETTY
MINISTER (FRANK)
OLD MAN (RIFF RAFF)
WIFE (MAGENTA)
DAUGHTER (COLUMBIA)
14 Transylvanians
6 Wedding guests
& 2 children

CAMERA DEPARTMENT
Chapman crane requi
Black & White Aca
Wide Screen (64)

**TUESDAY 22nd Oct.**

SET: EXT. DENTON CHURCH
SCENE NOS: 16 DAY
LOCATION Studio Lot
Weather Standby
INT. DENTON CHURCH 17 DAY

ACTION PROPS
Bouquet Wedding Ring Pitchfork

CAST AND CROWD
BRAD
JANET
OLD MAN (RIFF FAFF
WIFE (MAGENTA)
DAUGHTER (COLUMBIA

CAMERA DEPARTMENT
Black & white
Academy Screen

**WEDNESDAY 23rd Oct.**

SET: INT. DENTON CHURCH
SCENE NOS: 17 DAY
LOCATION Stage 2 Bray Studios
ACTION PROPS: Coffin
Black Rosettes &
White Rosettes

CAST AND CROWD
BRAD
JANET
OLD MAN (Riff Ra

CAMERA DEPARTME
Black & white
Academy Screen

**THURSDAY 24th Oct.**

SET: INT./EST. CASTLE (Monitor Shots)
SCENE NOS:
INT. JANET'S ROOM 83pt 85pt.
INT. BRAD'S ROOM 83pt 95pt.
INT. HALLWAY 112pt
INT. ZEN ROOM 114pt
EXT. CASTLE 108pt,110pt,95pt
INT. EMPTY HOUSE 95pt
INT. LABORATORY 85pt

LOCATION Oakley Court, Nr. Bray, Windsor

ACTION PROPS
4 Alsatian dogs
Dr. Scott's wheelchair

CAST AND CROWD
BRAD
JANET
FRANK

SPECIAL REQUI
Video camera
TV Monitor
Hairdressing:
Spec. FX: Rai

CAMERA DEPAR
Fish Eye len
Black and wh

**FRIDAY 25th Oct.**

SET: INT. LABORATORY
SCENE NOS: 69 NIGHT
56 (subliminal flash)
LOCATION Stage 1 Bray Studios

ACTION PROPS
Tank Microphone
Glasses of Champagne Hypodermic Needle

CAST AND CF
BRAD
JANET
FRANK
18 TRANSYL

SPECIAL RE
Practical

CAMERA DE
Colour

---

ROCKY HORROR PICTURE SHOW MICHAEL WHITE PRODUCTI

SHOOTING SCHEDUL

WEEK TWO

**MONDAY 28th Oct.**

SET: INT. LABORATORY
SCENE NOS: 70 NIGHT
58 (subliminal flash)
LOCATION: Stage 1 Bray Studios
ACTION PROPS
Hanging gymnast rings from chandelier

CAST AND CRO
BRAD
JANET
FRANK
RIFF RAFF

SPECIAL REQUI
Spec. FX. Tan
for

CAMERA DEPARTM
Colour wide

**TUESDAY 29th Oct.**

SET: INT. LABORATORY
SCENE NOS: 71,73,74,74a NIGHT
LOCATION: Stage 1 Bray Studios
ACTION PROPS: Gymnasium equipment
CAMERA DEPARTMENT:
Colour - wide screen
MUSIC PLAYBACK
Sword of Damocles/Whatever Happened
Charles Atlas Song/to Saturday Night

CAST AND CROWD
BRAD
JANET
FRANK
RIFF RAFF

SPECIAL REQUIRE
Art: Breakaway
Wardrobe: Costu
to fall into tan
Choreographer re

**WEDNESDAY 30th Oct.**

SET: INT. LABORATORY
SCENE NOS: 75 NIGHT
LOCATION: Stage 1 Bray Studios
ACTION PROPS: Harley Davidson motorbike
saxophone
CAMERA DEPARTMENT:
Colour - Wide Screen

CAST AND CROWD
BRAD
JANET
FRANK
RIFF RAFF
MAGENTA

SPECIAL REQUIREMEN
Bottles to smash wh
Spec. FX: Frozen ef

**THURSDAY 31st Oct.**

SET: INT. LABORATORY
SCENE NOS: 76 NIGHT
LOCATION: Stage 1 Bray Studios
ACTION PROPS: Harley Davidson motorbike
Saxophone
smashed bottles
ice pick
CAMERA DEPARTMENT
Colour. Wide Screen.

CAST AND CROWD
BRAD
JANET
FRANK
RIFF RAFF
MAGENTA

SPECIAL REQUIREMENTS
Lighting effects for
Spec. FX: Blood effec
Choreographer require

MUSIC PLAYBACK
Whatever Happened to S

**FRIDAY 1st Nov.**

SET: INT. LABORATORY
SCENE NOS: 77,78,79 NIGHT
137,(Still)
140 (Still)
LOCATION: Stage 1 Bray Studios
ACTION PROPS: Confetti
Ice Bucket
CAMERA DEPARTMENT:
Colour. Wide Screen

CAST AND CROWD
BRAD
JANET
FRANK
RIFF RAFF
MAGENTA

SPECIAL REQUIREMENTS
Makeup: Bloodied Eddie
Choreographer required

MUSIC PLAYBACK
I Can Make You A Man

# Time Warp

RIFF RAFF:

It's astounding. Time is fleeting.
Madness takes its toll.

MAGENTA:

Ahh.

RIFF RAFF:

But listen closely

MAGENTA:

Not for very much longer

RIFF RAFF:

I've got to keep control.
I remember doing the Time Warp
Drinking those moments when
The blackness would hit me.

RIFF RAFF and MAGENTA:

And the void would be calling.

GUESTS:

Let's do the Time Warp again.
Let's do the Time Warp again.

CHORUS—NARRATOR:

It's just a jump to the left.

GUESTS:

And then a step to the right.

NARRATOR:

With your hands on your hips.

GUESTS:

You bring your knees in tight.
But it's the pelvic thrust
They really drive you insane.
Let's do the Time Warp again.
Let's do the Time Warp again.

MAGENTA:

It's so dreamy—Oh, fantasy free me
So you can't see me—no, not at all
In another dimension—with
voyeuristic intention.
Well secluded I see all

RIFF RAFF:

With a bit of a mind flip

MAGENTA:

You're in for a time slip

RIFF RAFF:

And nothing can ever be the same.

MAGENTA:

You're spaced out on sensation.

RIFF RAFF:

Like you're under sedation

GUESTS:

Let's do the Time Warp again.
Let's do the Time Warp again.

COLUMBIA:

Well I was walking down the street
Just having a think
When a snake of a guy
Gave me an evil wink
Well it shook me up, it took me by surprise
He had a pick-up truck and the devil's eyes
He stared at me and I felt a change
Time meant nothing—never would again.

GUESTS:

Let's do the Time Warp again.
Let's do the Time Warp again.

CHORUS REPEAT—NARRATOR and GUESTS:

Let's do the Time Warp again.
Let's do the Time Warp again.

COLUMBIA (dancing):

Ah!
Oh Oh!
Ahhh!

GUESTS:

Let's do the Time Warp again.
Let's do the Time Warp again.

CHORUS REPEAT—NARRATOR and GUESTS:

Let's do the Time Warp again.
Let's do the Time Warp again.

JANET: Oh Brad, I'm frightened. What kind of a place is this?
BRAD: Oh, it's probably some kind of hunting lodge for rich weirdos.

RIFF RAFF: You've arrived on a rather special night. It's one of the master's affairs. — which one?

BRAD: Say! Do any of you guys know the Madison?

# TIME WARP

Words and Music by
RICHARD O'BRIEN

B
the black-ness would hit me
and the void would be call - ing
(All) F C G D A
Let's do the Time Warp a - gain
F C G
Let's do the
E
(Narrator) With your hand
(Trio)
D
But it's the pel - vic thrust
that real - ly drives you in -
A
sa - a - a - a - ane.
(All) F C G D A
Let's do the Time Warp a - gain.
F C G D A
Let's do the Time Warp a - gain
(Magenta) It's so
A
dream - y
oh fan-ta-sy
B
free me
So you can't
G
see me
D
no, not at
A
all
In an-oth-er di-men - sion

B G
with voy-eur-is-tic in-ten - tion_ Well se - clu - ded___
D A
I'll see all With a bit of a mind flip_ you're in-to the time
B G D A
___ slip_ Noth - ing_ can ev - er be the same_
3 3 B
You're spaced out on sen - sa - tion like you're un-der se - da - tion
(All) F C G D A F C G D
Let's do the Time Warp a - gain___ Let's do the Time Warp a -
A
Well I was tap-ping down the street just-a h
A7 D
vil wink, We-ell it shook me up
pick up truck_ and the de - vil's_ eyes_
E D
stared at me_ and I felt a change
A
Time meant noth - ing, nev - e
(All) F C G D A
would a - gain_ Let's do the Time Warp a - gain___
F C G D A
Let's do the Time Warp a - gain___

## Whatever Happened to Saturday Night

EDDIE:

Whatever happened to Saturday night
When you dressed up sharp and
You felt all right.
It don't seem the same since cosmic light
Came into my life and I thought
I was divine.
I used to go for a ride with a chick who'd go
And listen to the music on the radio
A saxophone was blowing on a
Rock and roll show
And we climbed in the back seat
And we really had a good time.

ALL:

Hot patootie bless my soul
I really love that rock and roll.

EDDIE and GUESTS:

Hot patootie bless my soul
I really love that rock and roll.
(Repeat three times.)

EDDIE:

My head used to swim
From the perfume I smelled.
My hands kind of fumbled with
Her white plastic belt.
I'd taste her baby pink lipstick and
That's when I'd melt.
And she whispered in my ear
Tonight she really was mine
Get back in front and put some hair oil on
Buddy Holly was singing his
Very last song
With your arm around your girl
You tried sing along
It felt pretty good, whooo—really had
A good time.

ALL:

Hot patootie bless my soul
I really love that rock and roll.
(Repeat.)

DEEP FREEZE

JANET: Oh oh you beast, you monster. Oh, what have you done with Brad?

FRANK: Eh well—nothing. Why? Do you think I should?

JANET: You tricked me—I wouldn't have—I've never—never—

FRANK: Yes, yes, I know. But it isn't all bad, is it? I think you really find it quite pleasurable.

FRANK: Oh come on, Brad, admit it. You liked it, didn't you? There's no crime in giving yourself over to pleasure.

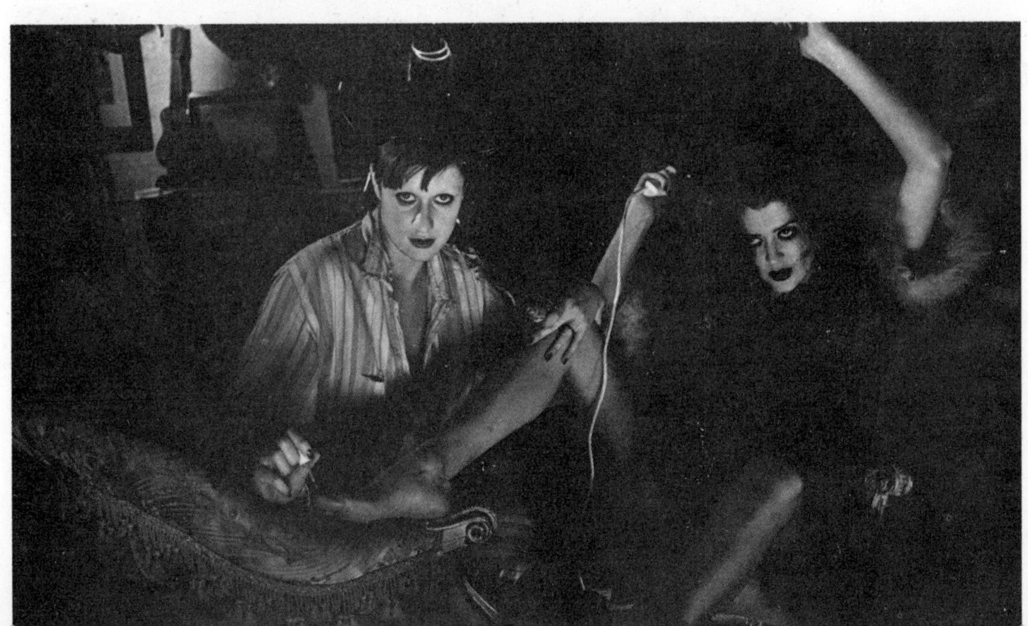

## Dammit, Janet

BRAD:

Hey, Janet.

JANET:

Yes, Brad.

BRAD:

I've got something to say. — *say it!*

JANET:

Uh huh.

BRAD:

I really loved the — *starts with an "S"* — skillful way — *what a genius!*

You beat the other girls *with a whip* to the bride's bouquet.

JANET:

Oh . . . oh Brad.

BRAD:

The river was deep but I swam it.

RIFF RAFF and MAGENTA:

Janet

BRAD:

The future is ours so let's plan it.

RIFF RAFF and MAGENTA:

Janet

BRAD:

So please don't tell me to can it.

RIFF RAFF and MAGENTA:

Janet

BRAD:

I've one thing to say and that's

Dammit, Janet, I love you.

JANET:

Ooh.

BRAD:

Here's a ring to prove that I'm no joker.

JANET:

Ohh.

BRAD:

There's three ways that love can grow.

That's good . . .

JANET:

Oh . . . oh . . . oh

BRAD:

bad or . . .

JANET:

Oh.

BRAD:

. . . mediocre.
Oh—Janet, I love you so.

JANET:

Oh. Oh! It's nicer than Betty Munroe had.

MAGENTA and COLUMBIA:

Oh Brad.

JANET:

Now we're engaged and I'm so glad

MAGENTA AND COLUMBIA:

Oh Brad.

JANET:

That you've met Mom and you know Dad.

WHOLE FAMILY:

Oh Brad.

JANET:

I've one thing to say and that's
Brad, I'm mad—for you too.
Oh Brad.

BRAD:

Oh Dammit.

JANET:

I'm mad. . . .

BRAD:

Oh, Janet.

JANET:

For you.

BRAD:

I love you too-oo-oo.

BRAD AND JANET;

There's one thing left to do-ah-ooh.

BRAD:

And that's go see the man who began it.

FAMILY:

Janet

BRAD:

When we met in his science exam—it

FAMILY:

Janet

BRAD:

Made me give you the eye and then panic.

FAMILY:

Janet

BRAD:

I've one thing to say, and that's
Dammit, Janet, I love you.
Dammit, Janet.

JANET:

Oh Brad, I'm mad.

BRAD:

Dammit, Janet.

BOTH:

I love you.

RALPH: Well, I guess we really did it, huh?

BRAD: I don't think there's any doubt about that. You and Betty have been almost inseparable since you sat in Dr. Scott's refresher course.

RALPH: Well, to tell you the truth, Brad, that was the only reason I showed up in the first place.

BETTY: Okay, you guys. This is it. Are you ready?

RALPH: Hey, Brad, Betty's going to throw her bouquet.

"She got hers, now he'll get his..."

JANET: Oh I can't believe that an hour ago she was plain old Betty Munroe, and now . . . now she's Mrs. Ralph Hapschatt.
BRAD: Yes, Janet. Ralph's a lucky guy.
JANET: Yes.
BRAD: Er. Everyone knows Betty's a wonderful little cook. — *She's the hottest baked potato in Denton!*
JANET: Yes.
BRAD: Gosh, Ralph, himself, he'll be lined up for promotion in a year or two. — *If he doesn't get busted.*

*Yeah, Denton— the home of happiness*

BE JUST
AND
FEAR NOT

## The Sword of Damocles

ROCKY:
The sword of Damocles is hanging over my head
And I've got the feeling someone's
Going to be cutting the thread
RIFF RAFF:
Oh!
ROCKY:
Oh woe is me—my life is a misery
Oh can't you see that I'm at the start
Of a pretty big downer.
I woke up this morning with a start when
I fell out of bed
GUESTS:
That ain't no crime.
ROCKY:
And left from my dreaming was a feeling
Of unnamable dread.
GUESTS:
That ain't no crime.
ROCKY:
My high is low—I'm dressed up with no place
to go. And all I know is I'm at the
start of a pretty big downer.
GUESTS:
Sha la la la
That ain't no crime
ROCKY:
Oh no no no no
GUESTS:
Sha la la la
That ain't no crime
ROCKY:
No no no no no
GUESTS:
Sha la la la
That ain't no crime
That ain't no crime

ROCKY:

The sword of Damocles is hanging over my head

GUESTS:

That ain't no crime

ROCKY:

And I've got the feeling someone's going
to be cutting the thread.

GUESTS:

That ain't no crime

ROCKY:

Oh woe is me—my life is a mystery
Oh can't you see that I'm at the start
of a pretty big downer.

FRANK:

Oh . . . oh . . . oh.

GUESTS:

Sha la la la
That ain't no crime

COLUMBIA, MAGENTA, RIFF RAFF, and GUESTS:

Sha la la la

GUESTS:

That ain't no crime

ROCKY:

No no no no.

GUESTS:

Sha la la la
That ain't no crime

COLUMBIA, MAGENTA, RIFF RAFF, and GUESTS:

That ain't no crime

GUESTS:

Sha la la la
That ain't no crime

ROCKY:

No no no no.

GUESTS:

Sha la la la
That ain't no crime

ROCKY:

No. No.

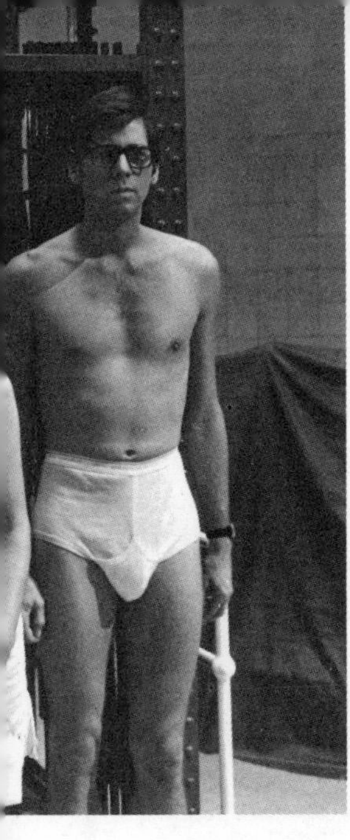

big

FRANK: How forceful you are, Brad. Such a perfect specimen of manhood. So dominant. You must be awfully proud of him, Janet.

JANET: Well, yes I am.

FRANK: Do you have any tattoos, Brad?

BRAD: Certainly not!

FRANK (*to Janet*): Oh well, how about you?

Show him the battleship, Janet!

Hey Frank, when's the orgy?

FRANK: Tonight my unconventional conventionists, you are to witness a new breakthrough in biochemical research. And paradise is to be mine. It was strange in the way it happened. Suddenly, you get a break. All the pieces seem to fit into place. What a sucker you've been. What a fool. The answer was there all the time. It took a small accident to make it happen. An accident!

What about the secret?

MAGENTA and COLUMBIA: And that's when I discovered—

FRANK: And that's when I discovered the secret. That elusive ingredient, that spark that is the breath of life. Yes, I have that knowledge. I hold the secret to life itself. You see you are fortunate. For tonight is the night that my beautiful creature is destined to be born.

Do you have that knowledge?

to what?

itself?

GUESTS:

Oohh oohh.

FRANK: Throw open the switches on the sonic oscillator. And step up the reactor power input three more points.

Peter Hinwood practices his suspension techniques in a waterless water tank.

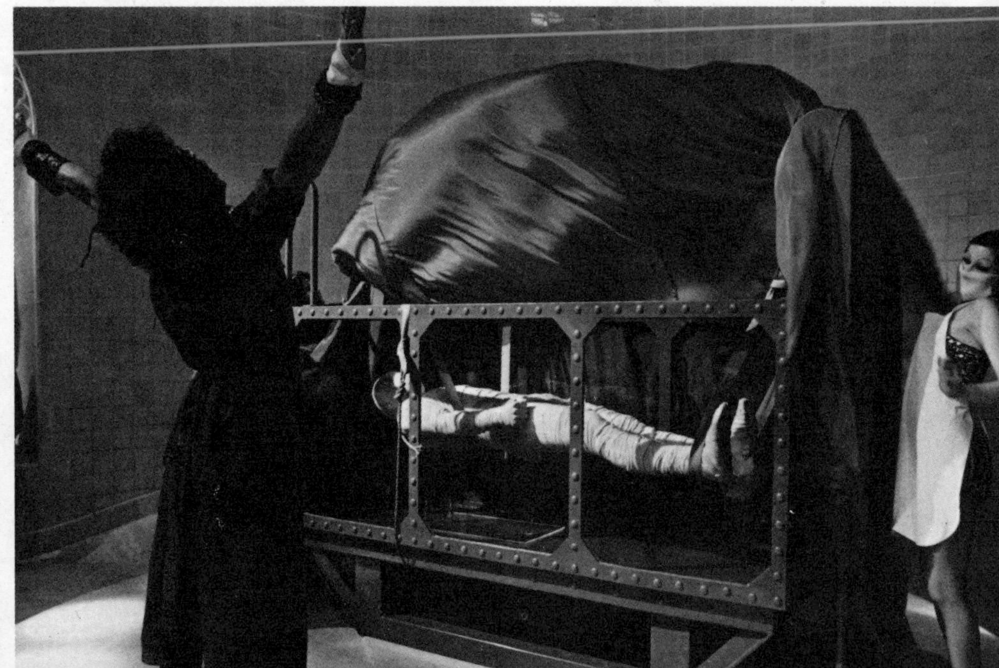

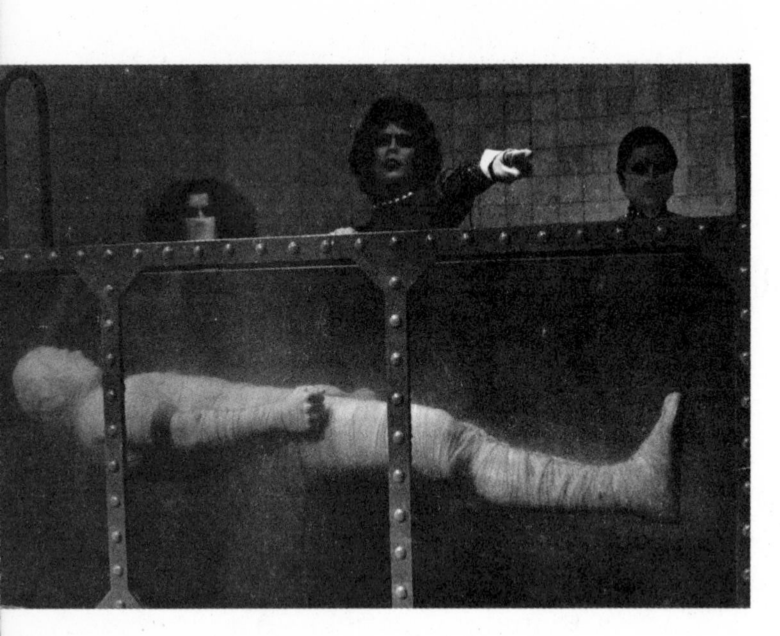

SONIC
OSCILLATOR
REACTOR
POWER
INPUT
MEDUSA

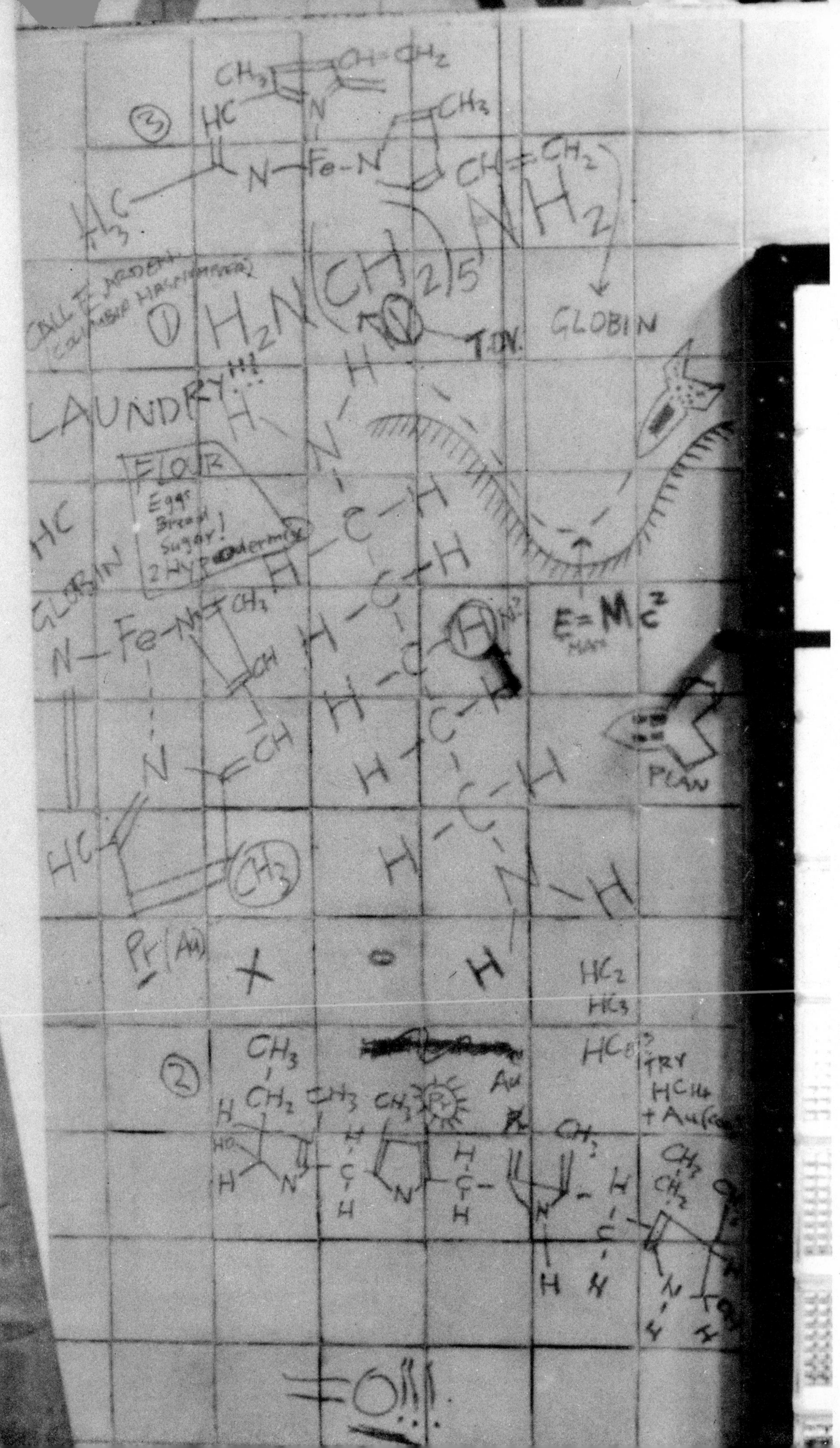

GLOBIN
LAUNDRY!!!
FLOUR
Eggs
Bread
Sugar!
GLOBIN
PLAN
TRY

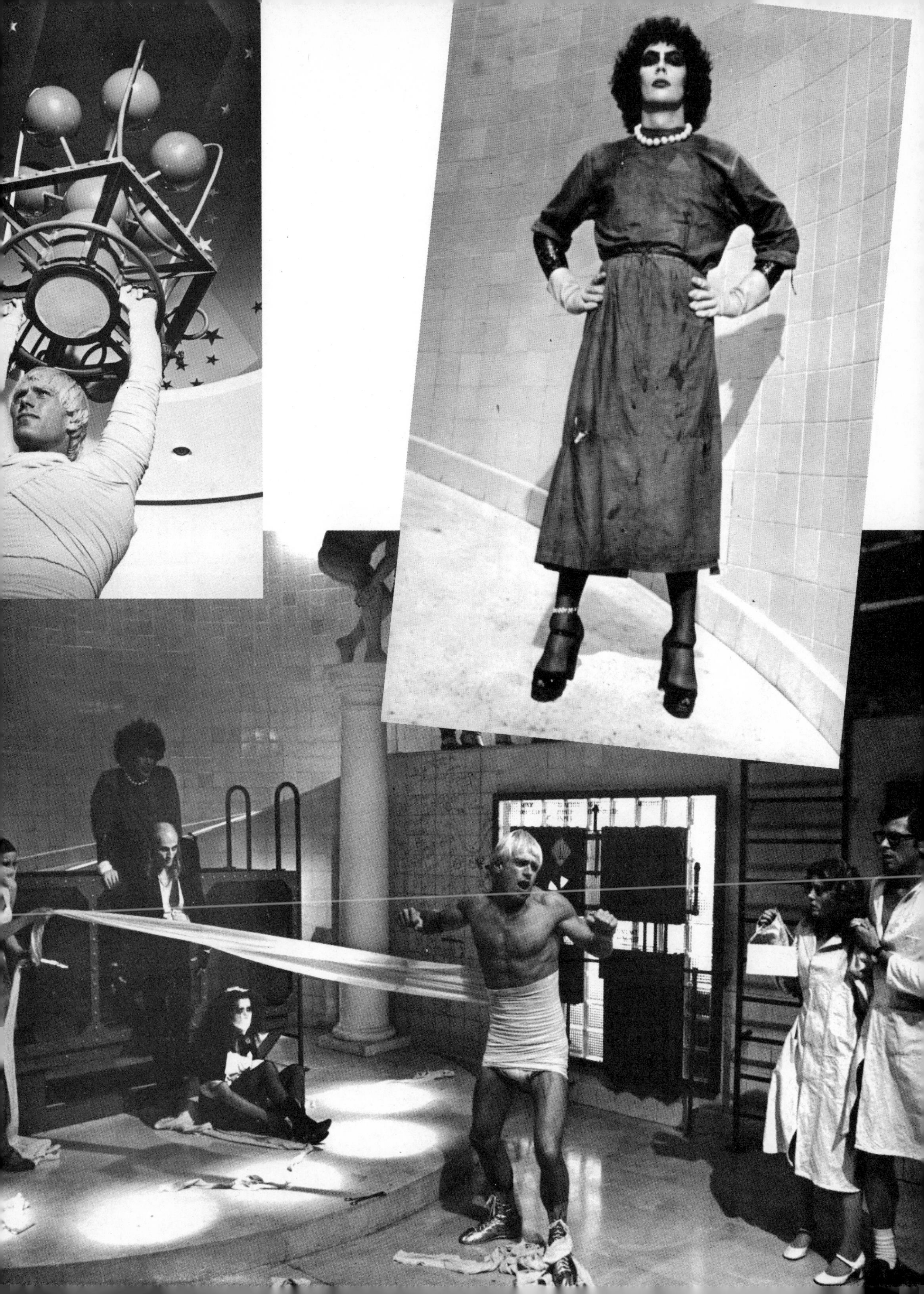

Try the castle!

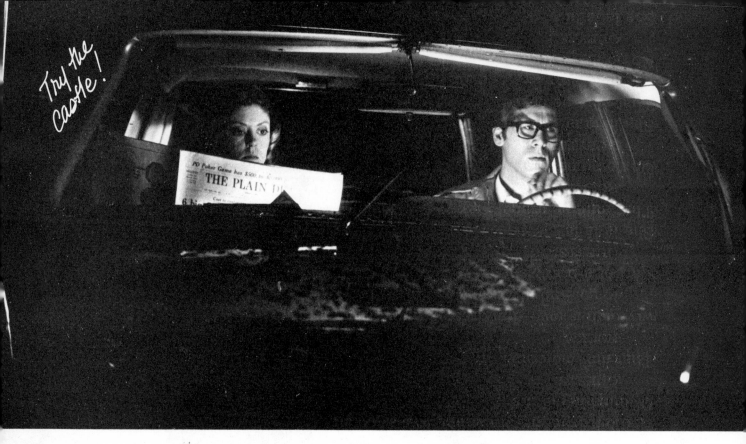

BRAD: Didn't we pass a castle back down the road a few miles?

Buy an umbrella, you cheap bitch!

## Over at the Frankenstein Place

JANET:

In the velvet darkness
Of the blackest night
Burning bright—there's a guiding star
No matter what or who you are.

BRAD and JANET:

There's a light.

PHANTOM VOICES:

Over at the Frankenstein place.

BRAD:

There's a light.

PHANTON VOICES:

Burning in the fireplace.

JANET:

There's a light . . . a light in the darkness
Of everybody's life.

RIFF RAFF:

Darkness must go
Down the river of nights dreaming
Flow morphia slow let the sun and light
Come streaming into my life
Into my life.

BRAD and JANET:

There's a light.

PHANTOM VOICES:

Over at the Frankenstein place.

BRAD and JANET:

There's a light.

PHANTOM VOICES:

Burning in the fireplace.
There's a light . . . a light.

BRAD and JANET:

In the darkness of everybody's life.

THER
wers
(28C)
(17C)
ge 23-E

# THE PLAIN DEALER

Dow Jones up 23.78

15¢ © 1974 Plain Dealer Publishing Co.

OHIO'S LARGEST NEWSPAPER

86 PAGES

CLEVELAND, THURSDAY, AUGUST 8, 1974

133D YEAR—NO. 220 ★★

## Urged to resign by own staff

# Nixon ponders decision to quit

© New York Times Service

WASHINGTON — Three Republican leaders indicated yesterday that President Nixon now is leaving open the possibility of resignation and said his decision would be based on the "national interest."

United Press International reported late last night that Nixon was preparing a formal resignation statement.

The President's state of mind was described late yesterday afternoon by Hugh Scott of Pennsylvania, the Senate Republican leader; Sen. Barry Goldwater of Arizona, and Rep. John J. Rhodes of Arizona, the House Republican leader, after a 30-minute meeting with Nixon in the Oval Office that began shortly after 5 p.m. EDT.

They met with Nixon as members of the White House staff said a movement was under way within the staff to persuade the President to resign. And pressure for resignation continued to mount in Congress.

Afterward, the three leaders told reporters on the White House lawn that they had come at the President's invitation to discuss the impeachment picture.

"We have told him the situation is very gloomy on Capitol Hill," said Scott, adding that they did not advise him what to do and that he did not tell them what he might be contemplating.

"No decision has been made," Scott said.

Rhodes, who announced Tuesday that he would vote for impeachment, said, "The President was in good spirits and good health, and as four old friends we talked over a very distressing situation."

Goldwater told Arizona newsmen by telephone late yesterday that he had informed Nixon he could count on no more than 15 certain votes for acquittal in the event of a Senate impeachment trial. The President also was told that there would

- Foreign newspapers' comment on Watergate is sudden and intense. Page 5-A.
- Atty. Gen. William B. Saxbe disputes claim that all cabinet members supported President Nixon's decision to stay in office. Page 7-A.
- Ford is prepared to asume the presidency. Page 10-A.
- Future immunity for President Nixon is debated. Page 6-C.
- Sen. Barry Goldwater says President Nixon could only count on 15 votes for acquittal if he was tried in the Senate. Page 8-C.

be perhaps only 10 votes against impeachment in the House, the Washington Post said.

The meeting followed a confused day of rumors that Nixon was on the verge of resigning, while the President, in seclusion with a few members on his staff and his family, maintained his public posture that he would not resign, but would let the constitutional process of impeachment run its course.

There were a number of indications, however, that the President has told a number of persons that he, indeed, is considering resigning.

(The Washington Post quoted three White House sources as saying that Nixon is nearing a decision to resign with the question now only one of timing. One informed source told the Post the decision would come within two or three days; one presidential assistant said: "It could be one day, it could be five days; he could change his mind tomorrow and say, 'To hell with it, I'm going to fight it.'")

Members of the White House staff said privately that a movement was under way within the staff to persuade Nixon to resign. They said pressures for resignation increased throughout the day and furthermore that the movement was led by Alexander M. Haig Jr., the President's White House chief of staff.

On the other hand, the President's family, who stayed with Nixon in his White House offices during what was described as "a day of agony" for all of them, urged Nixon not to resign.

Rabbi Baruch Korff, chairman of the National Citizens' Committee for Fairness to the Presidency, emerged from a meeting with the President yesterday afternoon with a grim face, and subsequently issued a statement saying that unless the White House is flooded with telegrams against resignation in the next few days, Nixon

Continued on Page 6-A

# House will drop impeachment mo if Nixon resigns

L.A. Times/Washington Post Service

could try the President onl

hawthorn books, inc. 260 MADISON AVENUE, NEW YORK, N.Y. 10016

TO Skip
FROM Sandy
RE

This is the wrong Cleveland Plain Dealer. The one in the film has a different headline. Please correct!

hawthorn books, inc. 260 MADISON AVENUE, NEW YORK, N.Y. 10016

TO Sandy
FROM Skip
RE

No. This is the right one — the one that came out on the eve of Nixon's resignation. The film people used the wrong one!

The castle of Dr. Frank-N-Furter was used as a refuge by General Charles de Gaulle during World War II.

RISK it!

## Charles Atlas Song

FRANK:

A weakling weighing ninety-eight pounds
Will get sand in his face when kicked to the ground.
And soon in the gym
With a determined chin
The sweat from his pores
As he works for his cause
Will make him glisten and gleam
And with massage and just a little bit of steam
He'll be pink and quite clean
He'll be a strong man
Oh, honey—

GUESTS:

But the wrong man.

FRANK:

He'll eat nutritious high protein
And swallow raw eggs
Try to build up his shoulders
His chest, arms and legs
Such an effort
If he only knew of my plan.
In just seven days

GUESTS, RIFF RAFF, MAGENTA, COLUMBIA, and FRANK:

I can make you a man.

FRANK:
He'll do press-ups and chin-ups
Do the snatch, clean and jerk.
He thinks dynamic tension must be hard work.
Such strenuous living I just don't understand.
When in just seven days—oh baby
I can make you a man.

REPRISE—FRANK:
But a deltoid and a bicep
A hot groin and a tricep
Makes me—ooooh—shake
Makes me want to take
Charles Atlas by the hand.

FRANK and ALL:
In just seven days—oh baby
I can make you a man.

FRANK:
I don't want no dissension
Just dynamic tension

JANET:
I'm a muscle fan.

FRANK and GUESTS:
In just seven days
I can make you a man.

FRANK:
Dig it if you can.

GUESTS:
In just seven days
I can make you a man.

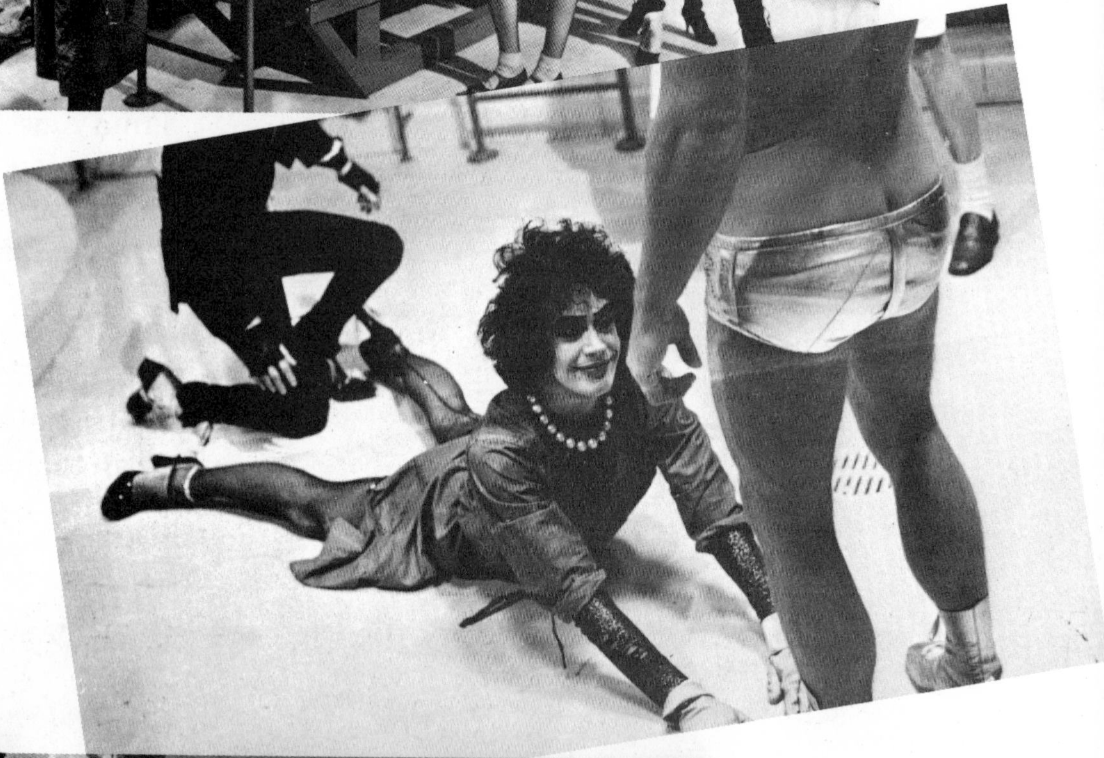

FRANK: He carries the

Charles Atlas seal of approval.

*And he didn't even take the lessons*

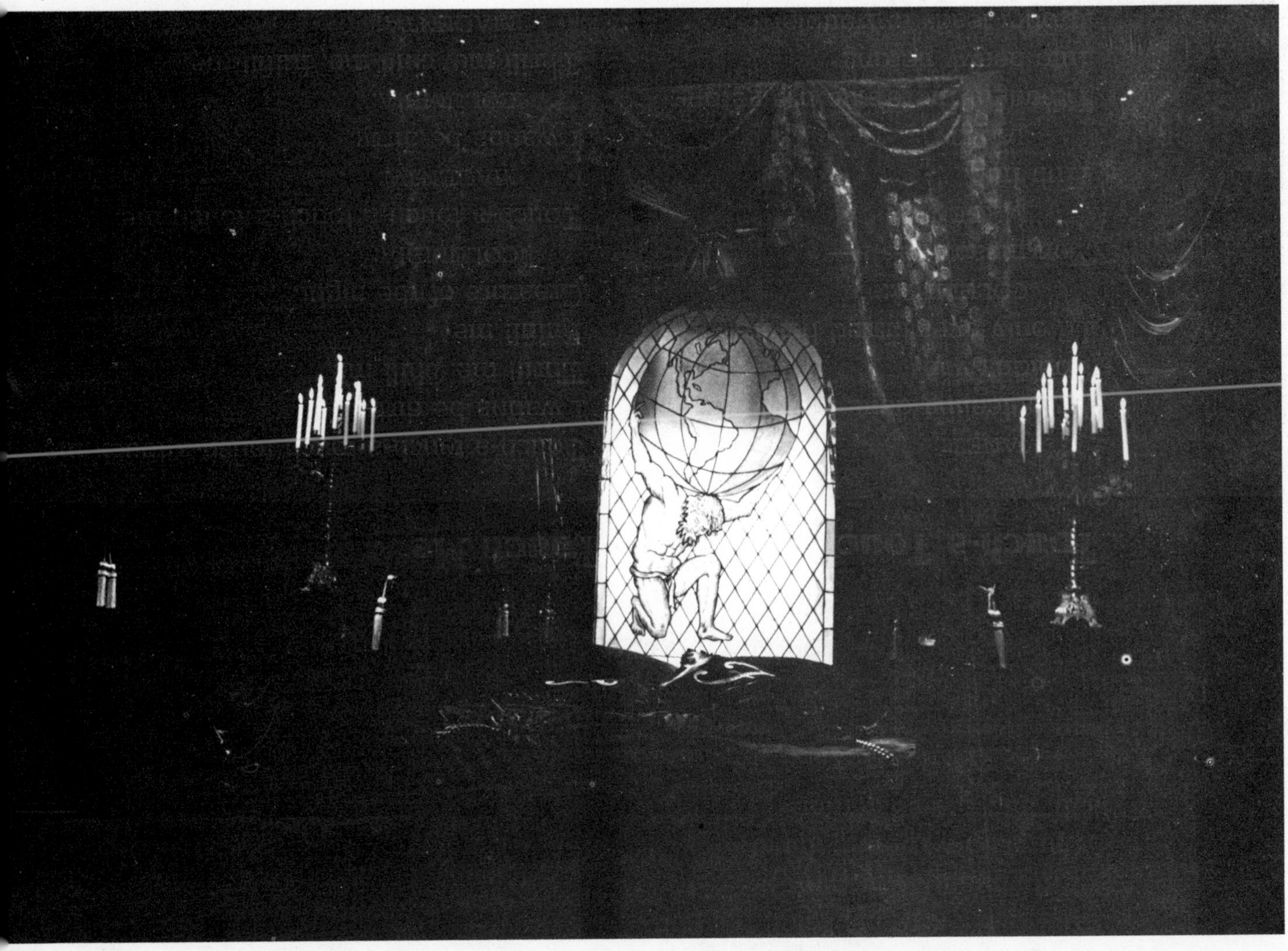

# Eddie's Teddy

DR. SCOTT:

From the day he was born, he was trouble.
He was the thorn in his mutter's side.
She tried in vain.

NARRATOR:

But he never caused her nothing but shame.

SCOTT:

He left home the day she died,
From the day she was gone—
All he wanted—
Was rock and roll porn, und a motor bike.
Shooting up junk.

NARRATOR:

He was a low-down cheap little punk.

SCOTT:

Taking everyone for a ride.

CHORUS—DR. SCOTT and ALL:

When Eddie said he didn't like his teddy,
You knew he was a no good kid,
When he threatened your life with a
switch blade knife.

FRANK:

What a guy.

JANET:

Makes you cry.

SCOTT:

Und I did.

COLUMBIA:

Everybody shoved him,
I very nearly loved him.
I said, 'Hey, listen to me,
Stay sane inside insanity,'
But he locked the door and threw
away the key.

SCOTT:
But he must have been drawn — Shabop, shabop, bop
In to something, — Skabop, skabop, bop
Making him warn me in
a note which reads

ALL:
What's it say? What's it say?

EDDIE'S VOICE:
I'm out of my head. — HED
Oh, hurry or I may be dead.
They mustn't carry out their evil deeds.
Yaaaow.

CHORUS—ALL:
(Repeat)

FRANK:
What a guy.

JANET:
Makes you cry.

SCOTT:
Und I did.

CHORUS—ALL:
(Repeat)

FRANK:
What . . . a guy.

ALL:
Woe woe woe.

JANET:
Makes you cry.

ALL:
Hey hey hey.

SCOTT:
Und I did.

ALL:
Eddie!

*(Photo credit: Argonaut)*

MONITOR
ey Frank, how's
your backhand?

What does Captain Kirk say to his chief engineer?

RIFF RAFF: Master, master, we have a visitor.
BRAD: Hey, Scotty! Dr. Everett Scott.
RIFF RAFF: You know this earthling—this person.
BRAD: I most certainly do. He happens to be an old friend of mine.
FRANK: I see. So this wasn't simply a chance meeting. You came here with a purpose.
BRAD: I told you, my car broke down. I'm telling the truth.
FRANK: I know what you told me, Brad, but this Dr. Everett Scott—his name is not unknown to me, eh.
BRAD: He was a science teacher at Denton High School.
FRANK: And now he works for your government, doesn't he, Brad? He's attached to the Bureau of Investigation of that which you call UFO's. Isn't that right, Brad?
BRAD: He might be.
FRANK: You . . .
BRAD: I don't know.
RIFF RAFF:
The intruder is entering the building, master.
FRANK: He'll probably be in—in the Zen Room.

Where could he be?

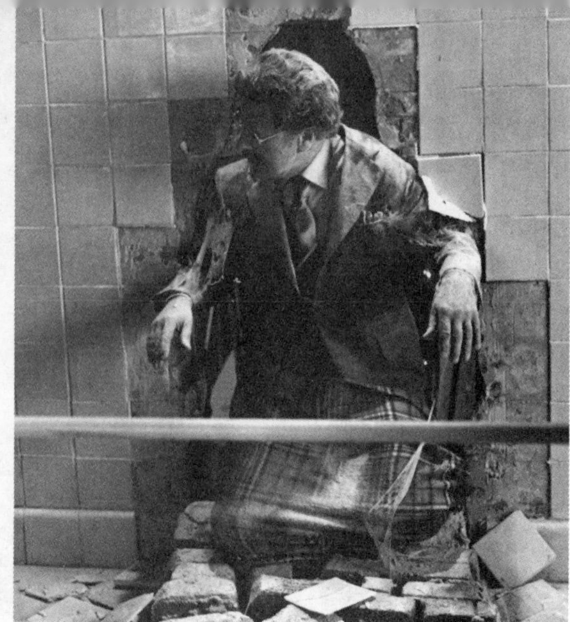

Gentlemen, start your engines

What's the matter, Columbia— you've eaten Eddie before!

↓

not with ketchup!

DR. SCOTT: Brad, what are you doing here?
FRANK: Don't play games, Dr. Scott. You know perfectly well what Brad Majors is doing here. It was part of your plan, was it not, that he and his female should check the layout for you? Well, unfortunately for you all the plans are to be changed. I hope you're adaptable, Dr. Scott. I know Brad is.
DR. SCOTT: I can assure you that Brad's presence here comes as a complete surprise to me. I came here to find Eddie.
BRAD: Eddie? I've seen him. He's—
FRANK: Eddie! What do you know of Eddie, Dr. Scott?
DR. SCOTT: I happen to know a great deal about a lot. You see Eddie happens to be my nephew.
FRANK: Oh! Oh! Oh!
BRAD: Dr. Scott!
JANET: (*from under covers*) Oh!
DR. SCOTT: Janet! — Mouseketeer Roll Call!
JANET: Dr. Scott!
BRAD: Janet!
JANET: Brad!
FRANK: Rocky!
ROCKY: (*stares*)
DR. SCOTT: Janet!
JANET: Dr. Scott!
BRAD: Janet!
JANET: Brad
FRANK: Rocky!
ROCKY: (*stares*)
DR. SCOTT: Janet!
JANET: Dr. Scott!
BRAD: Janet!
JANET: Brad!
FRANK: Rocky!
ROCKY: (*stares*)

## Touch-a Touch-a Touch-a Touch Me

JANET:
I was feeling done in
Couldn't win
I'd only ever kissed before.
COLUMBIA:
You mean she's a—
MAGENTA:
Huh huh.
JANET:
I thought there's no use getting
Into heavy petting
It only leads to trouble
And seat wetting.
Now all I want to know
Is how to go
I've tasted blood and I want more.
COLUMBIA and MAGENTA:
More, more, more!
JANET:
I'll put up no resistance
I want to stay the distance
I've got an itch to scratch
I need assistance.
Touch-a touch-a touch-a touch me,
I wanna be dirty.
Thrill me, chill me, fulfill me,
Creature of the night.
Then if anything grows
While you pose,
I'll oil you up and rub you down
MAGENTA and COLUMBIA:
Down down down
JANET:
And that's just one small fraction
Of the main attraction
You need a friendly hand,
Oh, and I need action.
Touch-a touch-a-touch touch-a touch me
I wanna be dirty
Thrill me, chill me,
Fulfill me
Creature of the night.
COLUMBIA:
Touch-a touch-a touch-a touch me,
MAGENTA:
I wanna be dirty.
COLUMBIA:
Thrill me, chill me, fulfill me.
MAGENTA:
Creature of the night.
JANET:
Oh, touch-a touch-a touch-a touch me
I wanna be dirty
Thrill me, chill me, fulfill me
Creature of the night.
BRAD:
Creature of the night.
FRANK:
Creature of the night.
MAGENTA:
Creature of the night.
RIFF RAFF:
Creature of the night.
COLUMBIA:
Creature of the night.
ROCKY:
Creature of the night.
JANET:
Creature of the night . . . oh . . .

Hey Janet—
wanna fuck?

ROCKY HORROR PICTURE SHOW — MICHAEL WHITE PRODUCTIONS LIMITED — 24.9.74

S H O O T I N G  S C H E D U L E

W E E K  F O U R

MONDAY 11th Nov.
SET: INT. DINING ROOM
SCENE NOS: 126,127,128,129, 130,131,132,133,135,136,137, 138,139,140 NIGHT
LOCATION: Oakley Court
ACTION PROPS: Photograph album, Electric carver, Wheelchair, Note
CAST AND CROWD: FRANK, BRAD, JANET, DR. SCOTT, COLUMBIA, RIFF RAFF, MAGENTA, ROCKY
MUSIC PLAYBACK: Eddie's Teddy
CAMERA DEPARTMENT: Colour - Wide Screen

TUESDAY 12th Nov.
SET: INT. DINING ROOM
SCENE NOS: 141,142 NIGHT
23a,24,25,26,27 NIGHT
LOCATION: Oakley Court
ACTION PROPS: Photograph album, Newspapers, Flag to fly on top of castle, Notice on gates, 3 Motorcycles, Glowing dome.
CAMERA DEPARTMENT: Dining Room: Colour - Wide Screen
Castle: Black & white Academy
CAST AND CROWD: FRANK, BRAD, JANET, DR. SCOTT, 3 Motorcyclists (Trans
SPECIAL REQUIREMENTS: Spec. FX: Rain
Lightning ef
MUSIC PLAYBACK: Eddie's Teddy, Wise Up Janet Weiss, Over AT The Frankenst

WEDNESDAY 13th Nov. EXTENDED DAY
SET: INT. COLUMBIA'S ROOM
EXT. CASTLE
SCENE NOS: 98,100,102,104,134 N.
28,29,30,31,32,33NIGHT
LOCATION: Oakley Court
ACTION PROPS: Newspapers, Glowing dome, Flag on castle
CAMERA DEPARTMENT: Columbia's Room: Colour. Wide Screen
Castle: Black & white. Academy
CAST AND CROWD: COLUMBIA, MAGENTA, RIFF RAFF
SPECIAL REQUIREMENTS: T.V. Monitor
Spec. FX: Rain
Lightning
MUSIC PLAYBACK: Touch A Touch Me, Eddie's Teddy, Over At The Franke

THURSDAY 14th Nov. EXTENDED DAY
SET: INT. CASTLE CORRIDORS
SCENE NOS: 116pt,143,165 NIGHT
35,36,37,91 NIGHT
LOCATION Oakley Court
ACTION PROPS: Wheelchair, Alsatians, Motorcycles
CAMERA DEPARTMENT: Corridors: Colour - Wide Screen Plus Sc.91
Castle: Black & white. Academy
CAST AND CROWD: JANET, FRANK, BRAD
SPECIAL REQUIREME
Wire set-up to pu
Lightning effect/
Spec. FX. Rain /
MUSIC PLAYBACK: Wise Up Janet We
Time Warp Introd

FRIDAY 15th Nove
SET: INT. ENTRANCE HALL, STAIRS and LANDING
SCENE NOS: 38,39,40 NIGHT
LOCATION: Oakley Court
ACTION PROPS: Practical vacuum cleaner, Portraits
CAMERA DEPARTMENT: 38-40 Black & white. Academy
CAST AND CROWD: BRAD, JANET
MUSIC PLAYBACK: Time Warp. Intr

---

ROCKY HORROR PICTURE SHOW — MICHAEL WHITE PRODU

S H O O T I N G  S C H E D U L

W E E K  T H R E E

MONDAY 4th Nov.
SET: INT. LABORATORY
SCENE NOS: 83,85,87 NIGHT
LOCATION: Stage 1 Bray Studios
ACTION PROPS: Collapsing mechanism for bed., Chains, Candelabra
CAMERA DEPARTMENT: Colour. Wide Screen
CAST AND C: RIFF RAFF, MAGENTA, ROCKY
SPECIAL REQ: T.V. Monito
Edited vide

TUESDAY 5th Nov.
SET: INT. LABORATORY 92H
SCENE NOS: 94,95,96,98pt,99, 100pt,101,102pt,103,104pt,105 NIGHT 60 (subliminal flash)
LOCATION: STAGE 1 Bray Studios
CAMERA DEPARTMENT: Colour. Wide Screen
MUSIC PLAYBACK: Touch A Touch Me
CAST AND CRO: JANET, ROCKY, RIFF RAFF, MAGENTA
SPECIAL REQUI
Makeup: Rocky
T.V.Monitor w
tape.
Wardrobe: Rep

WEDNESDAY 6th Nov.
SET: INT. LABORATORY
SCENE NOS: 106,107,108,109 110,111,112,113,114,115,116 to complete 117 NIGHT
LOCATION: Stage 1 Bray Studios
ACTION PROPS: Horse whip, Wheelchair
CAMERA DEPARTMENT: Colour. Wide Screen
CAST AND CROWD: FRANK, RIFF RAFF, BRAD C
SPECIAL REQUIRE
Practical lift
T.V. Monitor - E
Breakaway wall &

THURSDAY 7th Nov.
SET: INT. LABORATORY
SCENE NOS: 144,146,147
LOCATION: Stage 1 Bray Studios
ACTION PROPS: Statues
CAMERA DEPARTMENT: Colour. Wide Screen
CAST AND CROWD: FRANK, BRAD, JANET
SPECIAL REQUIREMEN: Lighting effects
MUSIC PLAYBACK: Wise Up Janet Weis, You're A Hot Dog

FRIDAY 8th Nov.
SET: INT. DINING ROOM
SCENE NOS: 119,120,122,123, 124,125 NIGHT
LOCATION: Oakley Court
SPEC. FX: Shooting Stage 1 Bray Studios.
INT. LABORATORY - TANK SHOTS 70pt.
CAMERA DEPARTMENT: Colour. Wide Screen
CAST AND CROWD: FRANK, BRAD, JANET, DR. SCOTT
MUSIC PLAYBACK: Eddie's Teddy
ACTION PROPS: Electric Carver, Side of Beef, Wheelchair, Photograph album

# Planet Shmanet Janet

FRANK:

I'll tell you once
I won't tell you twice
You'd better wise up, Janet Weiss.
Your apple pie
Don't taste too nice.
You'd better wise up, Janet Weiss.
I've laid the seed
It should be all you need
You're as sensual
As a pencil
Wound up like an 'E' or first string
When we made it
Did ya hear a bell ring?
Y' got a block
Take my advice.
You'd better wise up, Janet Weiss.
The transducer
Will seduce yah.
It's something you'll get used to
A mental mind-fuck can be nice.
Planet, schmanet, Janet!
You'd better wise up—Janet Weiss
You'd better wise up
Build your thighs up
You'd better wise up.

NARRATOR:

And then she cried out— MORE!

JANET:

Stop!!

FRANK:

Don't get hot and flustered.
Use a bit of mustard.

BRAD:

You're a hot dog
But you'd better not try to hurt her
Frank Furter.

DR. SCOTT:
You're a hot dog
But you'd better not try to hurt her
Frank Furter

JANET:
You're a hot dog. . . .

DR. SCOTT: You won't find earth people quite the easy mark you imagine. This sonic transducer—it is, I suppose, some kind of audiovibratory, physiomolecular transport device. . . .

BRAD: You mean . . .

A vibrator!

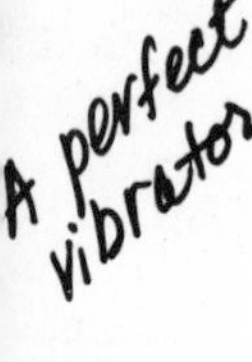


DR. SCOTT: Yes, Brad. It's something we ourselves have been working on for quite some time. But it seems our friend here has found a way of perfecting it. A device which is capable of breaking down solid matter and then projecting it through space, and—who knows—perhaps even time itself.

JANET: You mean he's gonna send us to another planet? — I'll go....

COLUMBIA: My God! I can't stand any more of this. First you spurn me for Eddie and then you throw him off like an old overcoat for Rocky. You chew people up then you spit them out again. I loved you. D'ya hear me? I loved you, and what did it get me? Yeah, I'll tell you—a big nothing. You're like a sponge—you take, take, take and drain others of their love and emotion. Yeah, I've had enough. You've got to choose between me and Rocky—so named because of the rocks in his head.

Whad'ya say?

Try Disneyland.

FRANK: It's not easy having a good time. Even smiling makes my face ache.

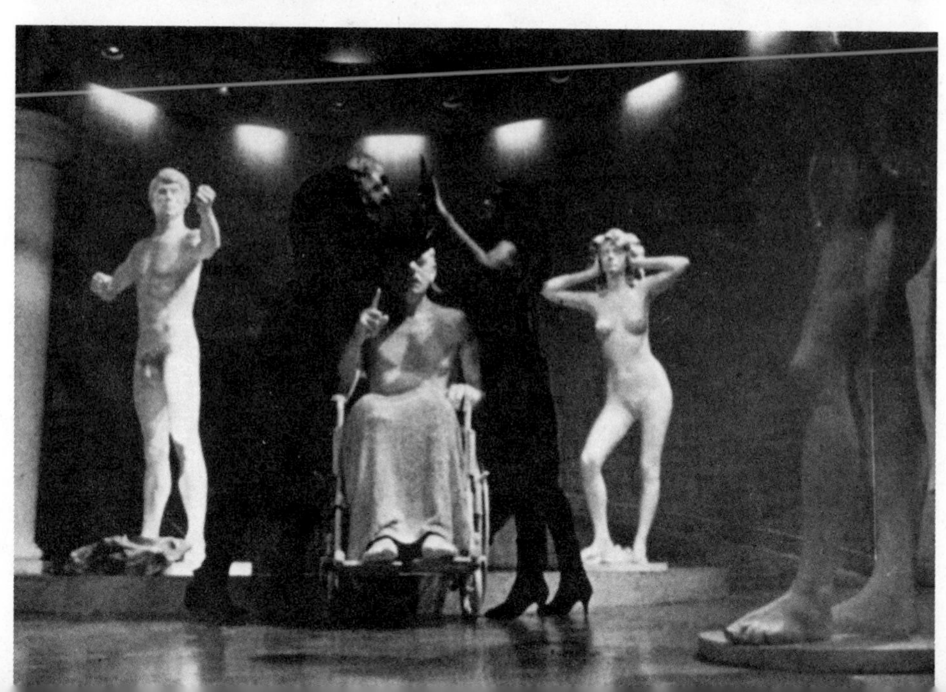

# Science Fiction/Double Feature

RICHARD O'BRIEN'S VOICE:
Michael Rennie was ill
The day the earth stood still
But he told us where we stand
And Flash Gordon was there
In silver underwear
Claude Rains was the invisible man
Then something went wrong



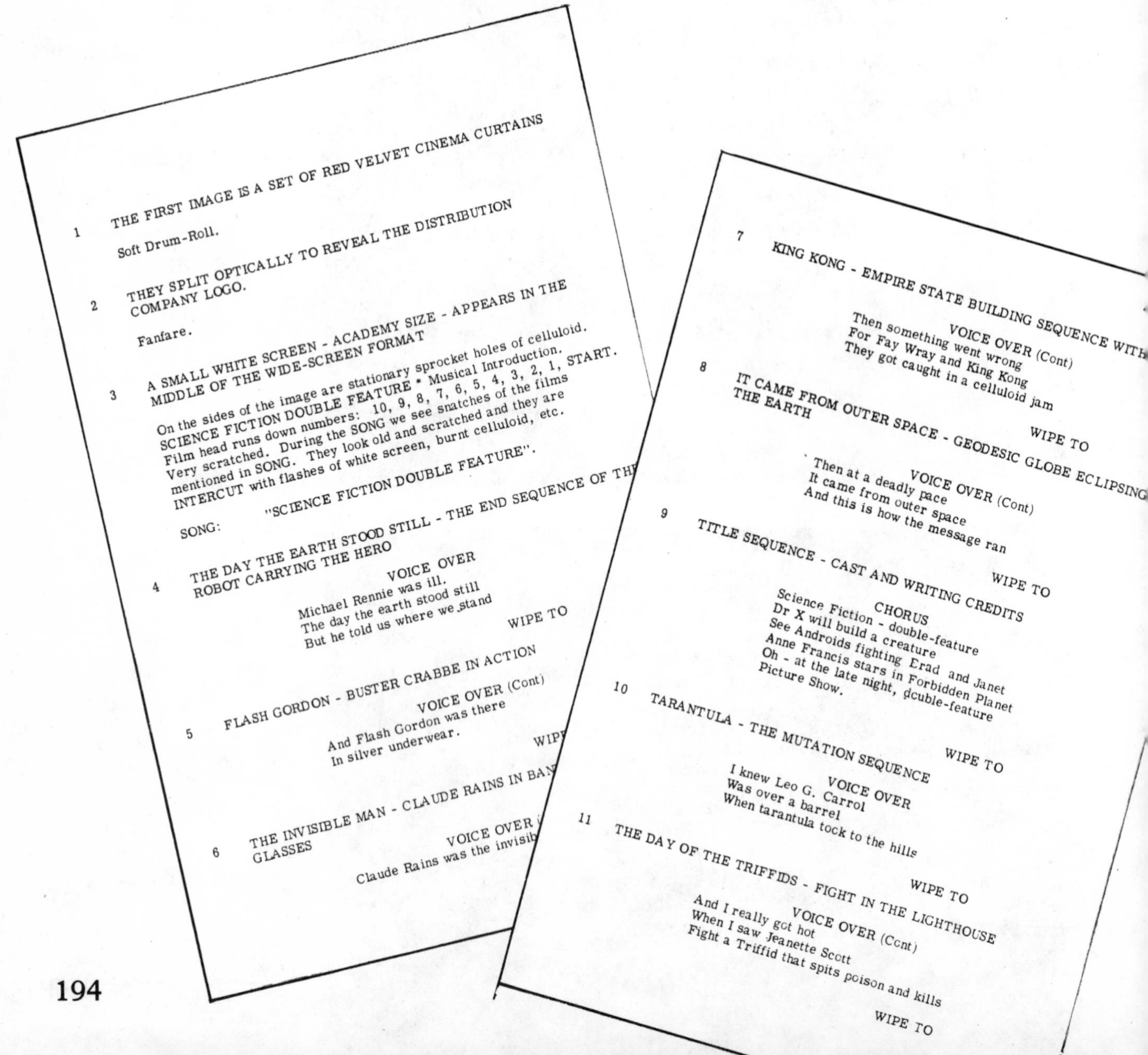

1 THE FIRST IMAGE IS A SET OF RED VELVET CINEMA CURTAINS

Soft Drum-Roll.

2 THEY SPLIT OPTICALLY TO REVEAL THE DISTRIBUTION COMPANY LOGO.

Fanfare.

3 A SMALL WHITE SCREEN - ACADEMY SIZE - APPEARS IN THE MIDDLE OF THE WIDE-SCREEN FORMAT

On the sides of the image are stationary sprocket holes of celluloid. SCIENCE FICTION DOUBLE FEATURE * Musical Introduction. Film head runs down numbers: 10, 9, 8, 7, 6, 5, 4, 3, 2, 1, START. Very scratched. During the SONG we see snatches of the films mentioned in SONG. They look old and scratched and they are INTERCUT with flashes of white screen, burnt celluloid, etc.

SONG: "SCIENCE FICTION DOUBLE FEATURE".

4 THE DAY THE EARTH STOOD STILL - THE END SEQUENCE OF TH ROBOT CARRYING THE HERO

VOICE OVER
Michael Rennie was ill.
The day the earth stood still
But he told us where we stand

WIPE TO

5 FLASH GORDON - BUSTER CRABBE IN ACTION

VOICE OVER (Cont)
And Flash Gordon was there
In silver underwear.

WIP

6 THE INVISIBLE MAN - CLAUDE RAINS IN BAN GLASSES

VOICE OVER
Claude Rains was the invisib

7 KING KONG - EMPIRE STATE BUILDING SEQUENCE WITH

VOICE OVER (Cont)
Then something went wrong
For Fay Wray and King Kong
They got caught in a celluloid jam

WIPE TO

8 IT CAME FROM OUTER SPACE - GEODESIC GLOBE ECLIPSING THE EARTH

VOICE OVER (Cont)
Then at a deadly pace
It came from outer space
And this is how the message ran

WIPE TO

9 TITLE SEQUENCE - CAST AND WRITING CREDITS

CHORUS
Science Fiction - double-feature
Dr X will build a creature
See Androids fighting Erad and Janet
Anne Francis stars in Forbidden Planet
Oh - at the late night, dcuble-feature
Picture Show.

WIPE TO

10 TARANTULA - THE MUTATION SEQUENCE

VOICE OVER
I knew Leo G. Carrol
Was over a barrel
When tarantula tock to the hills

WIPE TO

11 THE DAY OF THE TRIFFIDS - FIGHT IN THE LIGHTHOUSE

VOICE OVER (Cont)
And I really got hot
When I saw Jeanette Scott
Fight a Triffid that spits poison and kills

WIPE TO

For Fay Wray and King Kong
They got caught in a celluloid jam
Then at a deadly pace
It came from outer space
And this is how the message ran:

CHORUS:

Science fiction—double feature
Dr. X will build a creature
See Androids fighting Brad and Janet
Anne Francis stars in *Forbidden Planet*
Ah ha ha ho—at the late-night, double-feature
Picture show

RICHARD O'BRIEN'S VOICE:

I knew Leo G. Carroll
Was over a barrel
When tarantula took to the hills
And I really got hot
When I saw Jeanette Scott
Fight a Triffid that spits poison and kills — LICK IT!
Dana Andrews said prunes
Gave him the runes
And passing them used lots of skills
And when worlds collide
Said George Pal to his bride
I'm going to give you some terrible thrills
Like a— — Like what?

CHORUS:

Science fiction—double feature
Dr. X will build a creature
See Androids fighting Brad and Janet
Anne Francis stars in *Forbidden Planet*
Ah ha ha ho—at the late-night, double-feature
Picture show
By RKO . . . Oh ho ho.
To the late-night, double-feature
Picture show
In the back row. — Yeah, back row!
Oh ho ho.
To the late-night, double-feature
Picture Show.

3

12 THE NIGHT OF THE DEMON - SEQUENCE OF "RUNIC WRITING", FLYING INTO THE FIRE

VOICE OVER (Cont)

Dana Andrews said prunes
Gave him the runes
And passing them used lots of skills.

WIPE TO

13 WHEN WORLDS COLLIDE - ROCKET INVASION SEQUENCE

VOICE OVER (Cont)

And when worlds collide
Said George Pal to his bride
I'm going to give you some terrible thrills
Like a -

WIPE TO

14 TITLE CONTINUED - TECHNICAL AND PRODUCTION CREDITS

CHORUS

Science Fiction - double-feature
Dr X will build a creature
See Androids fighting Brad and Janet
Anne Francis stars in Forbidden Planet
Oh - at the late-night, double-feature
Picture Show
By RKO O - Oh
At the late-night, double-feature
Picture Show
In the back row
At the late-night, double-feature
Picture Show
I want to go.

DISSOLVE TO

15 EXT. A STILL FRAME OF DENTON CATHOLIC CHURCH DAY

CHORUS (Cont)

To the late night double feature
Picture Show.

The SONG ends with church bells ringing joyously as the IMAGE EXPANDS TO WIDE-SCREEN. The STILL FRAME bursts to life as the doors of the Denton Catholic Church are flung open and Mendelssohn's wedding march resounds from the church organ.

The original plans for film credits included clips from the movies named in the lyrics to "Science Fiction/Double Feature."

The picture disk

Not an Import!
A Different Set Of Jaws...
A Different Kind Of Rocky...
THE ROCKY HORROR PICTURE SHOW
The Original Soundtrack From The Original Movie
Available at Last

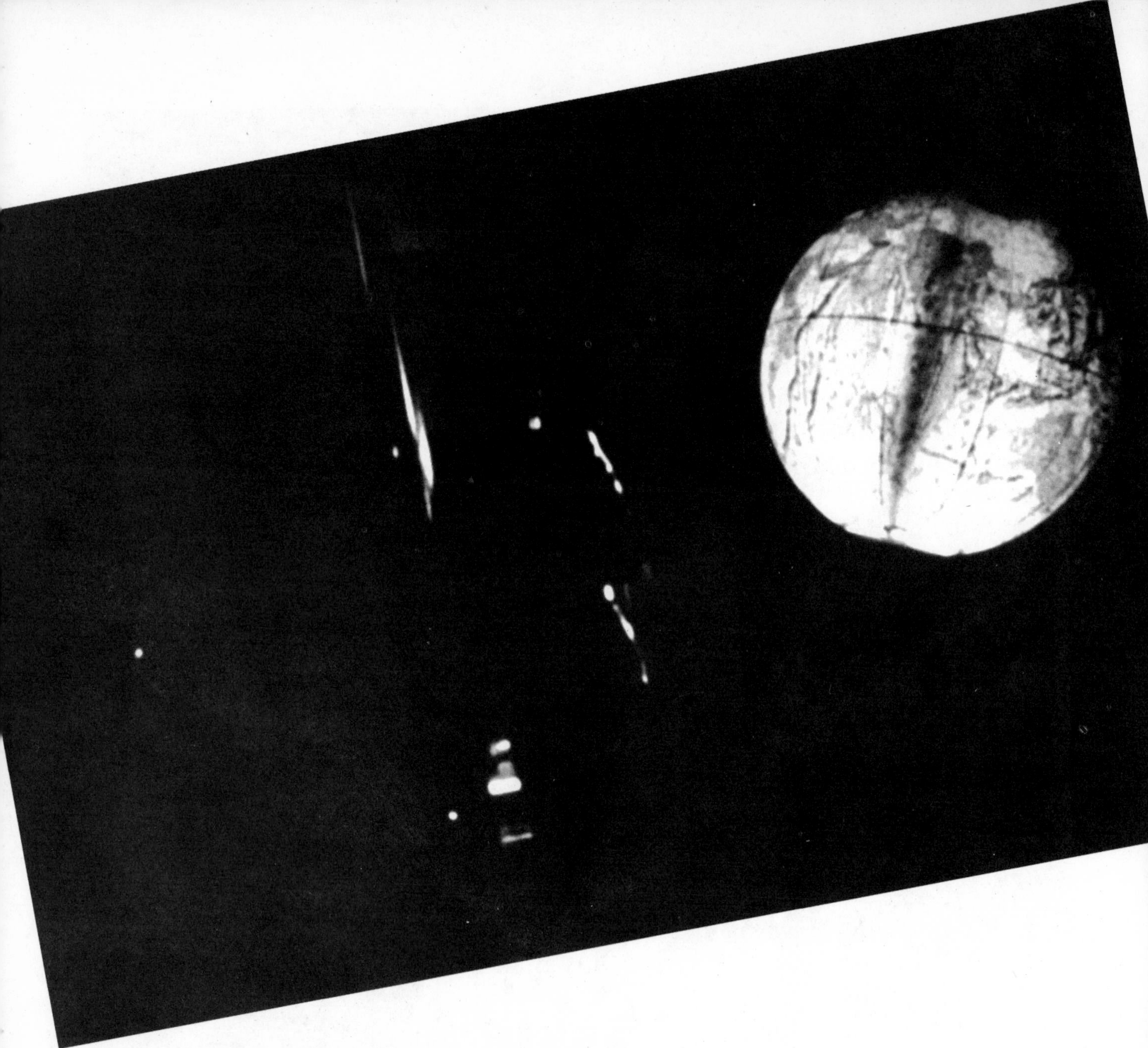

## Science Fiction (Reprise)

Science fiction—double feature
Frank has built and lost his creature.
Darkness has conquered Brad and Janet
The servants gone to a distant planet.
Oh, oh, oh, oh, oh,
At the late night double-feature, picture show
I want to go—oh oh
To the late night double-feature picture show.

## Super Heroes

BRAD:

I've done a lot
God knows I've tried
To find the truth
I've even lied
But all I know
Is down inside

ALL:

I'm bleeding

JANET:

And super heroes
Come to feast
To taste the flesh
Not yet deceased
And all I know
Is still the beast

ALL:

Is feeding

NARRATOR:

And crawling on the planet's face
Some insects called the human race
Lost in time
And lost in space

ALL:

And meaning.



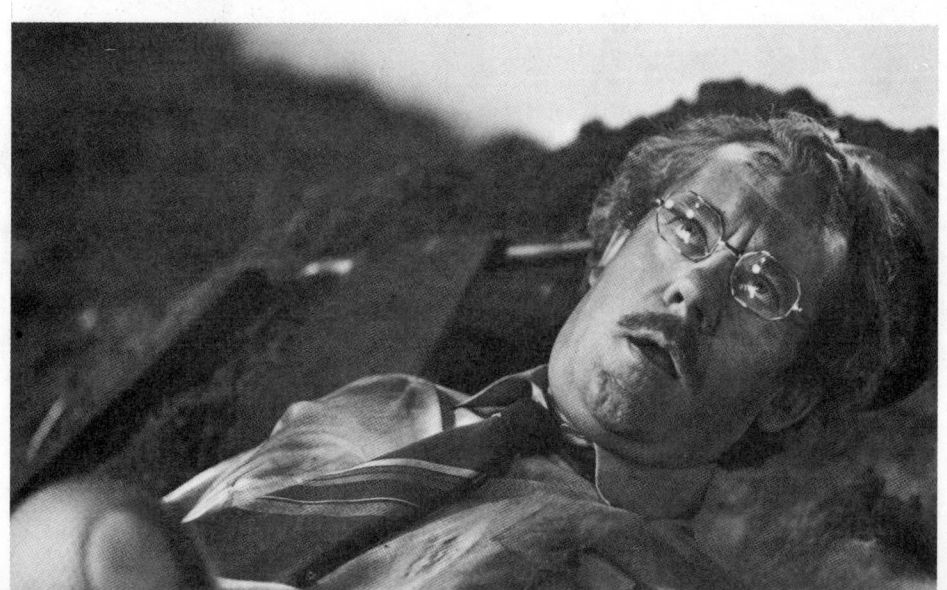

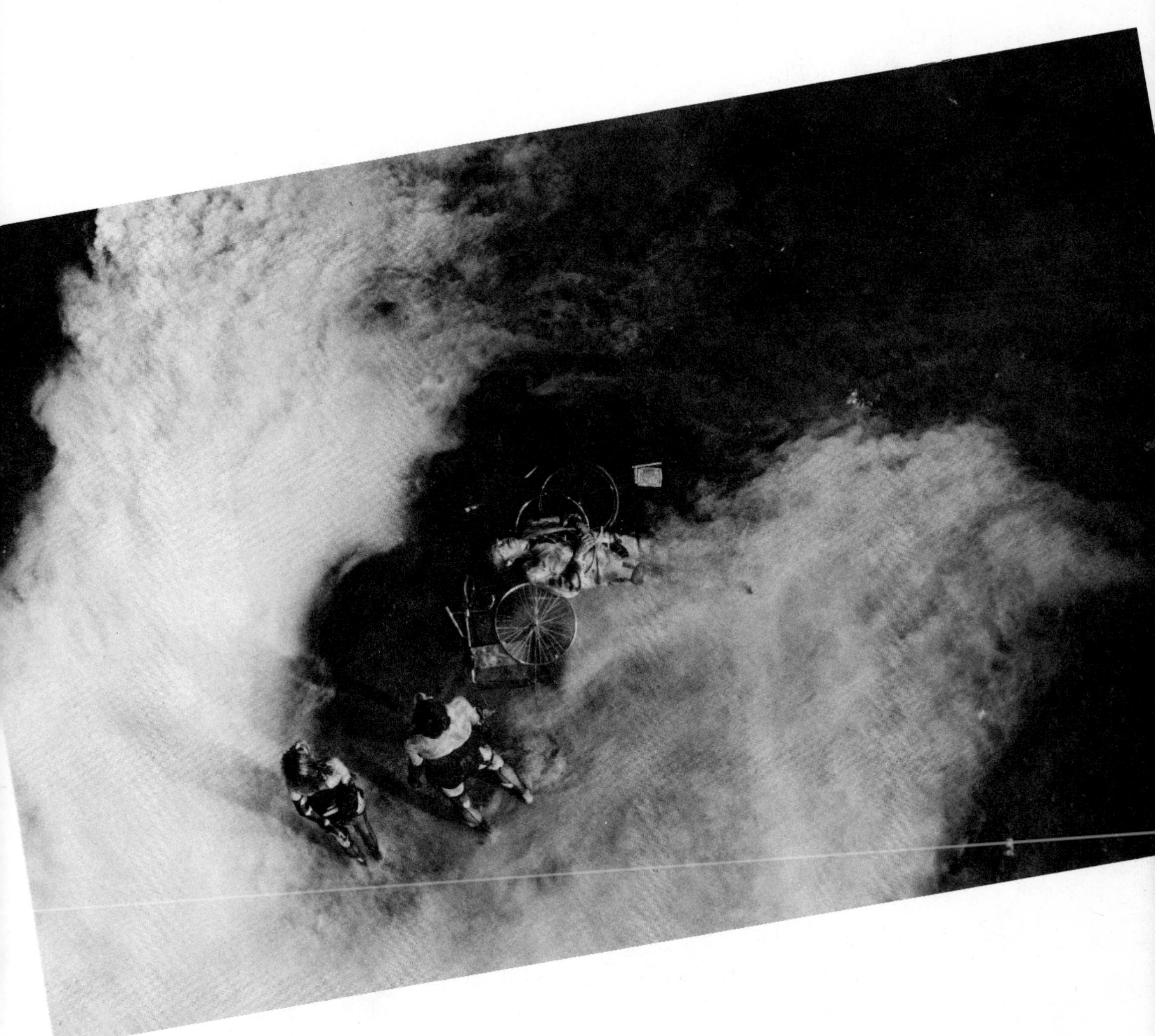

NARRATOR: And crawling on the planet's face
Some insects called the human race
Lost in time, and lost in space
And meaning.

## I'm Going Home

RIFF RAFF:
Frank-N-Furter
It's all over
Your mission is a failure.
Your life style's too extreme.
I'm your new commander
You now are my prisoner
We return to Transylvania
Prepare the transit beam.

*Can you explain this?*

FRANK:
Wait. I can explain—
On the day I went away
GUESTS:
Good-bye.
FRANK:
Was all I had to say
COLUMBIA and GUESTS:
Now I . . . I
FRANK:
I want to come again and stay

*So does Brad*

GUESTS:
Oh my, my
FRANK:
Smile and that will mean I may
I've seen—oh—blue skies
Through the tears in my eyes
And I realize I'm going home.
GUESTS:
I'm going home.
FRANK:
Everywhere it's been the same.
GUESTS:
Feeling
FRANK:
Like I'm outside in the rain.
GUESTS:
Wheeling
FRANK:
Free to try and find a game
GUESTS:
Dealing
FRANK:
Cards for sorrow, cards for pain
'Cause I've seen blue skies
Through the tears in my eyes
And I realize—I'm going home.
FRANK and GUESTS:
I'm going home
I'm going home.



RIFF RAFF: Our noble mission is almost completed, my most beautiful sister, and soon we shall return to the moon-drenched shores of our beloved planet.

MAGENTA: Ah—sweet Transexual—land of night—to sing and dance once more to your dark refrains. To take that step to the right . . . Ha.

RIFF RAFF: But it's the pelvic thrust. . . .

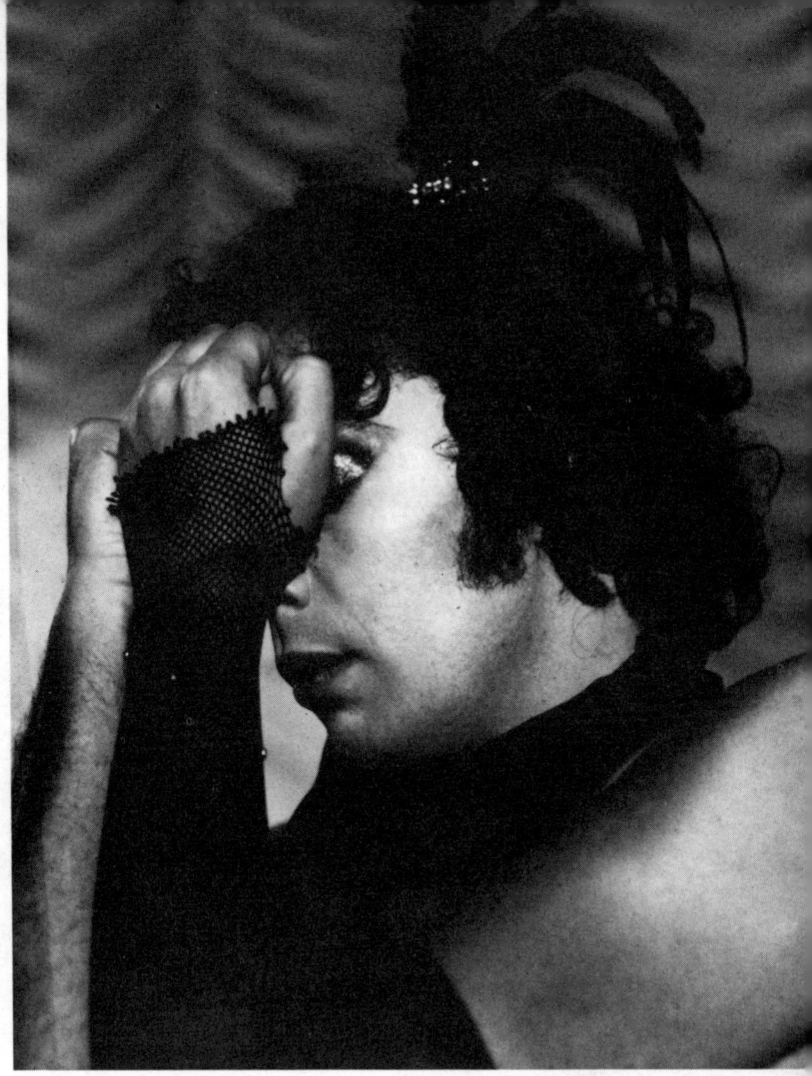

DR. SCOTT: Great Heavens, that's a laser.
RIFF RAFF: Yes, Dr. Scott. A laser capable of emitting a beam of pure antimatter.
BRAD: You mean you're going to kill him? What's his crime?
DR. SCOTT: You saw what became of Eddie. Society must be protected.
RIFF RAFF: Exactly, Dr. Scott. And now, Frank-N-Furter, your time has come. Say good-bye to all of this/ and hello to oblivion.

*Good-bye, all of this*

*Hi oblivion. How's the wife and kids?*

ROCKY HORROR PICTURE SHOW    MICHAEL WHITE PRODUCTIONS LIMITED    24.9.74

S H O O T I N G   S C H E D U L E

W E E K   F I V E

**MONDAY 18th Nov.**

SET: INT. JANET'S ROOM
SCENE NOS: 81,84,86 NIGHT
92,92b,d,f. NIGHT
LOCATION: Oakley Court

CAST AND CROWD
JANET
FRANK

ACTION PROPS: Practical bedlight
Netting around bed
CAMERA DEPARTMENT:
Colour - Wide Screen

**TUESDAY 19th Nov.**

SET: INT BRAD'S ROOM
SCENE NOS: 82,88,89,90 NIGHT
92a,c,g. NIGHT
LOCATION: Oakley Court

CAST AND CROWD
BRAD
FRANK

ACTION PROPS:
Practical bedlight
Netting around bed
CAMERA DEPARTMENT:
Colour - Wide Screen

SPECIAL REQUIREMENTS
T.V. Monitor with edited tape
Hairdressing, Wig for Frank

MUSIC PLAYBACK
Once in a While

**WEDNESDAY 20th Nov.**

SET: INT. VESTIBULE - LIFT
SCENE NOS: 55,57,59,61,63,65
67pt,68,87a NIGHT

CAST AND
BRAD
JANET
FRANK
RIFF RAF

CAMERA DEPARTMENT
53A Black & White Wide Screen
54 onwards Colour Wide Screen

LOCATION: Oakley Court

SPECIAL R
Practical
MUSIC PLA
Sweet Tra

**THURSDAY 21st Nov.**

SET: EXT. ROAD TO CASTLE
SCENE NOS: 19,20,21,22pt,23
62(subliminal flash)
LOCATION:
ACTION PROPS: Brad's car
Chocolates
Sign 'DEAD END'
Newspapers
CAMERA DEPARTMENT:
Black and white. Academy

CAST AND C
BRAD
JANET
MOTORCYCLI

SPECIAL REQ
Spec. FX. R
Low loader
Lightning e
Spec.FX: Ty

**DAY d .**

R E S T   D A Y   A F T E R   N I G H T   S H

**URDAY d**

Dance Rehearsal 2 p.m.

RIFF RAFF
MAGENTA
COLUMBIA
18 Transylvan

---

ROCKY HORROR PICTURE SHOW    MICHAEL WHITE PRODUCTIONS LIMITED

S H O O T I N G   S C H E D U L E

W E E K   S I X

**MONDAY 25th Nov.**

SET: INT. BALLROOM
SCENE NOS: 41,43,45,46,47 NIGHT
LOCATION: Stage 1 Bray Studios
CAMERA DEPARTMENT:
Black and White. Wide Screen

CAST AND CROWD
BRAD
JANET
RIFF RAFF

SPECIAL REQUIREMENTS
Choreographer required
MUSIC PLAYBACK
Time Warp - Chorus and So

**TUESDAY 26th Nov.**

SET: INT. BALLROOM
SCENE NOS: 48,50,52 NIGHT
LOCATION: Stage 1 - Bray Studios
CAMERA DEPARTMENT:
Black and White. Wide Screen

CAST AND CROWD
BRAD
JANET
RIFF RAFF

SPECIAL REQUIREMENTS
Choreographer required.
MUSIC PLAYBACK
Time Warp

**WEDNESDAY 27th Nov.**

SET: INT. BALLROOM
SCENE NOS: 53,54a, 67 NIGHT
LOCATION: Stage 1 Bray Studios
ACTION PROPS:
Red, Black & white streamers
CAMERA DEPARTMENT
53 Black & white Wide Screen
54a Colour Wide Screen

CAST AND CROWD
BRAD
JANET
RIFF RAFF
MAGENTA

SPECIAL REQUIREMENTS
Choreographer required
MUSIC PLAYBACK
Sweet Transvestite

**THURSDAY 28th Nov.**

SET: INT. BALLROOM
SCENE NOS: 149,150,151,152,
153,154,155 NIGHT
LOCATION: Stage 1 Bray Studios
ACTION PROPS:
Wheelchair Statues
CAMERA DEPARTMENT
Colour - Wide Screen

CAST AND CROWD
BRAD
JANET
FRANK

SPECIAL REQUIREMENTS
Choreographer required

MUSIC PLAYBACK
The Floor Show Part 1

**FRIDAY 29th Nov.**

SET: INT. BALLROOM
SCENE NOS: 156,157,158,159 NIGHT
LOCATION: Stage 1 Bray Studios
ACTION PROPS:
Wheelchair
CAMERA DEPARTMENT
Colour - Wide Screen

CAST AND CROWD
BRAD
JANET
FRANK

SPECIAL REQUIREMENTS
Spec. FX: Mist
Choreographer required
MUSIC PLAYBACK
The Floor Show Part 1

# Rose Tint My World

COLUMBIA:

It was great
When it all began
I was a regular Frankie fan
But it was over when he had the plan
To start working on a muscle-man.
Now the only thing that gives me hope
Is my love of a certain dope
Rose tints my world keeps me
Safe from my trouble and pain.

ROCKY:

I'm just seven hours old.
Truly beautiful to behold
And somebody should be told
My libido hasn't been controlled
Now the only thing I've come to trust
Is an orgasmic rush of lust
Rose tints my world keeps me
Safe from my trouble and pain.

BRAD:

It's beyond me.
Help me, Mommy.
I'll be good you'll see.
Take this dream away
What's this, let's see
I feel sexy
What's come over me. Whoa—
Here it comes again.

JANET:

Oh I—I feel released
Bad times deceased
My confidence has increased
Reality is here
The game has been disbanded
My mind has been expanded
It's a gas that Frankie's landed
His lust is so sincere

FRANK:

What ever happened to Fay Wray?
That delicate satin-draped frame
As it clung to her thigh
How I started to cry
'Cause I wanted to be dressed just the same.
Give yourself over to absolute pleasure
Swim the warm waters of sins of the flesh
Erotic nightmares beyond any measure
And sensual daydreams to treasure
forever—
Can't you just see it. Oh, oh, hooo. Oh.
Don't dream it. Be it.
Don't dream it. Be it.
Don't dream it. Be it.
Don't dream it. Be it.

ALL:

Don't dream it. Be it.
(Repeat four times.)

SCOTT:

Ach, we've got to get out of this trap.
Before this decadence saps our wills.
I've got to be strong and try to hang on
Or else my mind may well snap
Und my life will be lived for the thrill.

BRAD:

It's beyond me
Help me, Mommy.

JANET:

God bless Lili St. Cyr.

FRANK:

My my my my my my my my my . . .
I'm a wild and an untamed thing
I'm a bee with a deadly sting.
You gotta hit, and your mind goes ping
Your heart'll thump and your blood will sing
So let the party and the sounds rock on
We're gonna shake it till the life has gone
Rose tint my world
Keep me safe from my trouble and pain.

ALL:

We're wild and untamed things.
We're bees with a deadly sting.
You gotta hit and your mind goes ping
Your heart'll thump and your blood will sing
So let the party and the sounds rock on
We're gonna shake till the life has gone . . .
Rose tint my world
Keep me safe from my trouble and pain.
(Repeat)

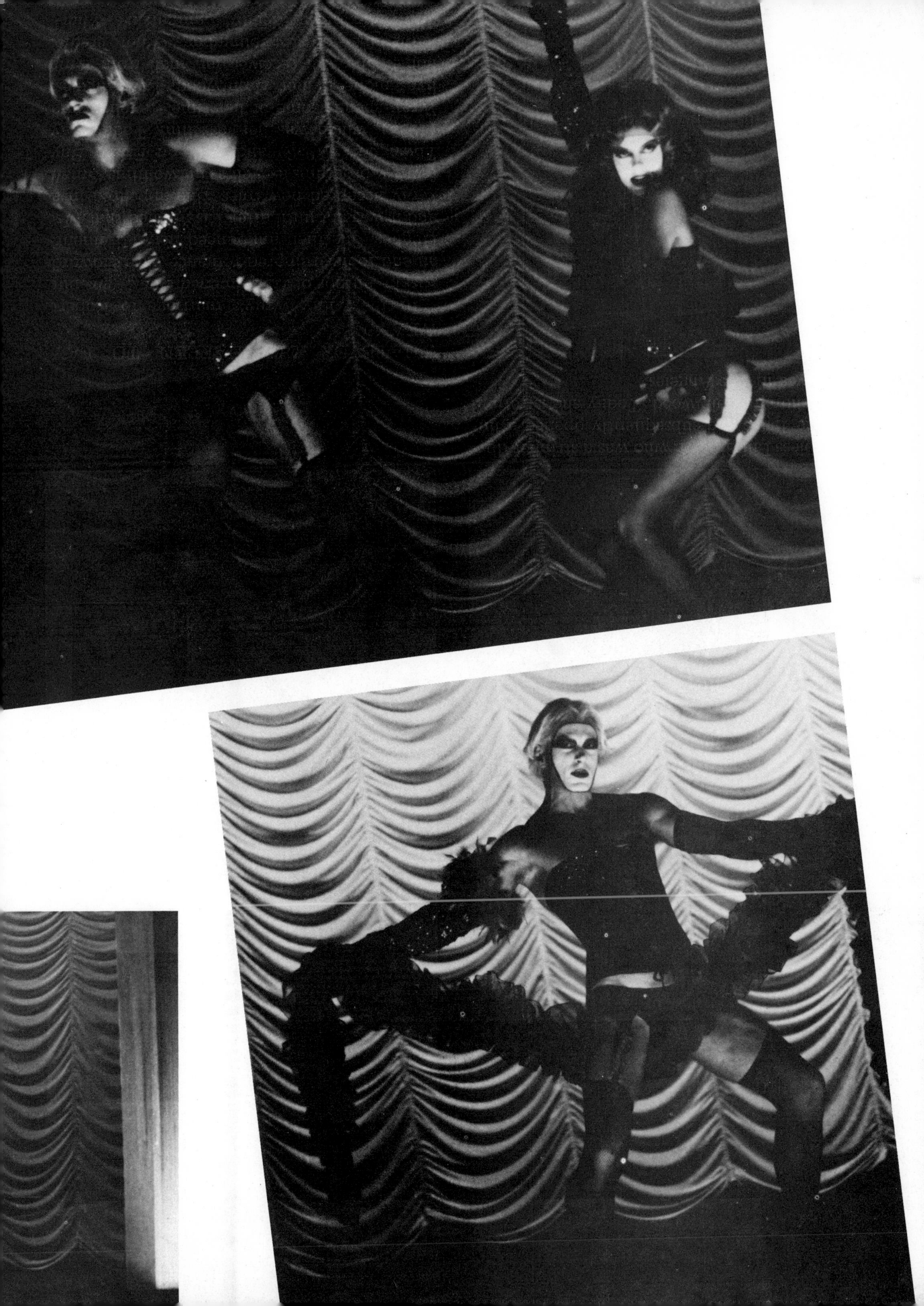

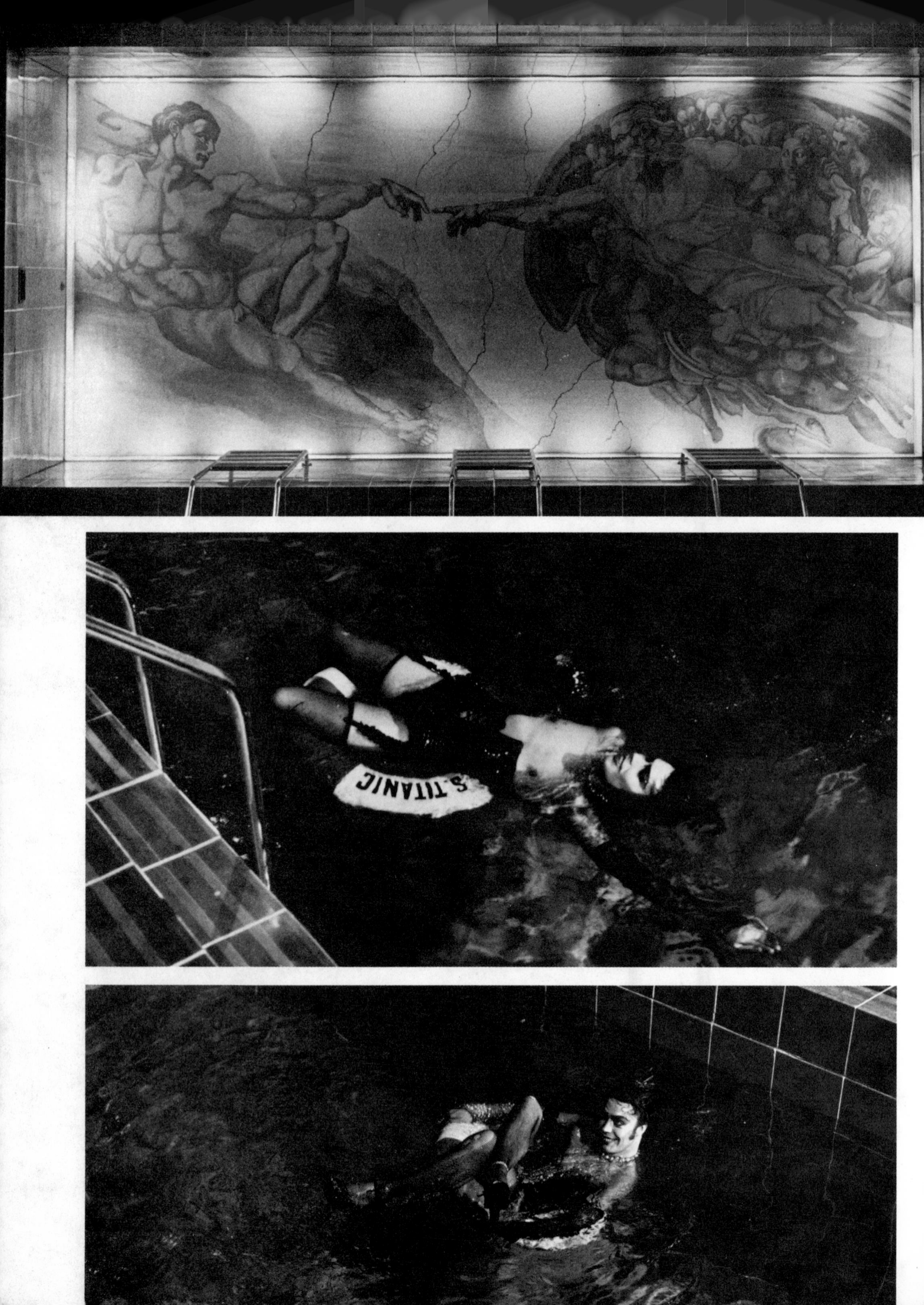
S. TITANIC

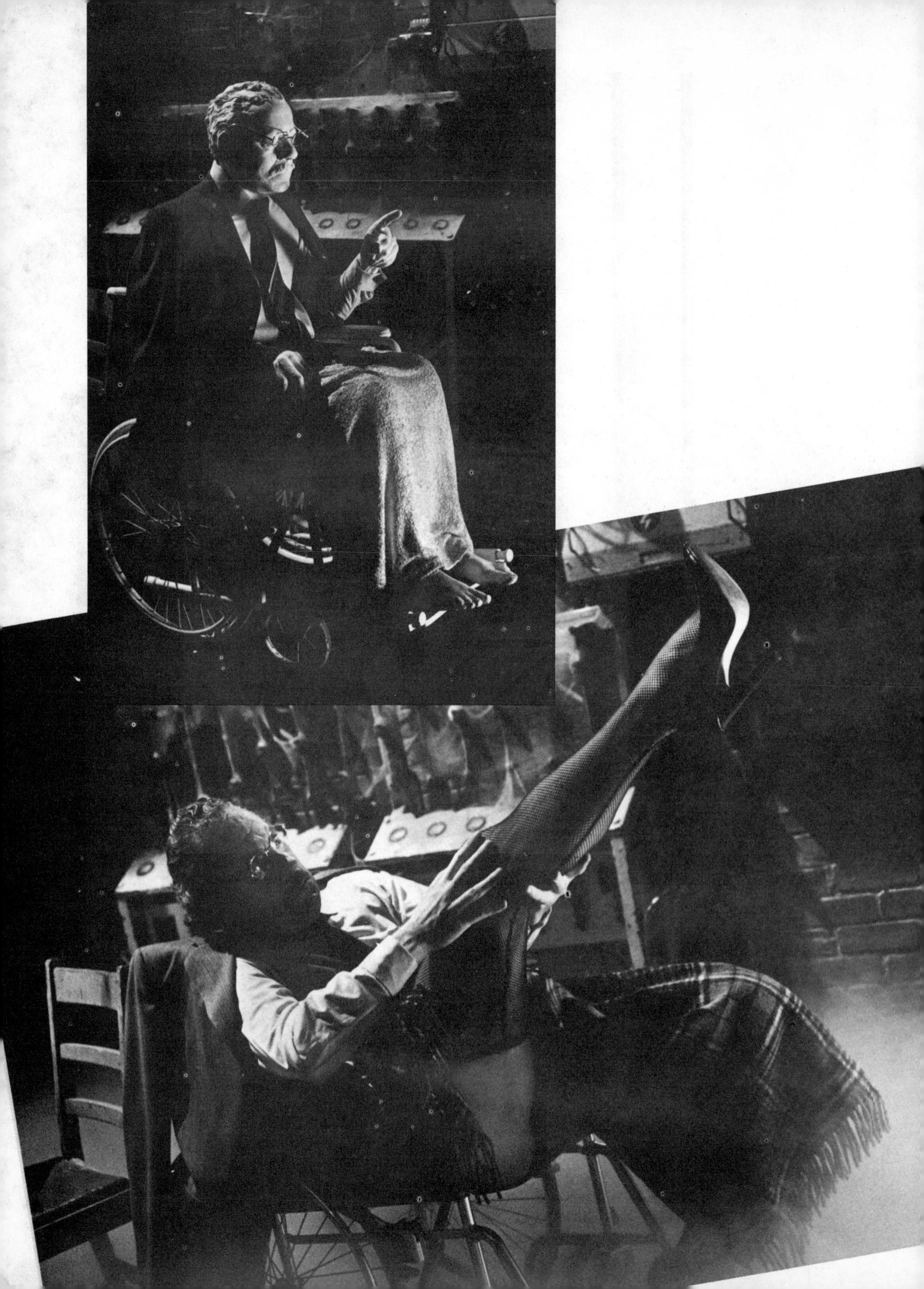

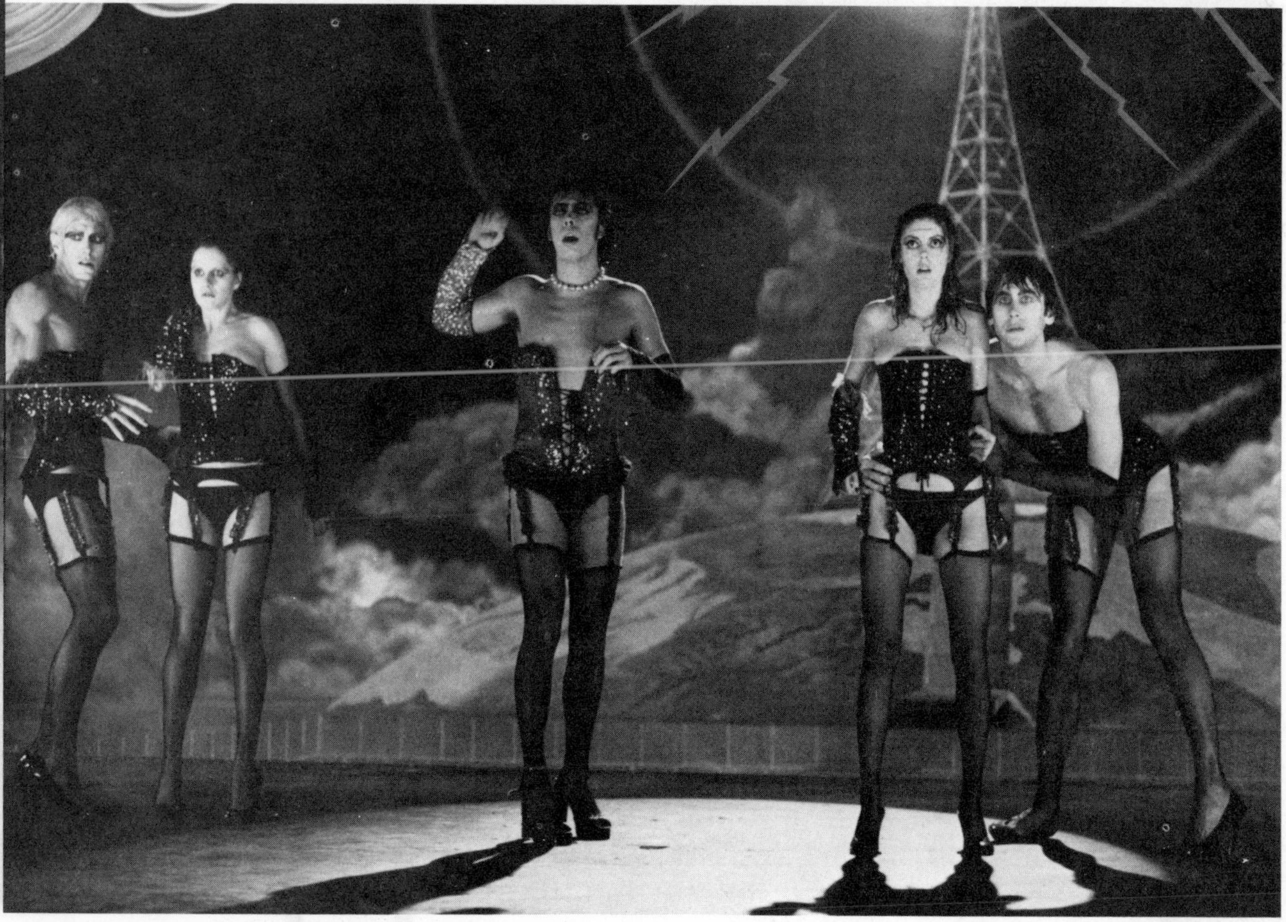

God bless Lili St. Cyr, who was a stripper during the 1940s and subsequently opened a lingerie shop in Hollywood. Today she is retired and lives in Los Angeles.

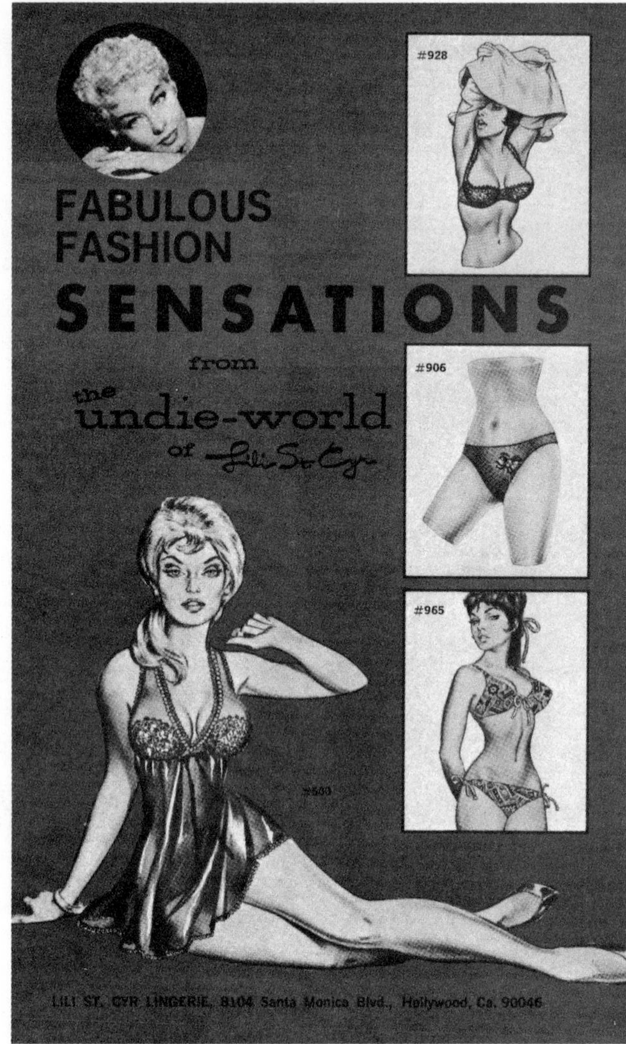


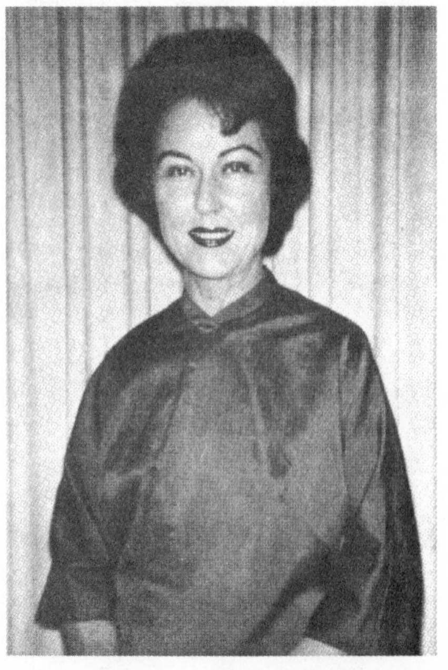

WHATEVER *DID* HAPPEN TO FAY WRAY?

In 1942, Fay Wray's marriage to Robert Riskin, author of *It Happened One Night*, put an end to her rumored romance with Howard Hughes. She then announced her retirement, and it was not until after Riskin died that Ms. Wray accepted new roles. She appeared in a few TV programs as well as in two films, *Small Town Girl* (1953) and *Hell on Frisco Bay* (1955), which was her last film. Today Fay Wray spends some of her time traveling and lives alone in her Brentwood, Los Angeles, home. She still receives fan mail from *King Kong* fans— mostly young boys. (*Photo credit*: *Jon Virzi.* From Richard Lamparski's *Whatever Became Of . . . ?*, reprinted with permission)

ROR PICTURE SHOW MICHAEL WHITE PRODUCTIONS LIMITED 24.9.74

S H O O T I N G S C H E D U L E

W E E K S E V E N

SET: INT. BALLROOM
SCENE NOS: 160,161,161a pt.
LOCATION: Stage 1 Bray Studios

CAST AND CROWD
FRANK
BRAD
JANET
ROCKY
DR. SCOTT
COLUMBIA

ACTION PROPS: Wheelchair
Chiffon drapes

CAMERA DEPARTMENT:
colour. Wide Screen

SPECIAL REQUIREMENTS
Spec. FX: Mist effect
Pool Wind Machine/chiffon flying
Choreographer required.
MUSIC PLAYBACK
Don't Dream It

SET: INT. BALLROOM
SCENE NOS: 161 pt.
LOCATION: Stage 1 Bray Studios

CAST AND CROWD
FRANK
BRAD
JANET
ROCKY
DR. SCOTT
COLUMBIA

ACTION PROPS: Wheelchair
Rostrum in Pool

CAMERA DEPARTMENT:
Colour. Wide Screen

SPECIAL REQUIREMENTS
Spec. FX Mist
Pool Wind Machine
Choreographer required
MUSIC PLAYBACK
I'm a Wild and Untamed Thi

CAMERA DEPARTMENT:
Colour. Wide Screen

SDAY SET: INT. BALLROOM
SCENE NOS: 162,163 NIGHT
LOCATION: Stage 1 Bray Studios
ACTION PROPS: Ray gun
Nail file
Deckchairs/Wheelchair

CAST AND CROWD
FRANK
BRAD
JANET
ROCKY

CAMERA DEPARTMENT
Colour. Wide screen

SPECIAL REQUIREMENTS
Choreographer required
Cloud effect
MUSIC PLAYBACK
Riff Raff's Recit.
I'm Going Home

RSDAY SET: INT. BALLROOM
SCENE NOS. 164pt. NIGHT

LOCATION: Stage 1 Bray Studios

CAST AND CROWD
FRANK
BRAD
JANET
ROCKY

ACTION PROPS: Wheelchair

Stunt Doubles:

CAMERA DEPARTMENT:
Colour - Wide Screen

SPECIAL REQUIREMENTS
Harness
Curtains collapsing

RIDAY
th
ec.

SET: INT. BALLROOM/SWIMMING POOL
SCENE NOS: 164 to complete (Ball)
165A NIGHT (Swim:Pool)

CAST AND CROWD
FRANK
BRAD
JANET
ROCKY

ACTION PROPS: Wheelchair

SPECIAL REQUIREME
Spec. FX: Mist
MUSIC PLAYBACK
Don't Dream It.

CAMERA DEPARTMENT:
Colour - Wide Screen

---

ROCKY HORROR PICTURE SHOW MICHAEL WHITE PRODUCTION

S H O O T I N G S C H E D U L E

W E E K E I G H T

MONDAY 9th December

SET:
SCENE NOS: 18,34,42,44,49,51
LOCATION: Oakley Court
ACTION PROPS:
Dossier: 'The Denton Affiar'
Chart with Time Warp dance steps

CAST AND CROWD
NARRATOR
MUSIC PLAYBACK
Time Warp
CAMERA DEPARTME
Black & White.

TUESDAY 10th December

SET: INT. STUDY
SCENE NOS: 72,80,93,97,118 NIGHT
LOCATION: Oakley Court
CAMERA DEPARTMENT
Black and White. Wide Screen

CAST AND CROWD
NARRATOR
MUSIC PLAYBACK
Sword of Damocle

WEDNESDAY 11th December

SET: INT. STUDY
SCENE NOS: 121,145,148,168 NIGHT
LOCATION: Oakley Court

CAST AND CROWD
NARRATOR

ACTION PROPS: Spinning globe
CAMERA DEPARTMENT:
Black and White - Wide Screen

SPECIAL REQUIREM
Light change
MUSIC PLAYBACK
Eddie's Teddy
Wise Up Janet Wei
Super Heroes

THRUSDAY 12th December

SET: EXT. CRATER
SCENE NOS: 167pt DAWN

LOCATION:

CAST AND CROWD
BRAD
JANET
DR. SCOTT
MUSIC PLAYBACK
Super Heroes

FRIDAY 13th December

SET: EXT. CRATER
SCENE NOS: 167 to complete

LOCATION:

CAST AND CROWD
BRAD
JANET
DR. SCOTT
MUSIC PLAYBACK
Super Heroes

SPECIAL EFFECT SHOTS

| | |
|---|---|
| 22 | Lighting strikes tree |
| 27 | Lightning in sky |
| 66 | Explosion (subliminal flash) |
| 165B | Castle explosion |
| 166 | Castle breaks up and vanishes |

STOCK SHOTS
1 - 14

STILL PHOTOGRAPHS

| | |
|---|---|
| 123 | Ext. High |
| 124 | Ext. Ceme |
| 125 | Int. Milk |
| 126.128 | Int. Toile |
| 127 | Ext. Stree |
| 130. | Ext. Bonfi |
| 131 | Ext. Shopf |
| 133 | Ext. Castl |
| 135 | Int. Truck |
| 137 | Int. Labora |
| 138 | Int. Eddi |